Warrior Mountains Indian Heritage

Student Edition

Rickey Butch Walker

© Copyright 2011
Bluewater Publications
Protected

All rights reserved. No part of this publication may be reproduced or transmitted in any form or by any means, electronic or mechanical, including photocopying, recording, or by any information storage and retrieval system, without prior written permission from the Publisher.

Published by:
Bluewater Publications
1812 CR 111
Killen, Alabama 35645
www.BluewaterPublications.com

Table of Contents

PREFACE I
LESSON 1 - INTRODUCTION 1
LESSON 2 – FAMILY HISTORY AND ANCESTRY 4
LESSON 3 – ECHOTA CHEROKEE TRIBE OF ALABAMA 9
LESSON 4 – PERIODS OF PREHISTORIC INDIANS 13
LESSON 5 – LIFESTYLES OF EARLY INDIAN PEOPLE 25
LESSON 6 – EARLY SURVIVAL NEEDS 32
LESSON 7 – REGALIA 40
LESSON 8 – CEREMONIAL ACTIVITIES 47
LESSON 9 – TENNESSEE RIVER 53
LESSON 10 – EUROPEAN CONTACT 59
LESSON 11 – FIVE TRIBES OF NORTH ALABAMA 66
LESSON 12 – CREEK TRIBE 72
LESSON 13 – CHICKASAW TRIBE 76
LESSON 14 – CHEROKEE TRIBE 79
LESSON 15 – SEVEN CLANS OF THE CHEROKEE 84
LESSON 16 – INDIAN TRAILS AND PATHS 88
LESSON 17 – INDIAN VILLAGES 105
LESSON 18 – LOCAL INDIAN LEADERS 125
LESSON 19 – INDIAN BATTLES 145
LESSON 20 – INDIAN TREATIES 155
LESSON 21 – INDIAN REMOVAL 161
LESSON 22 – TRADITIONAL CULTURAL PROPERTIES 167
LESSON 23 – STATE RECOGNIZED INDIAN TRIBES OF ALABAMA 180
INDEX 186

Preface

Warrior Mountains Indian Heritage curriculum was written for the academic and cultural enrichment of school students especially those of Indian Heritage. This work is a culmination of four years of research and development of educational plans that specifically address the reading and social studies objectives of education programs in the southeast. The lesson plans are designed to meet the state standards of Alabama and are based on the criteria required in the standardized assessment of all students in the state. Lessons are historically specific to the Indian heritage of the Warrior Mountains of North Alabama. These lesson plans were written from an Indian perspective for children in our schools with emphasis on those students of Indian ancestry.

In addition to the lessons, state standards, and standardized assessment criteria, Warrior Mountains Indian Heritage also contains individual performance reports, teacher-made pre/mid/post tests, activities for grades Kindergarten through seven, and a checklist for instructor improvement in team teaching. The state standards were taken from the August 2004 edition of the Alabama Course of Study. The standardized assessment criteria is based on Dynamic Indicators of Basic Early Literacy Skills (Dibels) for grades Kindergarten through three and the Stanford Achievement Test (SAT 10) for grades four through seven.

Warrior Mountain Indian Heritage has local, regional, and national significance since it addresses standardized assessment criteria used throughout the United States. The text can be a guide for other Indian programs across the nation who wish to develop their own lesson plans based on their specific history and culture. In addition, teachers of various grades can incorporate historically important details into their reading objectives.

LESSON 1 - INTRODUCTION

Prior to Indian removal, European people moved into Indian lands where they intermarried with Indian people. These mixed families lived in harmony until the United States government started forced removal. During these difficult years of removal, many of our ancestors started denying their Indian race and calling themselves Black Dutch or Black Irish. After the Trail of Tears ended in March 1839, our Indigenous ancestors remaining in Alabama began a long and tragic period of ethnic denial.

Many Indian people in the southeast assimilated into the general population in the early 1800's. Prior to 1840, many of our Indian people were forced from their homes in our area but many others hid their true identity. Both Creeks and Cherokees were removed from the southeast and passed through Alabama along the Tennessee River, or left here by the first railroad from Decatur to Tuscumbia, Alabama. During these times of removal, many of our Indian people escaped and avoided being sent west. Many of our ancestors went on the forced removal but later returned to their homelands in this area.

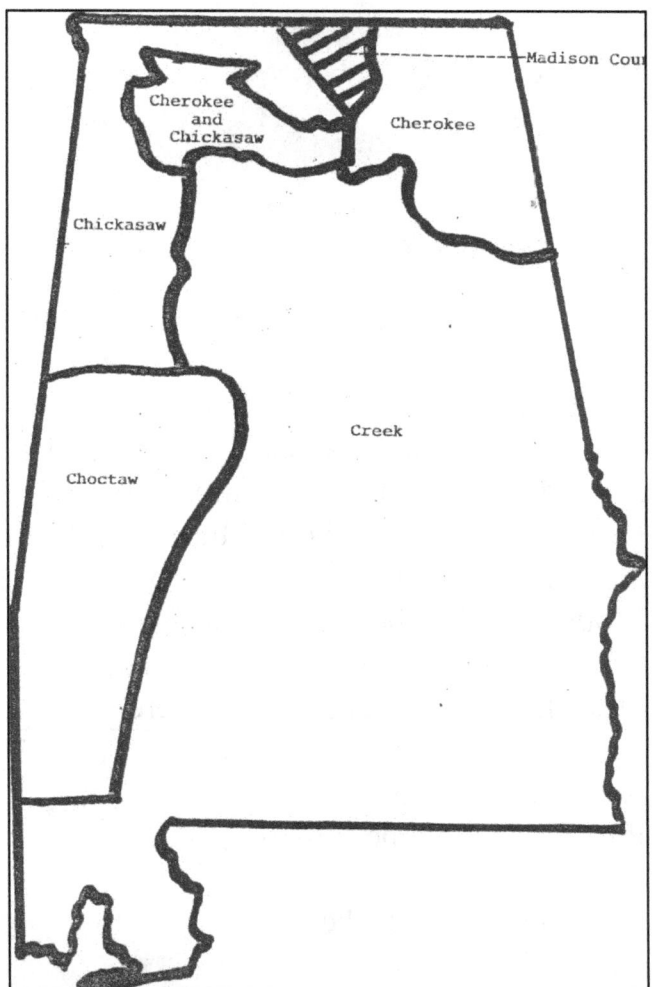
1806 Map of Alabama

From the early 1840's to 1968, it was illegal for people to be Indian in the State of Alabama; therefore, our Indian ancestors had to deny their rightful heritage. Sections two through seven of the Civil Rights Act of 1968 allowed people in Alabama to reclaim their Indian heritage. In 1972, the U.S. Congress passed the Indian Education Act which ultimately funded Indian programs across the country. The program primarily provided for cultural based education for Indian students. In 1981, the Echota Cherokee Tribe of Alabama was incorporated and organized by the descendants of Cherokee people who migrated into Alabama from the northwestern corner of Georgia. The Cherokee capitol in Georgia was at New Echota; thus, the Indian descendants with ties to this portion of the Cherokee Nation called themselves Echota Cherokee.

LESSON 1 - INTRODUCTION

Ceremonial Indian Mound at Oakville

In 1986, two members of the Echota Cherokee Tribe, Joe Stewart and Charlotte Stewart Hallmark, helped start their Indian education program for children that were members of the tribe. Rickey Butch Walker was hired as the first coordinator of Lawrence County Schools Indian Education program. Initially the program started an in-house Indian museum and in 1987 held the first Indian festival in Lawrence County. In 1990, the late Congressman, Tom Bevill, through the Appalachian Regional Commission funded an Indian Youth Leadership Project for Lawrence County Schools' Indian Education Program. During 1991, a land purchase was made for 26 acres containing two ancient Indian mounds and was named Oakville Indian Mounds Park. The facility was later renamed the Oakville Indian Mounds Education Center, which would complement and enhance our county's rich Indian culture and heritage. The Oakville museum and offices were opened in 1995 which was the year the Indian program was recognized as a National Showcase Project. Today, the Indian education offices and festival are held at the Center. Presently, the facility houses thousands of local artifacts and consists of some 116 acres. The majority of our Indian students or their parents are members of the Echota Cherokee Tribe of Alabama.

Burial Mound at Oakville

Review Questions

1. You are in this class because you, your parents, or grandparents are what race?
2. What Indian tribe are most of you a member?
3. Where is our Indian education program, museum, and mounds located?
4. What is an ancestor?
5. What clan are you a part of?
6. What is another name for the Indian Removal?

LESSON 1 - INTRODUCTION

7. What year did the Echota Cherokee Tribe become organized?
8. When did the Trail of Tears end?
9. How many Indian mounds are located at Oakville?
10. What two main tribes were removed from Lawrence County, Alabama?
11. What are the names used by Indian mixed bloods after removal?
12. What was the 1968 Act that recognized Indian people in Alabama?
13. What is folklore?
14. What years was it illegal to be an Indian in the State of Alabama?

LESSON 2 – FAMILY HISTORY AND ANCESTRY

Your ancestors are your direct family members who are older than you. For example: your parents, your grandparents, their parents and on and on. So, somewhere down the line you have an Indian ancestor and we want to teach you about how your Indian ancestors lived.

Most North Alabama Indian students are of mixed ancestry of Celtic and Indian. The Celtic (Kel'Tic') people are Irish, Scotch, Welsh, and/or Scots-Irish. The Indian people are mostly Cherokee, Creek, or Chickasaw. Celtic people are fair complected, blue eyes, red or blond hair, and sometimes have little spots called freckles. Indian people are olive complected, black eyes, and black hair. Indians in Alabama also mixed to some degree with African descendants. Anytime a question of race is asked, you should identify yourself as Indian. Be proud to claim your Indian ancestry, but also claim your other heritage since we are all mixed. It is important to understand that most of our ancestors are of mixed or metis ancestry. The word metis (pronounced as me'ta' or me'ti') means people of mixed European and American Indian ancestry.

Many of our North Alabama Indian students belong to the Echota Cherokee Tribe and is the reason they are allowed to attend Indian education classes. Most of our students are of mixed ancestry, usually Celtic and Indian. Celtic is a person of Irish, Scotch, Scotch-Irish, or Welsh ancestry and Indian is usually Cherokee, Creek, or Chickasaw.

Many people may question the fact that you are Indian. Some of our features do not meet their expectations of what an "Indian" looks like. Since most of our Indian students are of mixed Celtic origin, we are not supposed to look like full bloods. We have a unique culture here in North Alabama like no other in the world; therefore, be proud you are a mixed or metis Indian person. Being Indian is not based on what you look like. Television and movies have given society a false view of Indian people. All Indian people do not have dark skin, black eyes, and black hair. A great number of Indian people do but not all.

Look around the room at each other. How many of you have blue eyes? How about freckles? How about red or blond hair? Even though these are Celtic features, never deny your true Indian heritage. One of the most feared Cherokee warriors of the Appalachian frontier was the half-brother of Sequoyah, Robert Benge, also known as The Bench, or The Benge. Bob Benge was red headed, blue eyed, fair complected, and spoke perfect English.

It is important to understand that most of our ancestors were of mixed ancestry. As the southern portion of the United States became inhabited with Celtic people, intermarriage became common with the Indian races; therefore, the majority of our students are Celtic Indians.

LESSON 2 – FAMILY HISTORY AND ANCESTRY

By 1800, two of the three major tribes in Alabama were controlled by ½ Celtic and ½ Indian leaders. John Watts, Jr. was ½ Celtic (Scotch) and ½ Cherokee. Levi and George Colbert were ½ Celtic (Scotch) and ½ Chickasaw. Alexander McGillivary was ½ Celtic (Scotch), ¼ Creek, and ¼ French. Robert (Bob) Benge was the son of Scots trader John Benge and Wurteh Watts, who was ½ Cherokee and ½ Scotch; therefore, Bob Benge was ¼ Cherokee and ¾ Scotch. The Governor of Virginia presented a rifle for his red scalp.

During the 1600s, Celtic people came into the North Alabama area as traders for the English merchants in Old Charles Town, SC. They followed Indian trails and roads. These Celtic people were Irish, Scotch, Welsh, Cornish, or Scots-Irish descent. Many Celtic men married these young, beautiful Indian women. In the 1700s, many more Celtic men married Indian maidens and made their home here. The Chickasaws were the first to form communities of mixed ancestry. One such town was known as McIntoshville in northeastern Mississippi and another was known as **Breed Town** on the Coosa River in Alabama.

In 1729, James Logan Colbert, Scotch, married three Chickasaw wives who bore him many children. Over the years, mixed-blood settlements separated themselves more and more from primitive full bloods. By the 1800s, the mixed-bloods had completely taken over management of Chickasaw tribal affairs.

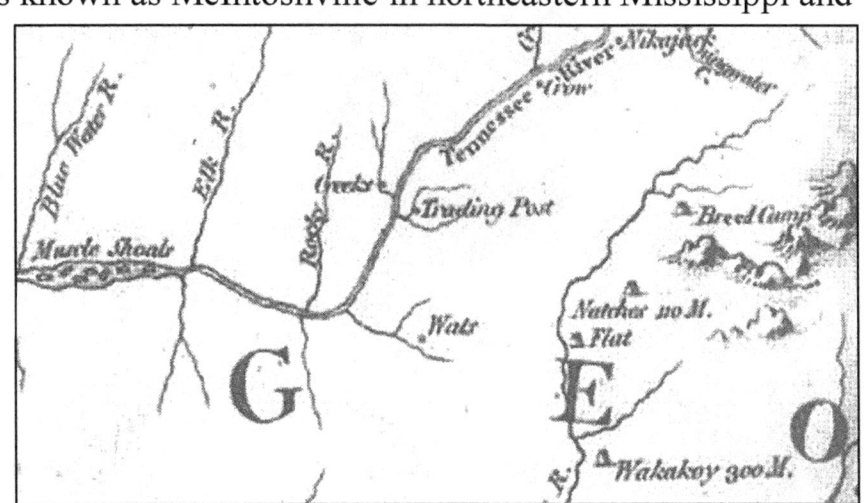

Chickasaw mixed bloods lived at Breed Camp and guided pack trains through North Alabama to the Chickasaw Towns on the Tombigbee.

John Melton, Irish, came into Lawrence County in the 1780s with the Cherokee Indians. He married a Cherokee woman. Melton had several children by his Indian wife, most of whom married white people. The Cherokee Indian Town of Melton's Bluff was named after John Melton. The town was located between Mallard Creek and Spring Creek on the south bank of the Tennessee River in Lawrence County, Alabama.

Most of you are members of the *Echota Cherokee Tribe of Alabama*, which has thousands of members in Alabama and in other states. Just think, you are a member of an Indian tribe, which has thousands of members. If you are an Echota Cherokee, you are also a member of a Clan. There are seven clans of the Echota Cherokee.

LESSON 2 – FAMILY HISTORY AND ANCESTRY

Most of our Indian students are members of the Echota Cherokee Tribe of Alabama; however, your Indian heritage may come from other tribes. To be a card carrying tribal member, most tribes require at least 1/32 American Indian blood. In 1980, a new tribe called the Echota Cherokee Tribe of Alabama was formed by people of Cherokee Indian heritage who lived in North Alabama that had migrated out of northwestern Georgia near the Cherokee capital of New Echota; thus, Echota Cherokees.

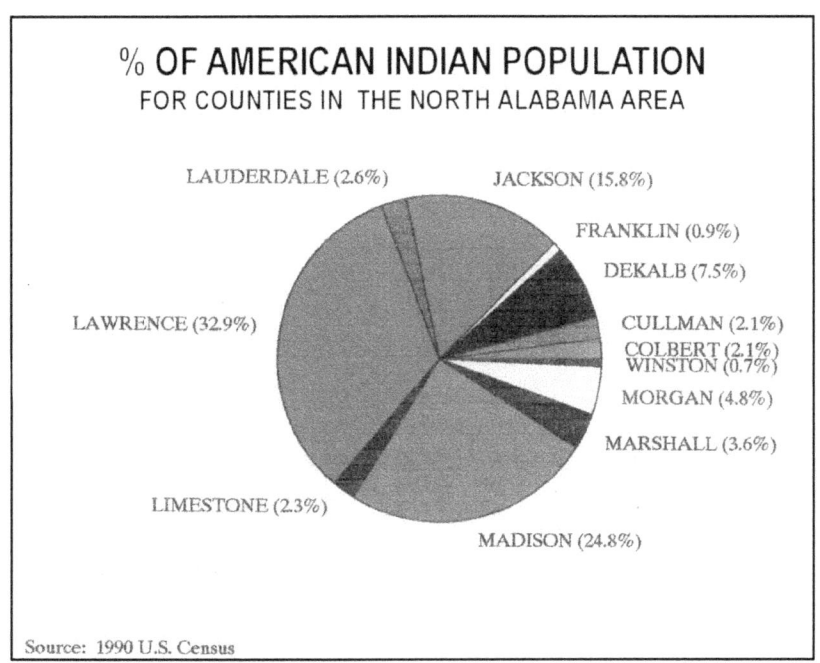

The Echota Cherokee Tribe is the largest and most active tribe in Alabama today. It has thousands of members in Alabama and surrounding states. According to the 1990 Census, Lawrence County has the highest population of Echota Indian people in Alabama with 6.7% claiming Indian heritage. In the 2000 Census, Lawrence County had the second highest Indian population with 5.2% claiming Indian heritage. The vast majority of Indians in Lawrence County are Echota Cherokees.

The Cherokee Indian people recognize the number "seven" as sacred because of the seven clans and the seven directions it represents. The seven clans of the original Cherokee were: Bird, Wolf, Deer, Paint, Long Hair, Wild Potato, and Blue. Out of these, the Blue Clan represents Lawrence, Walker, and Winston Counties. The seven directions of the Cherokee are East, North, West, South, Up, Down, and from within you as the center (where ever you are) because you are the center of your universe and only you can decide your eventual destiny. The direction you choose is your sacred direction from life to death. Only you can walk in your shoes down your path of life.

As children of mixed ancestry grew older, they were told of their Indian ancestors, but were not allowed to claim their rightful heritage. Since Indian removal, the degree of Indian blood of North Alabama's people has steadily diminished and will continue to do so throughout future generations. With the passage of Section 2 through 7 of the Civil Right Act of 1968, it became legal to be Indian and live in Alabama. Many Indian descendants of mixed ancestry began to seek and reclaim their Indian heritage, but for many it was too late. In 1972, the Indian Education Act passed the U.S. Congress. In 1980, the Echota Cherokee Tribe was organized. In 1986, the Lawrence County Schools' Indian Education Program began. In 1995, the Oakville Indian Mounds Education Center was completed.

LESSON 2 – FAMILY HISTORY AND ANCESTRY

Presently, about one-fifth (20%) of Lawrence County's children are state recognized Indians of mixed-Celtic ancestry and Cherokee, Chickasaw, or Creek bloodlines. As an Indian person, you have a right to claim your race as Indian and should do so, but never deny any of your other previous ancestors of different ethnic backgrounds.

Remarkable advancement of the Cherokee as a people came about largely through the mixing with Celtic families of Irish, Welsh, Scotch, Scots-Irish, and Cornish. During the Indian Removal, mixed-blood inhabitants remained in North Alabama because they were married to whites or were able to identify themselves with white ancestry. They sometimes called themselves Black Dutch or Black Irish in order to remain in the land they loved.

Fearing not only for their personal property but also their lives, the remaining Indian people in North Alabama denied their Indian race, held to white man's ways. As the times changed, both their Indian culture and Celtic culture blended in with the general population. Both cultures became assimilated into the general lifestyle of the North Alabama area.

Review Questions
1. How many clans make up the Echota Cherokee Tribe?
2. Which clan are the Echota Cherokee Indians living in Lawrence County?
3. What are the Indian traits?
4. A Celtic person is:
5. What Indian tribe do most of you or your parents belong?
6. Who was the Cherokee Indian town, Melton's Bluff, named after?
7. Who was one of the most feared, red headed, Cherokee warriors?
8. Celtic families sometimes called themselves what?
9. What is the name of the tribe that most of our Indian students are members?
10. Which Celtic man married three Chickasaw wives?
11. What number is sacred to our Indian ancestors?
12. What are the seven directions?
13. What is the name of a Celtic group?
14. What are the seven clans?
15. What was the name of the town named after John Melton?
16. Did the Civil Rights Act of 1968 make it legal or illegal for Indians to claim their heritage and live in Alabama?
17. Name one ½ Celtic and ½ Indian leader during the 1800's?
18. What is the largest tribe in Alabama today?
19. Explain why mixed-blood inhabitants (Celtic and Indian) called themselves Black Dutch or black Irish during the Indian removal:
20. In order to be an Echota Cherokee tribal member, a person must have at least what amount of Indian blood?

LESSON 2 – FAMILY HISTORY AND ANCESTRY

21. Who was the most feared Celtic Cherokee Warrior?
22. What are some traits of a Celtic Indian?
23. Name the law passed in 1968 that allowed Indians to claim their heritage and live in Alabama?
24. According to the 2000 Census, did Lawrence County have the second or fifth highest Indian population?
25. What tribe was the first to form communities of mixed ancestry?
26. Today, what tribe has thousands of members in Alabama?
27. What is the approximate percentage of Lawrence County's students that are state recognized Indians of mixed Celtic ancestry?
28. What county in Alabama has the largest population of Indian people according to the 1990 U.S. Census?
29. Indians in Alabama are mixed to some degree with what other race?

LESSON 3 – ECHOTA CHEROKEE TRIBE OF ALABAMA

Most North Alabama Indian students are members of the Echota Cherokee Tribe of Alabama, which represents Lawrence County; however, your Indian heritage may come from other tribes. To be a card carrying tribal member, the Echota Cherokee Tribe of Alabama requires at least 1/32 American Indian. In 1980, the Echota Cherokee Tribe of Alabama was formed by people of Cherokee Indian heritage who lived in North Alabama. Lawrence County Schools' Indian Education Program began in 1986 with some 600 Echota Cherokee children enrolled in our program. The Echota Cherokee Tribe of Alabama is recognized by the State of Alabama; therefore, if this is your tribe, you are a state recognized Indian.

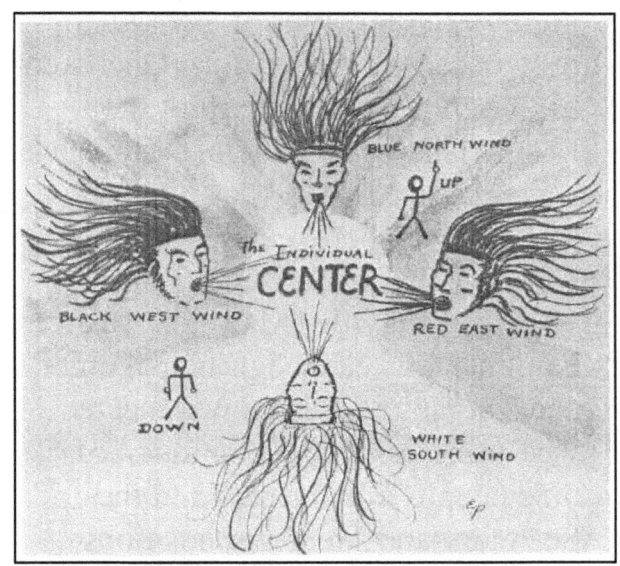

Cherokee Directions

The Echota Cherokee Tribe is the largest and most active tribe in Alabama today. It has thousands of members in Alabama and surrounding states. According to the 1990 Census, Lawrence County had the highest population of Indian people in Alabama with 6.7% claiming Indian heritage. In the 2000 Census, Lawrence County had the second highest Indian population in Alabama with 5.2% claiming Indian heritage. If you are a card carrying tribal member, you should always count yourself as Indian on the U.S. Census which is taken every 10 years.

The Cherokee Indian people recognize the number seven as sacred because of the seven clans and the seven directions it represents. The seven clans of the original Cherokee were: Bird, Wolf, Deer, Paint, Long Hair, Wild Potato, and Blue. Out of these, the Blue Clan represents Lawrence, Walker, and Winston Counties. The seven directions of the Cherokee are East (Red), North (Blue), West (Black), South (White), Up (Yellow), Down (Green), and from within you as the center (where ever you are) because you are the center of your universe and only you can decide your eventual destiny.

Most North Alabama Indian students are members of the Echota Cherokee Tribe and is the reason they are allowed to attend Indian education classes. It is very important to realize that we are people of mixed ancestry, usually Celtic and Indian. Anytime a question of race is brought up or asked, you should identify yourself as Indian and identify your tribe. Be

LESSON 3 – ECHOTA CHEROKEE TRIBE OF ALABAMA

proud to claim your Indian ancestry, but also be proud of your other lineage and other ethnic backgrounds.

The word Echota was originally derived from the over-hill town of our Cherokee Indian ancestors known as Chota. Chota was located on the Little Tennessee River in Monroe County of East Tennessee. Chota was the capitol of the Cherokee Nation until white settlers forced the Cherokees south and west into southeast Tennessee, northwest Georgia, and northeast Alabama. By 1800, all the Cherokees were forced out of the valley of the Little Tennessee River which they had called home for hundreds of years. The capital of the Cherokees was moved into northwest Georgia and was called New Echota. Since most of our Indian people were descendants of the Cherokees who lived in Cherokee County that comprised the northwestern quarter of Georgia, our tribe chose the name of the Cherokee capital of New Echota; thus, the Echota Cherokee Tribe of Alabama was organized.

The United Cherokee Tribe of Alabama was organized on June 14, 1978, at Daleville, Alabama. B. J. Faulkner was elected principal chief, and Thomas McCloski was elected vice-principal chief. A council of nine people was formed, and the Secretary and Treasurer positions were filled.

In 1978, Chief Faulkner opposed the development plans for an industrial park near Northport that would disturb a 1,000-year-old Indian village site and burial ground. In January of 1980, he sought the reburial of 3,000 Indians along the route to be flooded by the Tennessee - Tombigbee Waterway. In 1980, disenchanted members of the United Cherokee Tribe of Alabama formed a new tribe called Echota Cherokee Tribe, Inc.

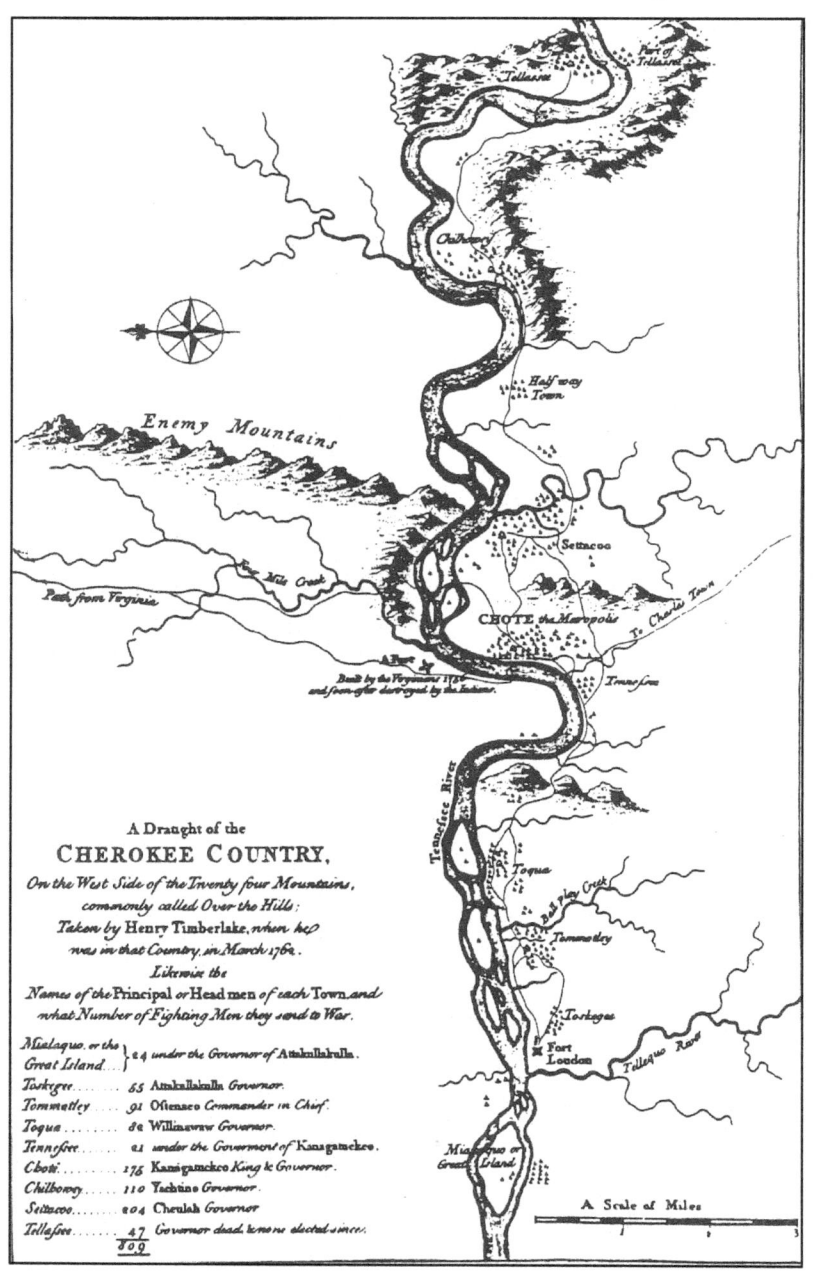

Map of Chota on the Little Tennessee River

LESSON 3 – ECHOTA CHEROKEE TRIBE OF ALABAMA

Joseph "Two Eagles" Stewart was elected principal chief, and Letter of Incorporation was filed in Shelby County and their seal was registered. The tribe filed for and received non-profit status and clans were organized over the State. A newsletter, "Smoke Signals", was mailed to members. Regular monthly meetings were held at the Alabaster Community Center. The governing body of the tribe, consisting of tribal council members, elected officers, principal chief and vice-principal chief, was set in to serve a four-year term. (Cromer, 1984)

Indian students enjoy friendship dance at annual Multicultural Event

The tribe has a land fund established for the purpose of purchasing land to build a Cherokee meeting ground and museum. Tribal members are active in voter registration drives around the state. The tribe, represented by the principal chief, is a member of the Alabama Indian Affairs Commission and the National Congress of American Indian (Cromer, 1984). The vast majority of North Alabama Indian students are members of the Echota Cherokee Tribe of Alabama.

Today, the Echota Cherokee Tribe of Alabama has their office on tribal land just south of Falkville, Alabama. The tribe is affiliated with several Indian education programs in Madison County, DeKalb County, Jackson County, and Lawrence County. These counties comprised historic Cherokee lands in the Tennessee Valley.

One of the most common characteristics of the true Warrior Mountains Celtic Indian people that are members of the Echota Cherokee Tribe is the direct line of descent from the Chickasaw, Cherokee, or Creek originating around the 1830's just prior to the Great Removal. Another common occurrence was the intermarriage within family units, where cousins married cousins, sisters of one family married brothers of another family, two different families intermarried over several years, and children from the same mother and different fathers took the mother's last name. One would be amazed at the number of people having the same great-grandparents on two sides of their family. An original Warrior Mountain Celtic-Indian, who is at least a quarter blood Indian, will many times have the same great-grandparents on more than one side of the family.

Another common thread is the migration of their Celtic ancestors from the Carolinas, to Georgia or Tennessee, and then into Alabama. Intermarriage between Celtic and Indian

LESSON 3 – ECHOTA CHEROKEE TRIBE OF ALABAMA

people most often occurred in the Carolinas, East Tennessee, North Georgia, and Northeast Alabama, which made up the Cherokee Nation until 1838.

The remnants of the Warrior Mountain Celtic Indian mixed-bloods survive in North Alabama under common family names. Today, the most common occurrence of surnames of Indian children in Lawrence County Schools are: Alexander, Black, Blankenship, Borden, Bradford, Dutton, England, Gillespie, Green(e), Hill, Hood, Jackson, Johnson, Jones, Kerby, Kelsoe, LouAllen, Owens, Parker, Riddle, Rutherford, Smith, Terry, Walker, White, and many other family names not as prevalent.

Review Questions

1. What tribe is the largest and most active in Alabama today?
2. Where is the capital, New Echota, located?
3. What river in North Alabama did our Cherokee ancestors live?
4. What are the seven clans of the Cherokee?
5. What are the seven directions of the Cherokee?
6. A person with mixed ancestry is part Celtic and what?
7. What is the name of the Cherokee capital located in Georgia?
8. What year was the Echota Cherokee Tribe formed?
9. What number is considered sacred to the Cherokee?
10. What is mixed ancestry?
11. How many Indians had to be reburied along the route of the Tennessee-Tombigbee Waterway?
12. What form of government recognizes the Echota Cherokee Tribe?

LESSON 4 – PERIODS OF PREHISTORIC INDIANS

Prehistoric Periods

Paleo Indians - The oldest group of people or the first known group to live in Alabama were called Paleo Indians because "Paleo" means "early" or "earliest". Paleo people were hunters.

- Cave dwellers
- Meat eaters
- Lived and traveled in small bands
- Spear points long and narrow with fluted sides
- More Paleo points found in Alabama than in western states
- Pleistocene overkill
- Lived on Tennessee River Valley of Lawrence County

Archaic Indians - The next group of people was called Archaic because that is a term commonly used to describe an early stage in the development of a civilization. Archaic Indian people were hunters and gatherers of wild food.

- Semi-permanent settlements
    a) Rivers during summer
    b) Caves, bluff shelters, and mountainous areas during winter
- Meat eaters and gatherers
- Foods: mussels (shell mounds), deer, acorns, and nuts
- Form of religion (burial of dead)
- Atlatl important weapon (throwing spears)
- Made soapstone and sandstone bowls
- First pottery made from clay
- Hides used as clothing
- Used hunting dogs
- Lived all over Lawrence County

Woodland Indians - The third group is called Woodland simply because that group lived in the eastern woodland section of North America. Woodland Indian people were hunters and gatherers, and they also built burial mounds, made pottery, and to a small degree practiced agriculture.

- Lived in more permanent settlements
- Improved pottery
- Began hunting with bow and arrow
- Meat eaters, gatherers, and farmers
- Grew and stored many vegetables

LESSON 4 – PERIODS OF PREHISTORIC INDIANS

- Began elaborate religious customs
- Mound building, Copena
- Most abundant points found in Lawrence County

Mississippian Indians - The fourth group of people or the last prehistoric group to live in Alabama were called Mississippian because archaeologists first identified its culture along the Mississippi Valley. Mississippian Indian people built platform mounds as bases for the buildings of their priests and rulers, made a distinctive kind of pottery, and, for food, depended heavily on agriculture. It was the Mississippian Indians that Desoto found when he came to Alabama in 1540.

- Permanent towns, fortified settlements and religious centers
- Fine pottery
- Excellent farmers---potatoes, corn, squash and beans
- Bow and arrow became very important weapon
- Small game hunted: deer, raccoons, turkeys, beavers, pigeons, opossums, mussels
- Mussel Shoals in Lawrence County on the Tennessee River extremely important

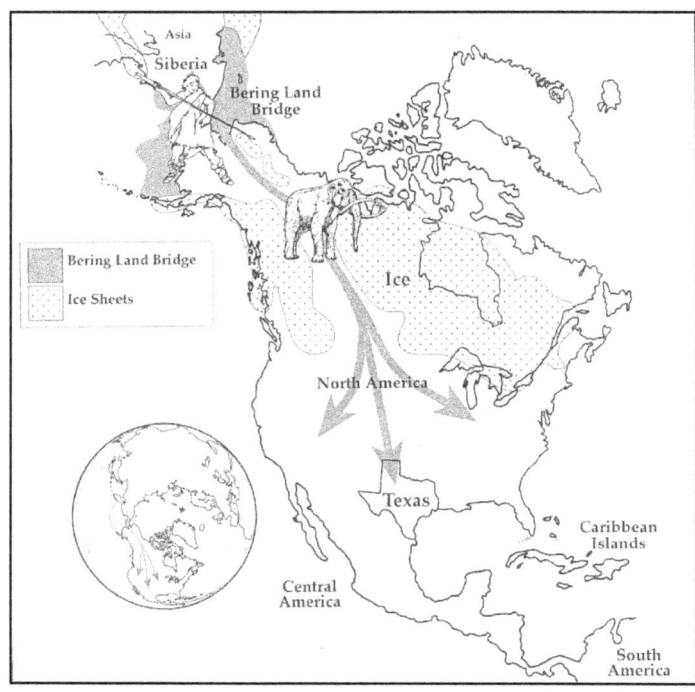

Beringa migration into America

Paleo - Our early Indian people lived during a period called "Paleo". About 12,000 years ago, Indian people and their families lived here in North Alabama, but they lived differently than we live today. They could not go to the grocery store for food or to the mall for clothes.

QUESTION: Where do you think our early ancestors got their food? (animals, berries, roots). Where do you think they got their clothes? (animal hides and woven plant fibers).

After a group of Indian people had lived in the same place for a while, they soon had to move because they had hunted all the animals around and they had eaten all the berries and roots; therefore, they had to move to look for more. What did they look for? (animals, nuts, berries, roots, and other foods). The early Paleo Indian people were called *nomads* because they *moved* around looking for food and animals. They came from a continent called Asia into North America. They followed the animals across a huge land bridge called the Bering Strait and known as Beringa.

LESSON 4 – PERIODS OF PREHISTORIC INDIANS

Today, we are going to learn about our very first Indian ancestors. They were called Paleo Indians. They came across the land bridge called the Beringa in the Bering Strait, from Asia. They were nomadic which meant they wandered from place to place searching for food. Around 12,000 years ago, Paleo Indians were living along the Tennessee River in Alabama; therefore, our Indian ancestors have been here thousands of years.

The Paleo Indians were hunters and meat eaters. They hunted large ice age animals like the mammoth, mastodons, wild horses, and saber-toothed tigers. The Paleo Indians usually traveled and lived in small bands. Typical bands were usually 20 to 25 people who were generally related. Both men and women within the band had particular jobs. Men were responsible for the preparation of tools and weapons as well as hunting. Women were responsible for childcare, crafts and cooking. The Paleo Indians did not live in permanent settlements, but were nomadic and moved from camp to camp. They located their camps where they could find plenty of animals--their primary source of food. Their shelters were natural caves and bluffs as well as lean-tos and skin tents.

The Paleo Indians were known as big game hunters. They hunted large animals by driving them into traps, over cliffs, or into enclosures. When hunting the animals, someone would distract the animal while others attacked with their weapons. Because of a lack of transportation and refrigeration, the animal had to be butchered on the spot and often eaten raw.

The early Indian people hunted the big wooly mammoths by driving them into traps and over big cliffs. After the animal was killed the Indians would cut the animal up with stone knives and eat it immediately. Some of it they would carry back to the village and use different parts to make clothes from animal skins. The brains were used to tan the hides and smooth the animal skins to make them soft.

After the animal was killed, all parts of the animal were used. Brains and bone marrow of the animals were eaten. Brains were used in curing the skins for use as clothing. Although the Paleo Indians are commonly recognized as big game hunters, they also included a wide variety of plants and animal foods in the diet.

The spear was probably the Indians' first weapon--The spear was made from flint rock that had been sharpened and attached to a long handle. Also, the early Indians hunted wild horses, camels, giant ground sloths, saber tooth tigers, rhinoceroses, deer, and bison; some of which are not extinct.

The Paleo Indians made spears from flint. They used a rock to chip off pieces until they formed a sharp point. The flakes of the flint stones were often ready to use as knives.

LESSON 4 – PERIODS OF PREHISTORIC INDIANS

Scrapers were made from the flakes by chipping a steep cutting edge. The scraper was used to prepare the hides. The scraper was also used in working wood, bone, and antler. Gravers were tools of small flakes with one or more finely chipped, delicate points. The gravers may have been used for engraving. Gravers were also used for punching small holes in skins to allow them to be laced together to make clothing and other equipment. The Paleo Indians had no known stone or ceramic vessels, but probably had baskets. Much evidence of Paleo habitation is found all across North Alabama, especially along the Tennessee River.

Now close your eyes and imagine how life was back then. Imagine how you would look, what you would eat, how you would live. Can someone tell me what this place would look like? Now, keep in mind that we are talking about a very long time ago. Have a picture of Bering Strait when they open their eyes and tell about Beringa.

Explain that our ancient Indian people walked from Asia to North America by a land bridge known as Beringa or the Bering Strait, which was covered with ice. If you went there today you would have to travel by water. Most of the land at that time was covered with ice.

The Paleo Indian people had to move each time the herd did. As you know, some of these animals are now extinct. How do you think they killed such large animals? Some members of the tribe could distract the animals while others would kill it. Another way would be to drive them over cliffs, drive them into traps or into enclosed areas.

Remember, we are talking about a long time ago. Sometimes, when the animals were killed, they were eaten on the spot because they didn't have refrigerators to keep the food from ruining and most often the meat was eaten raw. The meat they could carry and store was dried or placed in cool caves, underground, or in the cold spring water. Although, we are talking about a pre-historic time and a pre-historic people, they were very intelligent. They knew how to use every part of the animal. (Example: brains and bone marrow to eat). How many of you have eaten pig brains? Brains were also used to cure and tan skins, which were used for clothes. They also used bones for different tools and weapons.

For each time period that we cover, a different style of projectile point was used. Who knows what a point is? (stone projectile point-on end of spear or arrow. Show picture of Paleo points. Describe Paleo points--they have curved indentation on top that have been ground down smooth. They have a fluted depression, which is a groove out of the middle point.)

Spear points were made by the flaking process. First, a flat surface was made, using a hammerstone, they knocked off the edge of the flat stone making a long and narrow flake, which was razor sharp. Some of the tools made with flint included scrapers, knives, and gravers. Paleo Indians had no stone or ceramic vessels such as bowls, but they probably had

LESSON 4 – PERIODS OF PREHISTORIC INDIANS

baskets. Clovis points were named for a town called Clovis, New Mexico. These points have also been found throughout the Tennessee Valley.

Archaic - The last section we studied was the Paleo period. Today, we're studying about the Archaic period and how they were different. Based on artifacts, archaic people lived throughout North Alabama. They were the people who discarded mussel shells that eventually formed shell middens along the Tennessee River. The Archaic Indian people were forced to adapt to new and changing food sources, because the climate was beginning to get warmer. Although, the Archaic Indians continued to hunt, they no longer hunted large ice age animals.

Near the end of the Ice Age as the earth began to warm, the Archaic people no longer wandered over great areas. The mammoths and mastodons began to die out. The Archaic people were forced to change their eating habits. They became more of a gatherer than just a hunter. Now they found plants with nuts, seeds, roots, and berries, and they found other meats of animals such as deer, rabbit, mussel, fish, and squirrel. Deer became the most important game animal to Indians in this area. Chestnuts and acorns became important food sources for Archaic people as well as the deer. Chestnuts and acorns could be ground to make flour.

The change from eating Ice Age animals to smaller animals, nuts, and berries led to new methods of preparing the food. Nuts were cracked and picked, seeds and roots were ground, and even bark was beaten for fiber to eat. There are many more methods that were used in the production of foods.

Stone boiling was used to cook their food. They would heat rocks in the fire and then move them to a pit, which was lined with rawhide and filled with water. A soup mixture in this rawhide bowl was boiled by the hot rocks. Mortar, pestles, stone bowls, and nutting stones were some utensils used.

The largest animals hunted by the Archaic Indians were elk and bear. Other game was deer, rabbits, squirrel, wild turkey, fish, mussels, and grub worms. Also, they became gatherers of nuts, berries, seeds, roots, and other plants. Acorns became an important food, since they learned a method of making flour from the nuts. In addition, the American chestnut, which was destroyed by blight in the 1930s, was a major source of food to our Southeastern Indian ancestors. The American chestnut was the largest nut-producing tree in North America.

During the Archaic period, mussels became an important source of food. Mussels are found on riverbanks inside a shell. The Mussel Shoals starting in Lawrence County near Mallard Creek in the Tennessee River contained more mussels than any place in the world. This area consisted of four major Mussel Shoals: Elk River Shoals; Big Mussel Shoals; Little Mussel

LESSON 4 – PERIODS OF PREHISTORIC INDIANS

Shoals; and Colbert Shoals. Two other Shoals that could be navigated were Bee Tree Shoals and Waterloo Shoals.

Discarded mussel shells formed midden along with flood deposits which created shell mounds. Shell mounds became incidental burial spots. The mounds were created by centuries of activity. Many large shell mounds bigger than football fields were flooded by Wilson and Wheeler Dams on the Tennessee River.

Archaic people possessed a common burial ground. They were very careful with their dead implying emotions of strong affections as well as a belief in an afterlife. Sometime personal possessions were placed with the body (weapons, tools, or even bodies of their dogs). The graves were small circular pits dug into the shell mounds. The graves must have been marked in some way since they were seldom disturbed until later digging. These circular pits were usually sealed with a mud putty mixture consisting of clay, ash, and shell.

Archaic Indians developed new weapons, tools and utensils. The atlatl, a throwing lever, was probably the greatest improvement in weaponry. This allowed the hunter to throw a spear with greater force from a farther distance. The atlatl, or throwing stick, was made from wood, 2-3 ft. long with a deer bone or antler hook. There was a rock placed in the center of the throwing stick called a banner stone. The banner stone was either fixed or moved freely to give the spear more power. The spear was placed on the throwing stick against the antler hook. A quick flip of the lever gave the spear great power and distance.

The Archaic Indians also found it necessary to develop new weapons, tools and utensils as well as ornaments. One of the great weapon improvements was the Atlatl (At-lat-l). It allowed the hunter of the Archaic period to throw a long distance and with more force. A weight was placed in the middle of the throwing stick to give added power. The hunter held the spear resting on the atlatl and against the notched end; then he lifted the atlatl over his shoulder and with a whip like motion, sent the spear hurtling toward the target.

Archaic Indians had distinct characteristics. They seldom lived to be middle age and most died in their twenties and thirties. In appearance, there were at least two distinct types of Indian.

1. One was broad-headed, broad-faced, squared jaw and had a narrow, high-bridged nose.

LESSON 4 – PERIODS OF PREHISTORIC INDIANS

2. The other type had a narrower and longer head, a narrow face and was generally less rugged in bone structure.
3. The women had a more jutting jaw than the men and were smaller in size.

Archaic Indian people were probably the first to domesticate dogs. Skeletons of rather large dogs, possibly hunting dogs, have been discovered in burial sites. A need for material not found locally led to increased trade as well as social and religious interaction.

During each time period, changes occurred in the environment and also in Indian lifestyles. With each passing period, American Indian people became more civilized and settled. The Archaic people settled along the Tennessee River and consumed large quantities of fresh water mussels. The discarded mussel shells eventually formed large shell middens or heaps. These middens or heaps of shells became the first mounds to be built in North Alabama.

There is evidence of religion among Archaic Indians. The medicine man used a tube pipe for curing illness. Burials were accompanied with animals, possessions or ornaments. Burials indicate a form of religion. They felt the medicine man was a direct link to the Great Spirit.

Many of the tools were made from flint as in the Paleo period. Flint tools were used to work antler, bone, and hides. Flint could be sharpened for knives and scrapers. Also, it could be ground into a point to make a drill and a variety of weapon points. Fishnets, spears, traps, and hook and line were used to catch fish. Fishhooks were made from deer toe bones. Traps were made by weaving reeds and oak splints. Nets were made by fibers from plants. To create spears, cane was used with sharpened points.

In the late Archaic period, they began making pottery. For the first time, early man had lightweight waterproof containers to store food and water. With pottery, the Indian people were able to stabilize their food supply and settle in more permanent areas. The grooved ax was developed during the archaic time period from rocks tied to a wooden shaft. These axes were used to drive stakes, chop meat, dress hides, break animal bones for marrow, and chop charcoal from burned trees.

Projectile points during the Archaic period were unique because they were beveled, sharp on one side only, serrated on edges (depression), and notched end.

Woodland - We are learning about a more advanced period of our Indian ancestors. They are known as the Woodland Indian people. It is believed the Middle Woodland Indians, about the time of Jesus Christ, built the Oakville Mounds in Lawrence County.

LESSON 4 – PERIODS OF PREHISTORIC INDIANS

The third era of prehistoric time is called the Woodland period. The Woodland Indians were more advanced and lived in smaller settlements, which were more permanent than those of the Archaic period. Improvement of pottery, led to cooking by boiling. The saving, storing, and sowing of seeds to ensure the next years harvest encouraged the growth of more permanent groups of people. Based on artifacts, the Woodland people were very abundant in the Lawrence County area.

Ample food supply encouraged the growth of people living in towns and hamlets. Hamlets were farming families who shared hunting and gathering grounds. Towns had a market, a religious place, and administrative office. The Woodlands had a more formalized leadership. The local and regional leaders guided religion and settled disputes. In the beginning, leaders earned their leadership. Later, these leadership skills were passed to children.

Early Woodland Indians were farmers, gatherers, and hunters. Farmers grew gourds, beans, potatoes, squash, and corn. Vegetables could be stored or traded; therefore, surplus became possible. Storing and saving food allowed the people more time for trade, crafts, politics, or religion. Vegetables could be traded or easily stored in clay pots.

Burial customs were important to Woodland Indians. People were often buried with their personal possessions. A warrior was buried with weapons. A farmer was buried with agricultural tools. A woman was buried with household items. The grooved stone axes were replaced with ungrooved ones. Human skulls were one of their most treasured cult symbols.

During Woodland time, dugout canoes were made from yellow poplar or yellow pine. Poplar was more common because termites would not eat the poplar wood. The dugouts enabled Woodland people to travel on water for the first time and increase their trade routes. During the process of making a dugout canoe, the stone axes were used. Dugout canoes were made with a burning and scraping process. First, the tree was selected and clay was packed at the base of the tree. A fire was then started to burn the tree down. The ax was used to chip away the charred wood. It was also used to dig out the opening to the canoe . Some of the other tools used during the Woodland period were stone hoes, deer bone scrapers, grindstones, and flaked tools. The bow and arrow gradually replaced the spear as a hunting weapon.

Near their secluded village sites, the Woodland people constructed burial mounds to hold their dead. These relatively small mounds, often conical in shape, were sometimes near a river. Frequently there were two or more such mounds together. The number of burials in a mound varied from one to several dozen. Some were single interments; however, others were multiple burials on the same or different prepared surfaces. Some of the burial mounds were constructed over a period of time and built up in several layers. Occasionally shells,

LESSON 4 – PERIODS OF PREHISTORIC INDIANS

Cherokee town of Chota around 1762 (Tellico Archaeology)

clay, logs, or stone slabs separated the layers or were placed around the individual or mass graves. A prominent feature of this specialized burial custom was the placement of ornaments and tools with the bodies.

The tools and ornaments of the Woodland people were similar to those of the Archaic cultures, but they were more varied and often showed finer workmanship. Their tools included chipped drills, knives, celts, scrapers, axes, and a variety of smaller projectile points. The projectile points made during the Woodland period were stem based and cruder looking (example--Swan Lake or Bakers Creek).

Mississippian - They were a more advanced group, but the Mississippians improved all phases of life. Based on Mississippian artifacts, these people lived throughout North Alabama but seemed to be most abundant along the creeks and streams. The population increased and towns were larger and more permanent. The Mississippians were also known as the mound builders because all important religious practices were associated with their mounds. The Mississippians were known for their decorated pottery and stone pipes.

The last prehistoric time period we will cover is the Mississippian period. It was unique because of the distinctive form of pottery made with crushed shells and clay. During the Mississippian, the people became much more organized in their government and lifestyle. Houses became permanent structures made from cut saplings and branches. Religious ceremonies were connected with agriculture production. In other words, they had

LESSON 4 – PERIODS OF PREHISTORIC INDIANS

ceremonies for planting and harvesting foods. The Mississippian culture had planned communities. People were living in villages with public buildings, stockades, and plazas. Fortified settlements appeared during this time period. Wooden stockades surrounded the fort and often dry moats were built with thorn hedges placed in these.

Their houses contained only a single room measuring about 16 feet by 16 feet. Cane mats were used to divide the room. The houses had a hearth and sleeping benches that served as sofas. There was a centrally located fireplace to provide warmth in winter and protection from insects in the summer. The houses were formed by placing cut saplings in trenches and pulling over at the top to form a roof. The walls were woven with cut branches, covered with clay, and the roof was covered with grass or bark. The cooking was done outside or in a cooking shed.

The Mississippian people were involved in long distance trade. Fortified settlements appeared during the Mississippian period. The Indian mound at Florence, Alabama was a fortified village.

Religious ceremonies were very important to the Mississippian Indians. In early times, family members were buried in a shallow hole in the floor of the house with each burial, the floor rose higher. Ceremonial pipes were among the most sacred possessions of a tribe. The pipe was carved from stone and decorated with animals or human figures. The ceremonial pipe was passed around the council and each member took a puff before handing the pipe to the person on his left. The pipe came to be referred to as a peace pipe because they often smoked with former enemies as a peace treaty was made. Another belief relating to the spirit world concerns the black drink. It was brewed like tea from the leaves of the holly plant. The black drink contained large amounts of caffeine and when heated and drunk in large quantities caused vomiting. They believed that by emptying their stomachs, they rid themselves of evil.

Indian people considered the land sacred and could not be bought or sold. This idea was difficult for the white man to understand. Indians believed that tobacco was a sacred plant. They believed it was a gift from the spirit world with mystical powers. They smoked to ward off evil spirits. They smoked to curb appetites and cure infection. They smoked before they waged war.

The most important ceremony was the Green Corn Ceremony. The festival was like our Thanksgiving and New Year rolled into one. It was a time to give thanks for a successful harvest, to settle differences, and to begin a new year.

Games were an important part of Indian culture. Indians spent much of their time farming. They grew corn, beans, squash, pumpkins, and sweet potatoes. Art forms were more

LESSON 4 – PERIODS OF PREHISTORIC INDIANS

advanced than that of the previous culture.

Mounds were built around the plaza with some for temples and some for burial. The temples were usually divided into two rooms and contained images of animals or birds on the entrance. One room was for worship and one for burials. The Southern Indians believed the universe was made of three separate but related worlds - the upper world, lower world, and this world.

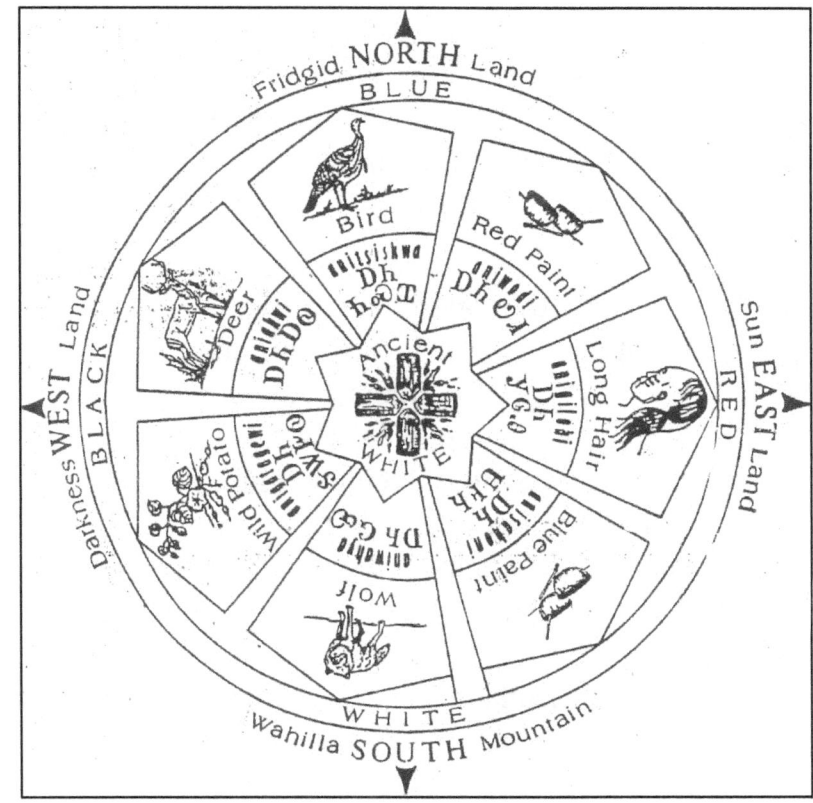

During ceremonies each of the four directions were recognized.
1. East was associated with the color red, according to the Cherokee doctrine, because it was the direction of the rising sun. East was also associated with the sacred fire, blood, and the color of success.
2. North was the direction of the cold winds of winter and its color was blue (sometimes purple) and it represented trouble and defeat.
3. West was the moon segment and because it was associated with the setting of the sun and the absence of warmth, it was thus associated with the color black, which was the region of the souls and of death itself.
4. South was the direction of the warm winter sun, its color was white, and it was associated with peace and happiness.

Vegetables, wild fruits, nuts, wild animals, and fish were main sources of food. Hunting took second place to farming. Indians grew corn, beans, squash, pumpkins, potatoes, and sweet potatoes. They also gathered nuts, seeds, roots, and fruits and stored them.

The men showed skill in stalking and killing game. Fishing was done with spears and arrows, but most often by dragging seines made of brush fastened together with vines. Seine means to drag the bottom of a lake or pond with a net to get the fish out.

Clothing of the Mississippian was very decorative. Among the Southeastern Indians, young children ran unclothed until their tenth or twelfth birthday. This was accepted in their society just as wearing clothes are expected in our society.

LESSON 4 – PERIODS OF PREHISTORIC INDIANS

Mississippian religious symbols were engraved, painted and sculptured on shells and dyed cloth. The points during this time period were small and triangular because hunting was second to farming. The bow and arrow were the primary weapons. The Mississippi triangles were the most prevalent point during this time period.

Review Questions

1. What did the Paleo people live in?
2. What group used dogs for hunting?
3. What group grew and stored vegetables?
4. What group were excellent farmers?
5. What group hunted ice age animals?
6. What time period used the bow and arrow?
7. Which was the most advanced time period?
8. What did the Woodland Indians hunt with?
9. What custom was considered important to the Woodland Indians?
10. Name one characteristic about the Paleo Indians?
11. Who lived in permanent towns?
12. What is the Green Corn Ceremony?
13. What period of early Indians were farmers, gatherers, and hunters?
14. What period of early Indians were known as mound builders (Explain why)?
15. What is one characteristic of the Mississippian people?
16. What style of projectile point was most prevalent during the Mississippian period?
17. Which group of Indians did Desoto find when he came to Alabama in 1540?
18. What did the Archaic people live in?
19. What group improved pottery?
20. Who had fortified settlements?
21. Name the four prehistoric time periods in order from the oldest?
22. What group used the spear as a weapon?

LESSON 5 – LIFESTYLES OF EARLY INDIAN PEOPLE

There were five Indian tribes of early North Alabama. They were the Yuchi, Creek, Shawnee, Chickasaw, and Cherokee. The Creek, Chickasaw, and Cherokee all lived for a long time in North Alabama. The Cherokee and the Chickasaws both lived in the northern part of our state and shared their land.

Early Cherokee Houses

Indian people were from different tribes but they were a lot alike. Many people think that Indian people just went to war and hunted, but they did much more than that. Every village had big gardens. Men and women both worked in the garden and the food was for everyone in the village. Can anyone tell me what they think our Indian ancestors probably grew? (potatoes, corn, and beans). After working in the gardens, the men and women had different jobs. The men would hunt, build buildings, and make weapons and tools to work with. The women raised children, cooked and made clothing.

Some of the Cherokees that moved into North Alabama had big farms with lots of livestock. They also planted crops for money such as cotton and corn. The Cherokee Chief Doublehead owned a lot of livestock and had some 40 slaves at the time of his death.

Settlements - Our Cherokee Indian people lived in houses not tipis. They had two types of houses: a summer house-"ge-tsa'di" and a winter house-"asi'." The summer house was like a long shed built from small trees, which they lived in during the hot summer months (show picture). The winter house, also built from logs, had a cone shaped roof. Clay was packed on the outside of the logs to fill in the cracks and keep out the cold air. A fire was built in the center of the room with beds lining the walls.

The Cherokee of North Alabama lived in farming villages which consisted of either log cabins or plank houses. These Cherokees were living similar to the settlers with houses containing chimneys and fireplaces.

Cherokee Parents - Cherokee fathers were responsible for providing food by hunting and fishing. He also made tools and weapons and helped protect his family and village. The mother tended the garden, cooked, made clothes, made crafts, cleaned the house and raised

LESSON 5 – LIFESTYLES OF EARLY INDIAN PEOPLE

the children. The children were primarily the responsibility of the mother. The mother disciplined the girls and was responsible for their up-bringing. The elders of the village took responsibility for the care and instruction of the boys. Traditionally, boys were disciplined by the oldest uncle of the mother's family, not their father.

Cherokee Indian Family

The Cherokee mother had more responsibility in the upbringing of the children than the father. Why do you think that the mother was responsible more than the father? The father was busy hunting, farming and sometimes defending his village. The mother was at the village cooking and making clothes for the family. Indian girls were disciplined by their mothers and the boys were disciplined by their uncle which was the mother's brother.

The Cherokee Indians believed that the children were only kin to the mother's family, probably, because the mother gave birth to her children. The woman owned the home. Today, our mothers and fathers are equal in the raising of the family.

When Cherokees moved into North Alabama, many Cherokee women were married to Celtic traders of Scotch, Irish, or Scots-Irish ancestry. The Celtic men tried to teach the children the ways of the Europeans. Most all of you are descendants of these people.

Cherokee Clan - The clan was a unit of family, kin folks, or relatives and the most important aspect in the life of our Cherokee people. A person belonged to his mother's clan. His only kinsmen were those who could be traced through his mother. The most important and powerful man in a Cherokee's life was his mother's brother. The maternal uncle was responsible for the discipline of his sister's child. The uncle was the one who taught the child to hunt and wage war. The woman owned the dwellings. An ousted husband simply went back to his clan until he remarried. His children remained with his wife.

Since kinship was matrilineal, Cherokee women probably decided the matter of adoption and often had the power to determine the fate of captives. The Beloved Woman, Nancy Ward, saved the life of Mrs. William Bean who was about to be burned at the stake. The

LESSON 5 – LIFESTYLES OF EARLY INDIAN PEOPLE

Cherokee extended the same privileges to those who married or were adopted into the tribe as those who were born into the tribe.

Mary Hughes eventually married her husband's murderer and refused to leave the tribe even after she was ransomed. Twenty boys captured during the French and Indian War cried and refused to eat when they were returned to their families. Some captives were never adopted into a clan. These people, called the atsi nahsa'i, had no personal or legal protection. Their very existence depended on their master's good will.

Clan membership was essential to one's existence as a human being within the Cherokee society. Since clans were divided into peace or war clans, a Cherokee's clan determined his political alignment and his role in society.

Children's Toys and Games - Cherokee girls had dolls made of cornhusks and the boys had other toys like balls and shells. They also had dogs to play with. The children played games. Usually the games helped develop skills that could be used later on: counting and throwing, for example. At the first Thanksgiving feast in 1621, Indian people there taught the settlers their games, and together they raced, wrestled, sang, and danced.

Deer - How many of you have a dad or granddad that likes to hunt? What kind of animals do they hunt? (example: deer, rabbit, raccoons, squirrel, birds) Have any of you ever seen a deer? Where? (zoo, forest) Long ago, our Indian ancestors hunted many different kinds of animals for survival. Deer was their main source of meat and hides (skins). When a Cherokee hunter killed a deer he always asked its spirit for pardon (this was to show honor). During early European settlement, long rifles were used by our metis Indian people to exploit a trade in deer skins. Thirty deer skins could be traded for a new rifle.

Our Cherokee people not only used the deer for food and clothing, they used all different parts of the deer to make tools and weapons. The points of antlers were used to make wedges to pry things apart, to split wood into thin layers for basket making, and to chip flint arrowheads. Antlers were also used to make garden rakes.

Deer bones were made into scrapers, needles, awls, and fishhooks. Bone scrapers had many uses. Deer jaws could be used to scrape green corn from the cob. This tool was used to take the hair from hides being tanned. Bone needles were made from the ribs. They were large, flat, and curved. The hole was in the middle. These were used for sewing rush mats. Fine pointed bone awls were used for embroidery stitches and sewing clothing.

Fishhooks were made from round deer bones. First, the bones were sliced with flint knives. Then, the slice was cut into two half-inch circles. Each half was rubbed on sandstone until it

LESSON 5 – LIFESTYLES OF EARLY INDIAN PEOPLE

was shaped and sharpened. Other fishhooks were made from bone splinters. They were much easier to make than the rounded ones.

Can anyone tell me what glue is used for? (to hold things together). Our Indian folks made glue from boiled deer hooves. This glue was used to secure sinew. Sinews (or tendons) are the tough fibers that hold a muscle to a bone. The long band of sinew was taken from a deer leg or from the top of the deer's back. It was dried to use as thread. Sinew was used for making moccasins, bowstrings, arrows, and to hold axes to their handles.

Warrior Mountains - We are going to talk about a very special place! A place filled with majestic mountains, peaceful valleys, and very special people. Let's talk about some special features of the Bankhead Forest, also called the Warrior Mountains, which is a national forest. Sometimes we don't stop to think about how lucky we are to have a national forest near our home. The Bankhead Forest serves many purposes for us here in North Alabama.

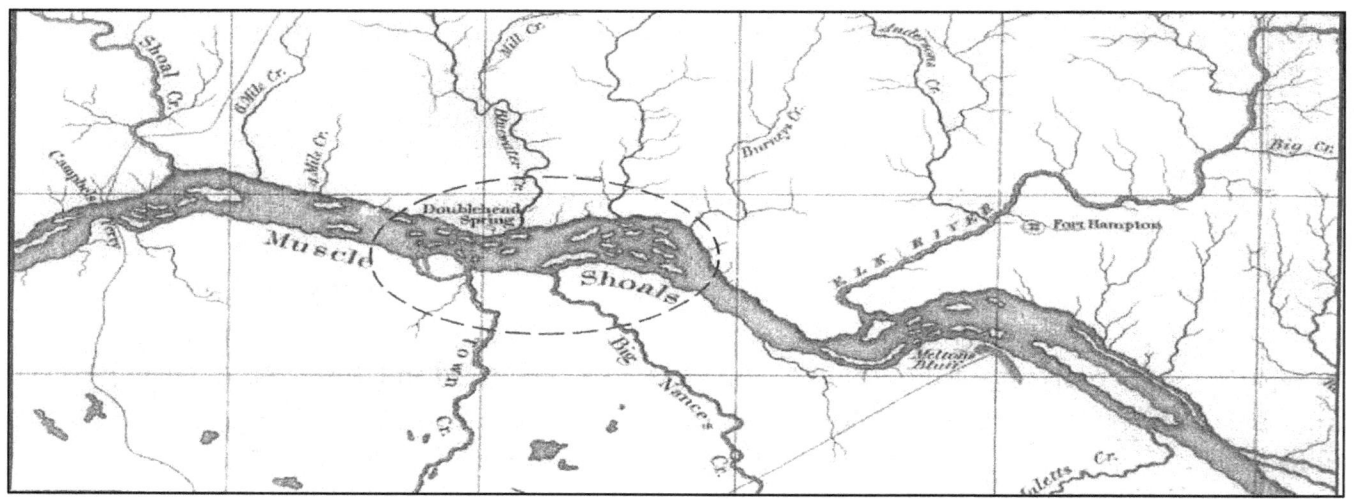

Map of Shoal Town on Big Muscle Shoals

Our Indian ancestors also enjoyed the mountains and their beauty, but more importantly they needed the mountains for their survival. The mountains had natural caves and bluffs that provided shelter for our Indian people. Many prehistoric bluff shelters exist throughout the county, but mainly in the Warrior Mountains. Many sites of prehistoric Indian villages have been found in North Alabama. Bluff shelters, usually facing a southern direction, were used during winter months. Numerous bluff shelters are located in Bankhead National Forest where the gathering of nuts, fruits, and other foods were practicable. Some of the many bluff shelters in Bankhead National Forest are known as Kinlock, McDougal, and Corral. Petroglyphs (rock drawings) are found on rocks in some shelters. A total of 237 Indian sites were identified in Wheeler Basin. These sites give insight into the times and lifestyles of Indians that once lived in and around the North Alabama area.

LESSON 5 – LIFESTYLES OF EARLY INDIAN PEOPLE

Mussel Shoals - Many of the early stone tools used by Indian people were chipped and flaked from flint found at Elk River Shoals and Big Muscle Shoals. The Tennessee River played an important part in providing the things our ancestors needed to survive. The Tennessee River was used as a major transportation route through North Alabama. From the river, the early man could obtain a great variety of plants and animals that were a major source of food. There was also rich soil suitable for farming.

The freshwater mussels found in the shoals were an important food supply for the tribes that settled in this region. This bountiful supply of mussels caused many Indian tribes to settle in this area along the Tennessee River. Large shell mounds or middens have been found along the banks of the Tennessee River. The Paleo Indians and the shell-mound Archaic Indians were among the earliest Indians in North Alabama. Early Alabama Indians were shell-midden people and bluff dwellers. Shell middens were primarily used during the summer months when low water levels made the gathering of mussels easy.

Foods - The foods our Indian ancestors ate are very different from the foods you eat today. Mainly because of the way it was prepared. They did not have grocery stores, microwaves, refrigerators, stoves, electricity, and many more conveniences we have today. Vegetables, wild fruits and nuts, wild animals and fish were their main sources of food. Deer was their main source of meat.

Our Indian ancestors used common food preservation methods. Drying was the most common preservation method. Beans were dried in the pod or shelled. Pumpkins and squash were cut into strips and put in the sun to dry. Meat was dried over the fire, and they also smoked their meats to preserve them.

Indian people spent much of their time farming. They grew corn, beans, squash, melons, pumpkins, and sweet potatoes. Indians made mush, dumplings, hominy, and succotash from corn. Corn was the main food for Indians. Corn could be used in many different ways. The women and girls spent many hours grinding corn. Corn could be parched, boiled, roasted and made into corn cakes. Corn was stored in cribs built of poles about eight feet off the ground.

Cherokee Plowing With a Steer

LESSON 5 – LIFESTYLES OF EARLY INDIAN PEOPLE

Cooking - Cooking was done over fires built having forks of wood driven into the ground, a stick laid across it, and a pot in which meat boiled hung from a stick. The Indians cooked their food in clay pots and they also put pieces of meat on a stick and held it over a fire. Boiling was the most common method of cooking with different foods combined to make a thick stew. Bread and sometimes meat was baked by wrapping the food in cornhusks or leaves and covering it with hot coals.

Historic Farming - By the time the first Cherokees moved into North Alabama , they were using farming methods adopted from the Europeans. These Cherokees had metal plows, mules, horses, cattle, hogs, sheep, goats, and chickens. Some Cherokees were plantation owners with many slaves. At the time of his death, Doublehead owned some 30 slaves and much livestock.

Review Questions

1. Who owned the home and was responsible for the children in early Indian time?
2. What were the two homes called?
3. What were early historic homes made from?
4. What is another name for Bankhead National Forest?
5. How many different kinds of homes did the Cherokees live in?
6. Name the only job men and women worked together?
7. Who was responsible for providing food by hunting and fishing?
8. Who was mainly responsible for raising the children?
9. The elders of the village took responsibility for care and instruction of whom?
10. Did the Cherokee believe the children were only related to the mother's side of the family or father's family?
11. What were the Cherokee dolls made from?
12. What animal was important to the Cherokees?
13. Name some of the Cherokees important foods?
14. What were fish hooks made from?
15. Who cooked, made clothes, and raised the children?
16. Identify the father's responsibilities:
17. Name two animals the Cherokee farmed with?
18. What river played an important role in providing things our ancestors in North Alabama needed to survive?
19. Name two of the five tribes of North Alabama?
20. What did our ancestor's houses look like?
21. Who disciplined the boys?
22. Who disciplined the girls?
23. What were found in the shoals that were food supply to early Indians?
24. Identify several important characteristics of the mother:

LESSON 5 – LIFESTYLES OF EARLY INDIAN PEOPLE

25. What were needles made from?
26. How many deer skins were traded for a new rifle?
27. Kinlock in the Bankhead National Forest is known as a :
28. What part of the deer was used to make a rake?
29. What material was used to make moccasins and bowstrings?
30. What did our Indian ancestors cook their food in?
31. How did our Indian ancestors make glue?
32. When was the first thanksgiving?
33. Who was known as the "Beloved Woman" that saved the life of captive, Mrs. William Bean, who was about to be burned at the stake?

LESSON 6 – EARLY SURVIVAL NEEDS

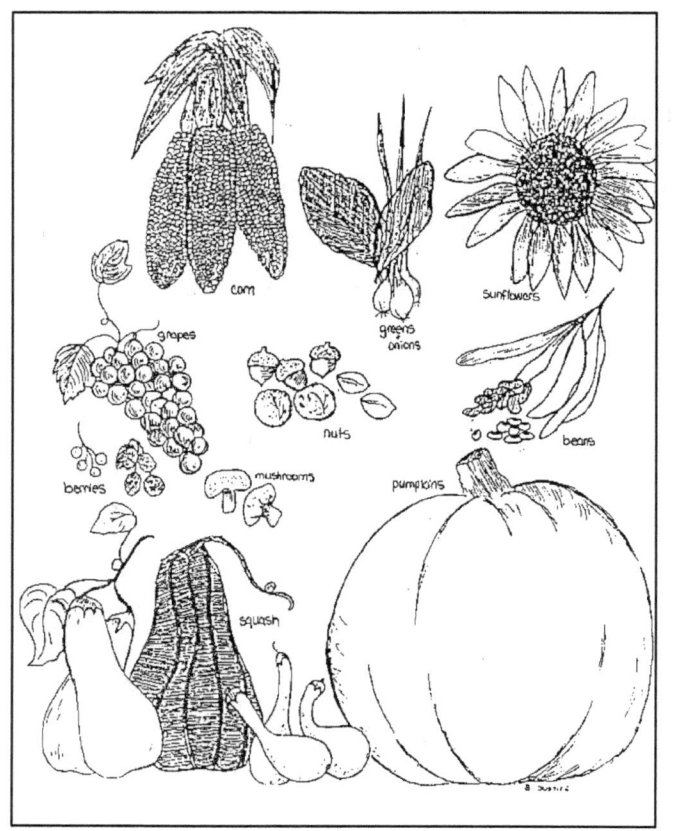

Cherokee Foods - We are going to talk about the Cherokee Indians who were ancestors to most of you. The Cherokee were farmers and grew beans, pumpkins, squash, and *most importantly corn and potatoes.* Some food they gathered was wild grapes, persimmons, plums, blackberries, chestnuts, walnuts, hickory nuts, acorns, and wild onions.

The Cherokee hunted smaller animals for food such as deer, wild turkey, bear, squirrel, rabbit, and quail. The main source of meat and hides was deer. (Do color sheet of animals they hunted). Some of the rivers and streams produced foods for the Indians such as fish, turtles, and mussels. Indians used fish hooks made of bone. They also used nets, traps, and spears to catch fish.

Cherokees in North Alabama were farmers who raised all kind of crops. Some also had livestock including horses, cattle, hogs, and chickens.

Indian survival depended on a generous supply of food. The Southeastern environment had many sources to offer. Crops of beans, pumpkins, squash, cucumbers, radishes, and most importantly corn and potatoes were utilized in their daily diet. Corn was used for various foods. It could be ground for corn meal. Hominy, grits and several methods of cooking corn provided a variety of tastes. Many plants yielded fruits, berries, and nuts. Some of these include wild grapes, persimmons, plums, blackberries, chestnuts, walnuts, hickory nuts, and acorns. Acorns could be pounded into a powder and processed for flour. Foods were preserved with a drying process.

Animals provided a meat source to their diet also. Deer, rabbit, bear, squirrel, wild turkey and quail were commonly hunted. Their main source of meat was deer. How many of you have ever tasted deer or rabbit meat? Do any of you have a relative that hunts for meat today? It's important to remember the Indian people respect animals and never hunted just for sport. Every part of the animals killed was put to use.

The cattail was like the supermarket of the swamp. The roots of the cattail were dried then pounded into flour (show a cattail stalk that has been split open). The white substance was

LESSON 6 – EARLY SURVIVAL NEEDS

pounded for flour. Young plants were eaten like celery. Also, the yellow pollen was used with corn flour to make very good bread.

Cherokee Homes - Our Indian ancestors in North Alabama lived in villages. They always located their villages near a spring, creek, or river, which provided an abundant water supply, and forest. Why do you think they wanted to be near water? Why do you think that our Indian people wanted to live near a forest?

What kind of houses did our early Indian people have? Smaller branches were woven around the saplings. A mixture of clay and grass was used to plaster the walls. The roof was covered with bark or thinly split wood shingles. The door, which was the only opening except for the small hole in the roof, was about two feet wide.

The winter house had walls built of logs standing on end and woven together with white oak strips that made solid walls. The roof was cone shaped. A clay mixture was used to plaster the inside and outside of the house which was covered with bark or grass. A fire burned in the center of the house with beds lining the walls. The door of the winter house was about four feet high, and it was so narrow that only one person could enter at a time. A small peephole

Cherokee Dwelling

was level with the ground so the enemies could be seen. The summer home was called "ge-tsa'di". The winter home was called "Asi'".

After the Cherokees moved into North Alabama , they lived in log cabins or plank houses. Some wealthy Cherokees and Chickasaw had plantations with slaves. They owned horses, mules, cattle, hogs, sheep, goats, and chickens. They also raised cotton, corn, and other crops.

Our Cherokee Indian people lived in villages of several homes built close together. The Cherokee Indians never lived in tipis. The roofs of early Cherokee homes were built in the shape of a cone and outside walls were either round or square. (draw on board or show picture)

LESSON 6 – EARLY SURVIVAL NEEDS

The time the Cherokees were living in North Alabama, they were living in log cabins or plank houses. Both Chief Doublehead and Chief George Colbert lived in two story plank houses with fireplaces. Some early Cherokees had plantations with slaves.

In the Cherokee family, the father was responsible for hunting animals for their food. The mother's responsibility was to take care of the children, prepare the food, and to make their clothes.

Tools and Weapons - We are going to talk about tools and weapons used by our early Indian people so they could survive. One of the main hunting weapons of early Indian people was the bow and arrow. How many of you have ever seen a bow and arrow? They made the bow from some type of wood. The guts of a bear were used as the string for the bow. The arrows were made from cane. The sharp point on the arrow was made primarily from flint rock.

The favorite weapons of the Cherokee were the bow and arrow and blowgun

The blowgun was made from a piece of cane cut to a length of seven to nine feet. The cane was hollowed out by dropping hot coals into the cane or by drilling a hole with a smaller cane to which was fixed a flint drill. The cane had to be hollowed out so a dart could be blown through it. The blowgun darts were made of hardwood splinters. The blowgun was used to hunt small animals like rabbits, squirrel, turkey, or birds. Some people think the Cherokees used poison on their darts but there is no evidence of that.

Our Indian people had many tools they used. One important tool was a stone ax made from a flint rock attached to a handle. They also used mussel shells for scraping. Other tools they had were made from flint rocks, which had been shaped into arrowheads. Does everyone know what an arrowhead is? If you ever see a rock that is shaped like this, you will know it was probably made by an Indian.

Stones were used to heat their water. The stones would be placed into a fire to get hot, and then put into the water to heat it.

Some of the tools they used were the stone ax and deer antler rake. Since our ancestors could not go to the grocery store as we do today, they had to make big gardens. The stone ax and antler rake were used for this purpose. Their very survival depended upon the skillful making and use of their tools and weapons. Early weapons used were spears and the atlatl.

LESSON 6 – EARLY SURVIVAL NEEDS

Indian people found it necessary to develop new weapons. One of their great improvements was the atlatl which was an extension of the spear. The atlatl allowed the hunter to throw with great force and to keep at a safe distance from animals. The main part of the atlatl besides the spear shaft was the throwing stick. Attached to the throwing stick was a banner stone and deer antler hook.

A lot of time was spent hunting animals for food. The main hunting weapon during the Mississippian Period was the bow and arrow. The bow was made from many types of trees and the arrow from mountain cane.

When our Cherokee ancestors moved into North Alabama , they were using weapons made of metal. Long rifles and metal knives were used by Cherokees who lived in this area.

How do you think the early Indians made their clothes? They used sharp pointed pieces of bone called awl were used for sewing leather clothes.

Cutting tools and weapons used by early Indians were chipped from flint. Flint also has another name chert. Flint (chert) was used to make a variety of weapon points. One very important point made was called an arrowhead or spear point. The arrowhead was made by using two methods called pressure flaking and percussion. In percussion flaking, the flint is battered into shape with skillful blows from a hammer stone. In pressure flaking, a pointed tool of antler or bone is pressed against the edge to remove small flakes. After the arrowhead was completed, it was tied on the end of a piece of cane.

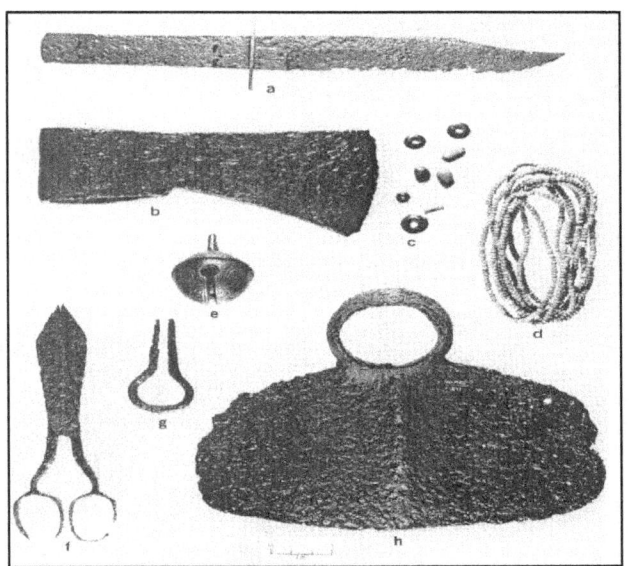

Early metal tools used by Cherokee *(Tellico Archaeology)*

Metal Tools - The first North Alabama Cherokees were out of the Stone Age. Their weapons, made of steel, were long rifles and knives. By the time they moved to North Alabama, our Cherokee people were using plows and metal tools like the settlers used. By the time our first Cherokee people came here, they were using metal pots and pans. The metal cookware was an important trade item of the British.

By the time the Cherokees moved into North Alabama, their favorite weapon was the long rifle. Lawrence County Cherokees used long rifles to hunt and fight with. Thirty deerskins could be traded for a rifle. Metal tools were also an important trade item that Indians got from the British and later the Americans.

LESSON 6 – EARLY SURVIVAL NEEDS

Pottery - Remember, Archaic Indian people first developed stone pottery; however, clay pottery was fiber, sand, or shell tempered, which means that fibers (grass, roots, Spanish moss and other materials), sand, or crushed mussel shells were placed in the clay. The clay was then dried and strengthened by firing.

Pottery from the Overhill Cherokee Towns *(Tellico Archaeology)*

Pottery making was one of the best known Cherokee crafts. There were three basic forms of traditional Cherokee pottery: the bowl; the pot; and a large jar. Most clay used for making Cherokee pottery was found around creek or river banks. It was dug, dried, ground, and sifted. Using an axe head and stone pestle, the lumps of dry clay was broken into fragments, ground to fine flour, and sifted in a basket to remove pebbles. The fine dried clay powder was mixed with water. It was worked with stone and kneaded with the hands. Plant fibers, coarse grit, sand, or crushed shells were added as a tempering agent to aid in hardening. Clay for making pottery had the consistency of putty. Clay has been used for hundreds of years to make cooking vessels.

To begin, a ball was formed and then pressed into the desired beginning shape, like a small bowl. The edges were pressed thin and then built up with rows of clay formed into long thin rolls, in a coiling manner. The last coil formed the rim and was sometimes notched. The firing was done outside. A hot fire was built and the vessel was put close into the embers and covered with dry bark. Heat was added until the vessel turned red. Cornhusk or dried corn cobs were placed inside and allowed to blaze up. The vessel was turned upside down until all the flaming material was burned up. This made it waterproof on the inside. These vessels were extremely important in food preparation and cooking.

LESSON 6 – EARLY SURVIVAL NEEDS

The gorget was made of clay but sometimes from stone during the Woodland period. The gorget was used as decoration for the body such as a neck or an arm piece of jewelry. The word gorget means neck armor. During the Mississippian period, shells were used to make beautifully designed gorgets.

Clothing - Prehistoric Indians wore clothes made from animal skins. Clothing was usually leather or fur depending on the climate. Men wore a breechcloth which was a strip of skin or cloth about six feet long and one foot wide. The breechcloth was worn between the legs and looped over the belt at the waist. The ends hung down in front and back to the knees. The main item of clothing for the woman was a short, deerskin skirt or dress hanging to the knees. In cold weather, both men and women wore leggings made from buckskin. The woman's leggings usually came to the knee while the man's leggings usually reached from the heel to the hip.

Removal Era Clothing

By the time the Cherokee came into Alabama, they had already made contact with the English settlers. Through trade, the Indians were replacing their clothing made from hide with cloth brought by the traders. By the 1800's, all southeastern clothing was made from trade cloth, or from cloth made by Indian women using looms.

The traditional clothing worn by today's Cherokees is similar to that made during the removal. The women wear a tear dress made from calico material. During the removal on the Trail of Tears the Indians were unable to trade for materials so they used what was available to them. They used the calico sacks, which flour and meal came in. They would tear the sacks into the pieces that they needed and would sew them together. The men would wear a ribbon shirt. The shirt has bright colored ribbons sewn on it.

Weaving - Some of the first weaving involved the use of animal hair. The weaving loom was made from wood. It was square shaped with strings running from top to bottom. Animal hair was woven in and out of each string. Then a brush was used to pack the hair into place and make it tight. Plant fibers were also used to make yarn. Cotton and wool are still used to make clothing and yarn today. Look at the label in some of your clothes at home.

LESSON 6 – EARLY SURVIVAL NEEDS

Fingerweaving - Fingerweaving without a loom is very old and widespread. Generally only fingers are used but needles or weaving frames may be used. Sashes woven in bright geometric patterns were major items made by finger weaving. Before contact with white traders, the sashes were woven of vegetable fibers mixed with animal hair. Wool sashes became popular when yarn and trade sashes were acquired.

Ornamental sashes were worn around the waist with the long fringes trailing or hung over one or both shoulders in bandoleer fashion. They were also wrapped around the head like a turban. Short pieces were tied around the arms or worn on the legs as garters. Sometimes they were used to tie or carry medicine bundles or to decorate a weapon. Glass beads were often woven into the sashes or threaded on the long fringes at each end.

Plants - Perhaps one of the greatest contributions of the American Indian was the use of medicine made out of herbs or plants. Most Indian tribes had a medicine man, which provided not only for the spiritual needs, but also for the medical needs of his people. The place and ritual differed in different tribes and areas of the continent, but to most tribes the gathering and preparation of the herbs or plants was entrusted to the skills of the well trained individual-the medicine man.

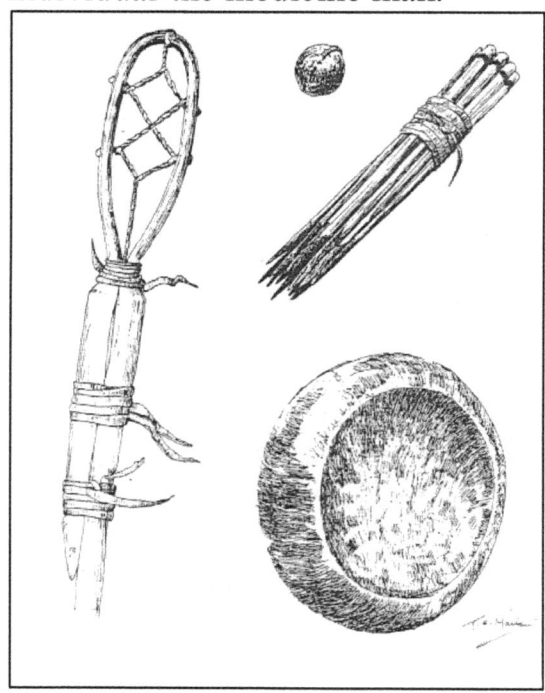

Cherokee Games

The medicine man carried a pouch made out of leather to transport and store fragile plants from the woods to his home. Then, he would gather all needed to begin the process of making his medicine. He would measure, chop, grind, or boil to ensure just the right method of preparation.

Games - Chunkey, stickball, guessing games, stick dice, bowl catch, Cherokee ball game, and other games prepared boys for hunting.

Discuss with class how the games prepared boys for hunting and how games were sometimes used to settle arguments instead of going to war. Describe some of the games to your class and ask if any games played today are similar to those played by Indians.

Review Questions
1. What did men and women wear in the winter?
2. Cherokee owned what animals?
3. What is a bow made from?
4. What are the names of the homes of our Cherokee ancestors?

LESSON 6 – EARLY SURVIVAL NEEDS

5. The Cherokees most important crops were what?
6. Name three animals the Cherokees hunted:
7. What kind of bone did the Cherokee use to make fish hooks?
8. What were two reasons the Cherokees used water?
9. What tool did early Indians use to sew leather clothes?
10. After European contact, what type of homes did the Cherokees live in?
11. What was their pottery made from?
12. What object was used by our early Indian ancestors to cook food?
13. What was the string on a bow and arrow made from?
14. Describe an important tool used by our early ancestors:
15. What was a game the children played?
16. Identify an important trade item of the British:
17. What was used to heat water in early Indian times?
18. Name some tools our ancestors used?
19. What were some early weapons used?
20. What were some weapons used by the first North Alabama Cherokees?
21. Who provided medicine for our ancestors?
22. What was the favorite hunting weapon of the Mississippian Indians?
23. What was used to settle arguments instead of going to war?
24. Some early weaving involved the use of what?
25. What was the main item of clothing for women?
26. After European contact, what did Indian women make their clothes from?
27. The sharp point on the arrow was made primarily from what?
28. In most early Indian tribes who provides for the spiritual needs of the people?
29. What were the homes located near?
30. Explain the importance of games:

LESSON 7 – REGALIA

The early Indian men and women didn't have clothing like we do today. You may be wearing something that is made out of leather or buckskin. Do you know what leather or buckskin is? (Leather or buckskin is something we get from different kinds of animal skins. Buckskin is made from deer hides.)

A long time ago, our Indian people used many kinds of animal skins to make leather and buckskin such as: deer, rabbit, bear, beaver, buffalo, and elk. How do you think our ancestors made leather or buckskin? First, they would take the animal skin and scrape all the fur off. Next, they would wet it, stretch it, and let it dry. Then, they would take a rock and rub it over the skin until it became smooth and soft. Then they rubbed the skin with the animal's brains. The brain of an animal was enough to tan its hide.

Our Indian ancestors used leather and buckskin to make their clothes, shoes, blankets, and bags to carry water from the stream. What are some things we have now that are made from leather or buckskin? (Your mom may have a purse made out of leather. Your dad may have a billfold or belt made out of leather). Can you think of anything else that is made out of leather? (saddles, bridles, furniture, car seats, gloves, shoes)

Early Indian Clothing *(History of Alabama for Junior High Schools)*

Buckskin Clothes - Our early Cherokee Indian people made their clothes out of deer skins. The women made all of the clothing for the family. The Cherokee men wore three different kinds of clothes; a breechcloth, buckskin leggings, and a jacket made of buckskin. Buckskin leggings were made in pairs and covered the whole leg, but were not sewn together. A buckskin jacket, which hung to the knees, and leggings were worn in the winter and a breechcloth was worn in the summer to stay cool. The Cherokee women wore a short deerskin skirt, which hung to the knees.

They had to kill animals to get their clothes. When the Indians killed an animal, they would use every part. Nothing was wasted. Most of their hides came from deer and bear. The men would kill and skin the animals. The women would start the process of hides. Sometimes they would wear a deerskin or woven mantles to show that they were important. In winter months, the men would add a deerskin shirt and leggings tucked into the high, laced moccasins worn by everyone.

LESSON 7 – REGALIA

The clothing of our early Indian people was different from what you wear. The breechcloth was a strip of skin or cloth about six feet long and one foot wide. They wore buckskin leggings as protection from the underbrush and from the cold in winter. They fitted the whole length of the leg and were held up by a cord tied to the waist string. A jacket made of buckskin, reaching to the knees, was also worn; in cold weather a bearskin or blanket was thrown around the shoulders.

Leather came from animal hides. Hides were processed and fashioned into clothing and footwear. They were, also, responsible for preparing the hides. Women were probably engaged almost continuously in the processing of hides (show picture of woman working hide on rack).

Preparation of Skins - Leather today comes mostly from cow or pig. People usually buy their leather from companies that buy large quantities. Today, hides are tanned by machines. It took a lot of work to prepare an animal hide so that it could be used as clothing, footwear, or blankets. (1) The flesh was removed with a stone, bone, or antler scraper; (2) The hair of the hides was removed with flint scrapers; (3) Tanning was merely a matter of smearing the hide with fat, brains, and liver; (4) The hides were then soaked in water; (5) The skin was sometimes smoked; (6) The hide was then stretched on a framework to dry; (7) The leather was finally made pliable by working between the hands or sliding back and forth across a pole. Hides were processed and fashioned into clothing and footwear. (1) Women were responsible for making the clothes from hides; (2) Women were probably engaged, almost continuously, in the processing of hides.

Historic Clothes - By the time Cherokees moved into North Alabama, they were wearing traditional clothing of the settlers and pioneers. Cherokee women learned to make clothes using looms. They traded with the British and later Americans for cloth, shoes, hats, shirts, pants, dresses, and other clothing items. Some dressed like rich plantation owners in fine clothes of the planters and society. By the time our Cherokee people moved into Lawrence County, they were wearing clothes made of cloth. Today, you are an Indian and look at your clothes.

The first Cherokees in North Alabama wore clothes made from cloth. The cloth was a trade item of the British. Indian women using a loom also weaved cloth for making clothes.

Our Indian people did not always wear skins, but for thousands of years they did. Skins (also called leather) provided the best type of clothing they could find until the Europeans arrived in North America and started trading with Indian people. The Europeans wore clothing made of cloth (like we wear today). When the European traders traded with our Indian ancestors, they would swap cloth for skins. This is how they got cloth material to make their clothes. Indian women also had looms that they wove their own cloth to make

LESSON 7 – REGALIA

clothes. Many Indians and Celtic people intermarried in this area of Alabama; therefore, their clothing changed to a blend of Indian and Celtic.

Today, Cherokee women wear tear dresses as tribal regalia. The dress is made from cotton with a small floral design. The dress is trimmed with bright ribbons or a diamond design appliquéd to the fabric. The men wear shirts decorated with brightly colored ribbons. This is called a ribbon shirt. We have talked about the different dress of our ancestors but, remember you are Indians, but you are wearing the clothes that are in fashion or comfortable for you.

Jewelry - Jewelry has always been important to our Indian people. Both men and women wore jewelry for decoration. The men liked to wear necklaces to show that they had a good hunt and were proud. Our Indian people used different things to make necklaces such as beads, animal teeth and bear claws. They also wore earrings and bracelets to show they had won a fight against other people. Do you have any jewelry that you like to wear? Maybe you have a special person in your life that you really like a lot. You might want to make them a bracelet or necklace and give it to them to let them know that they are special to you. Sometimes we call these friendship bracelets or necklaces.

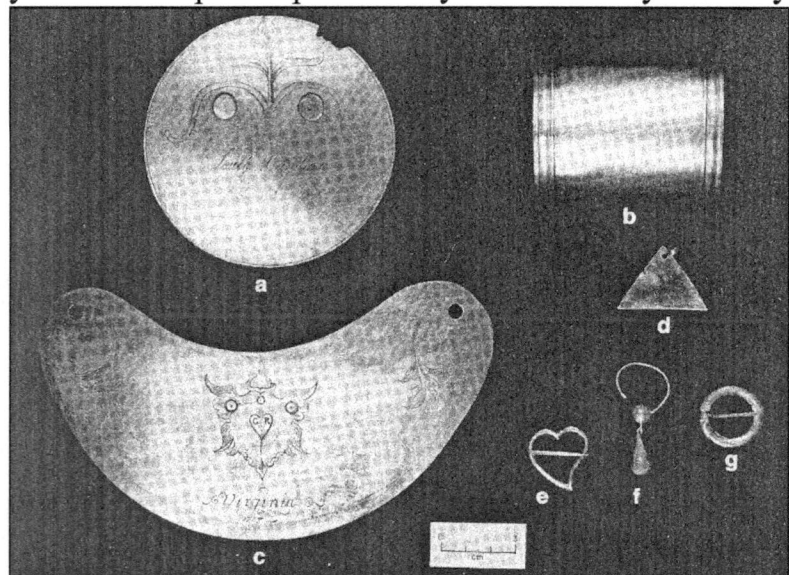

Silver Cherokee Jewelry and Body Ornaments (*Tellico Archaeology*)

Our Indian ancestors used another way to decorate themselves and their belongings. They used different things to make paint such as, sand rocks, different kinds of berries (blackberries, blueberries, strawberries, plums, and cherries), and different plants (bloodroot and yellow root). The paint was used to decorate their faces and bodies before going to war or if they had won a battle. Also, Indians used paint to make pictures on animal skins. Silver ornaments became important to wear by Cherokees. Sequoyah was considered a great Cherokee silversmith.

The earliest of our ancestors decorated their bodies with ornaments and tattoos. This usually demonstrated their position in society. This still has some effects on people today. Some people believe you need to wear name brand jeans or certain T-shirts to fit in. You should remember that it is important to be yourself. But we all like to dress up because it makes us feel good. How many of you are wearing a ring or watch? This is an example of jewelry. But where did your ring or watch come from?

LESSON 7 – REGALIA

The first jewelry or ornaments were made from things in nature. For example, the Indian people used shells, rocks, and even clay. They also used plants to create dyes for tattoos on their body. Another source for jewelry was from teeth, claws, and bones of animals that were killed. After European contact, the Indian people began to trade for various glass beads; therefore, making their adornment even more colorful.

Beads - They also used beads as money. They called their money wampum. The different colors represented their value. The purple beads were the most valuable because they were harder to get.

Cherokee men and women wore jewelry and used tattooing as adornment. How many of you have thought about wearing jewelry or having tattoos? As a matter of fact, that was the way the men could show that they had been successful in battle or hunting. It was like having trophies.

Who can name some things that our Indian ancestors might have used to adorn themselves? A lot of you may think that all our people wore a feather head dress, but they didn't. Only a few did. Other things they used were animal bone, teeth and shells.

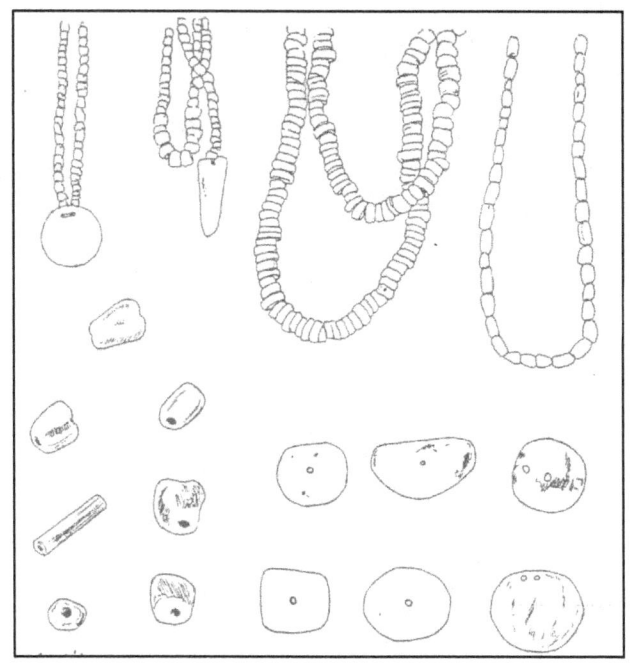
Early Beads

Body Paint - Sometimes Cherokee Indians would paint their faces and bodies for different reasons such as battle or a cause of celebration. Where do you think they got their paints and dyes? They found berries, bark from trees, and from sand rocks. They also used paint for pictures on stones to tell stories.

Tattooing - The men also used tattooing as a mark of personal identification and to designate honors.

Tattooing was common among Cherokee men. Designs of animal figures, serpents, stars, the moon, the sun, and scrolls were used. Designs were made by pricking the skin with a sharp object like a garfish tooth, bone, or a needle. Sometimes they would paint their faces or body with paint. Where did they get their dye or paint? They had to make it. They would mix iron ore with bear grease, berry stain or ashes from the fire. Face and body painting was seen as a means of obtaining magic. The colors and symbols make them look and feel powerful. Different face paint colors meant different things to different tribes.

LESSON 7 – REGALIA

Hair - Boys and Girls, you all look very nice today! I'm looking around the room and I see many different types of clothing and hairstyles. We all wear our hair and our clothes the way we have been taught, don't we. Well, today, we are going to discuss how our Indian ancestors dressed and wore their hair. They also dressed the way they had been taught. And let's remember, they didn't have clothing stores, barbershops, or beauty shops like we do.

Indian men plucked or pulled all the hair from their bodies except for their eyebrows, and sometimes they removed their eyebrows. However, since this was a custom from childhood the nerves became accustomed to the shock and little pain was experienced. The items used in removing the hair was tweezers made from attaching two mussel shells together, sharp side of a mussel shell, rocks and projectile points. Burning the hair with hot stones was also used.

Reasons for Cutting Hair

1. Cleanliness--The hair became tangled and dirty. It would get caught on limbs and branches, OUCH!!
2. Certain hairstyles represented a custom from certain tribes (example-Mohawk, Cherokee, and other examples of different tribes and their hairstyles).
3. A symbol of belief or superstition in a magical power.

Dyes and Colors - Look around the room and count how many different colors you see. The Native American people loved beautiful and colorful things. The clothes we have today are dyed cloth with various colors and patterns. Our ancestors also learned ways to dye the various objects they wore. How do you think they did this? Well, they used things that were natural to their surroundings. For example, how many of you have ever picked some blackberries and it turned your fingers purple? Blackberries were just one of the many things used for dyeing. Also, green walnuts make a great dye that will last a long time.

Native Americans used plant materials to make beautiful, soft colors to dye wool, cotton, and other fibers. They made almost every color, though shades of yellow were the easiest to produce. Listed below are some of the plants Native Americans used for coloring. As a general rule, if the plant part is hard, like bark or sticks, pound or grind it to loosen the fibers; if it's soft, like flower petals or berries, use it as is.

Wash the plant material first. Then put it, ground up or whole, in a large pot and fill the pot with water. Boil until the color is a little darker than you'd like. Strain the dye material out and add a little salt and baking soda to the colored water of dye bath. For a more permanent dye, add a teaspoon of alum, available from a hardware or crafts store.

LESSON 7 – REGALIA

To dye wool or heavy cloth, soak it in warm water before putting it in the dye bath. Let it boil in the dye bath for about an hour and then let it cool in the pot. To dye raffia, thread, or thin cloth, soak them in the dye bath for several hours. Rinse all dyed materials several times in cold water. Then hang them up to dry, away from direct sunlight or heat, which may cause bleaching.

Color--Plant Material
- Blacks--wild grapes, hickory bark, alder bark, and dogwood bark.
- Blues--larkspur petals, alfalfa flowers, sunflower seeds.
- Browns--walnut shells, birch bark, oak bark.
- Greens--moss, algae, lily-of-the-valley leaves, cedar berries.
- Purples--blueberries, raspberries, blackberries, and rotten maple wood.
- Reds--sumac berries, dogwood berries, beets, cranberries, bloodroot.
- Yellows--onion skins, goldenrod stems and flowers, sunflower petals, dock roots, marigold petals, moss, peach leaves, birch leaves, sagebrush, yellow root.

Some of the common plants used for color from the Warrior Mountains include bloodroot and yellow root. Bloodroot has a very deep red color and yellow root has a golden color. These were dug from the ground and boiled to produce their color.

Pottery - Early Cherokee Indians used the coiled method, which is still used by many Cherokee potters today. Amanda Swimmer, noted Cherokee potter, explains the process: "For coiled pottery, start with a disk of clay, placing ropes of clay on top of each other until you reach the desired height. Then you mold these coils together using your fingers. Now, set the pots out in the sun to dry. When they become dry, polish them with smooth river stones. Make your design, then let them dry to a chalky white. First preheat the pottery until it becomes bluish in color. It then should be put directly into the fire until the fire goes out. The type of wood you use in the firing determines the color of the finish. For the lighter colors you use hardwoods, which give off more flames and less smoke, while for dark colors use a softwood, which gives off more smoke and less flame."

Review Questions

1. The Cherokee Indian clothes were made from what animal?
2. What part of an animal was used to tan its hide?
3. Where did leather come from?
4. What was used to give our Indian ancestors purple?
5. What was a form of money, also called wampum?
6. What was jewelry made from?
7. Explain reasons for the men cutting their hair?
8. Why were tattoos important?

LESSON 7 – REGALIA

9. What are leggings made from?
10. Why did the men and women wear jewelry?
11. What color was the most valuable bead?
12. Where did our Indian ancestors get their dyes?
13. What type of dress do Cherokee women wear today?
14. What did the men wear that was about six feet long and 1 foot wide?
15. What determined the color of pottery?
16. Who was a famous Cherokee silversmith?
17. Identify the various plants used to make shades of red:
18. What were some things our ancestors used to tattoo themselves?
19. What type of wood was used in order to get a lighter color of pottery?
20. What were things our Indian ancestors used to make paint?
21. Who did our ancestors trade cloth for skins with?
22. How did our ancestors remove their hair?
23. What gave our ancestors the color yellow?
24. What was the hardest color bead to get?
25. What method did the early Cherokee Indians use that many Cherokee potters still use today?
26. Who was engaged in the processing of hides:
27. Name the steps our ancestors followed to prepare the animal skins for clothing, footwear, or blankets:
28. How did they make dye or paint?

LESSON 8 – CEREMONIAL ACTIVITIES

Our Indian ancestors always had lots of work to do such as hunting, cooking, growing, gathering food, and fishing. But besides all their work, our folks also had lots of fun and enjoyed their lives. They loved making music and playing games just like we do today.

Cherokee Music - Our Indian ancestors had many musical instruments such as drums, flutes, whistles, and rattles, but the most important instrument was the drum.

Drums were made from hollowed out logs and wet skins were stretched across the ends. The drum was a sacred instrument to our people. They believed the beat of the drum carried their prayers to heaven.

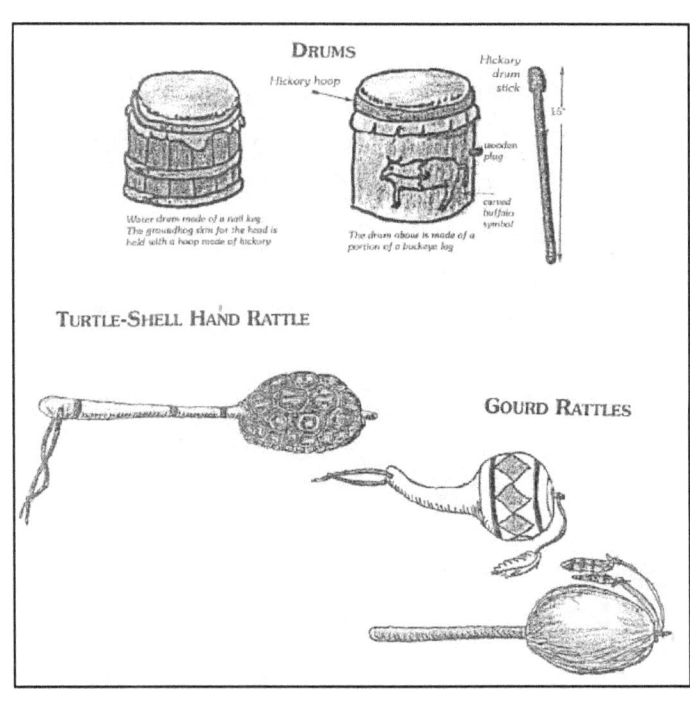

Cherokee Musical Instruments

Most Indian dancers shook rattles to the rhythm of their dances. The rattles were made from dried gourds or even turtle shells. The gourd has seed inside the rattle when you shake it. Traditional Cherokee songs are chants made with a gourd rattle. Gourds and rattles were used to show that Indian dancers were keeping beat to the drum. Rattles were also thought of as objects of great power to be used to summon good spirits or drive away evil ones. Turtle shells were used as rattles in the corn dance. Different types of turtles were used to make the rattle including the snapping or mud turtle, the box turtle, and the water turtle. The shells were laced together to keep the stones from falling out. The Creek woman, prior to performing a dance, would fasten the turtle shells to the calves of their legs.

Flutes were made from cane. They made beautiful music with their flutes.

Indian Mother Carrying Infant

Oh, how our Indian people loved music! They used musical instruments as a part of their ceremonies as well as for personal enjoyment, such as games.

LESSON 8– CEREMONIAL ACTIVITIES

Indian men and women seemed to enjoy life. They held athletic events, played games, danced, held feasts, told stories, and played musical instruments. Many times rattles were carried by dancers as a part of their ceremonial dress.

Cherokee Games - Cherokee Indian boys and girls had lots of work to do. The maternal uncle taught the boys how to fish and hunt and the mothers taught the girls to cook and make crafts, but they still had time for games and music. The girls made dolls from corn cobs. Have you ever seen a corn cob doll? They enjoyed playing with dolls just like you do today. The Indian mother carried her baby on her back in a cradle board.

Games were an important part of our early ancestor's culture. They played a variety of games, such as ballgames and guessing games. Their favorite game was stickball where two teams played against each other using ball sticks to try to score. Another ballgame they played was called "chunkey" where they threw a pole to see who could throw closer to a stone disk called chunkey stone. Chunkey was a favorite game, which utilized a round stone (like a biscuit) that was rolled.

Another game was the basket and bean game. Each bean would be burned on one side and the other side left white. The six beans were tossed into the air and caught in the basket. If all of the beans land white side up, they got points. Our Indian people enjoyed this on long winter nights.

Besides ballgames, they also played guessing games with moccasins or shells. Blow gun competitions as well as stickball, were important gatherings for the Cherokee towns.

Although the Indians worked very hard to do their chores in the village, they also took time out to play. One of the first games Indian people played was called "stickball" or "ballplay." Stickball or the ballplay is one Cherokee sport that has lived on throughout the years. Even though today it has been changed to erase some of its dangers, everyone still loves the ball game. The Cherokee in Cherokee, N.C. still play stickball at their Fall festival.

The day before the ball game is played is a day spent in preparation. Special sequences of events are followed to prepare participants for the game. The ball dance, going to water (dipped themselves seven times), and scratching are carefully done to bring strength, speed, courage, endurance, and purification to your team and to weaken your opponents. Sometimes players will draw a cross or a semicircle with a dot in it on their upper body as a sign of good luck. Slippery elm is chewed and the spit was rubbed on their bodies to make themselves slippery.

In the ball game, there are two teams. One village or clan plays against another village or clan. They play in a large field with a goal at each end for each of the teams. The

LESSON 8– CEREMONIAL ACTIVITIES

equipment needed to play consists of two ball sticks for each player and a game ball made from soft animal skins, about the size of a walnut.

The object of the game is to be the first team to score twenty points. You score one point each time the ball crosses your goal post. You can only move the ball with your ball sticks. Sometimes it takes all day long for a team to win. Today, the points have been cut back and twelve points wins the game.

Everyone anxiously awaits the signal from the Medicine Man that he has finished the rites and is coming up from the water. One team yells three short calls that are repeated by the opposing team. They are ready to get onto the field. The Medicine Man begins the game by tossing the ball into the air and then the players try to get to the ball, by using their sticks, to score points for their team.

Green Corn Ceremony

Many would go home with broken arms or legs, cuts, or bruises. Sometimes, players even died in their eagerness to prove their clan was the most skilled. Today, rules are given to help prevent the players from getting hurt.

Before the game began, everyone would bring their possessions to bet with. Ladies would put on all of their clothing and wager skirt against skirt, blouse against blouse with the opposing team's women. Men would wager weapons, animals, whatever they had.

Cherokee Masks - How many of you have ever been trick or treating on Halloween? Did you dress up in a costume? Most children who go trick or treating will wear some kind of mask to cover their face.

A long time ago, our Indian ancestors wore masks for different reasons. They loved to have ceremonies. A ceremony is like a big celebration or party. During these ceremonies, Indian people wore different kinds of masks while they were dancing. Some wore masks while they hunted to give them good luck so they might find many animals to kill for food. Sometimes when hunting deer, they would use a whole deerskin to cover their body so they could get closer to the animal without scaring it away.

LESSON 8– CEREMONIAL ACTIVITIES

Our Indian people made many different kinds of masks. Some of these masks were carved from trees or made out of animal furs and some masks, such as the Booger Mask, were made from gourds. Do you know what carved means? It means to cut away pieces of wood from a tree. The wooden masks were carved into the shape of a man's face and they were pretty ugly. The Cherokee have wooden masks that represent each of the seven clans.

Cherokee Ceremonies - Can you name a ceremony that we might celebrate today? One of the most important ceremonies for the Indian was the Green Corn Ceremony. The festival was like our Thanksgiving and New Year rolled into one. It was a time to give thanks for a successful harvest, to settle differences, and to begin a new year. The ceremony took place in July or August depending on when corn ripened. The sacred fire and corn ritual was part of the Green Corn Ceremony. Logs were laid in the form of a cross around a new fire, which the medicine man had started by twirling a fire drill. Then, the medicine man placed four ears of corn in the fire as an offering of thanksgiving to the Breath Maker for another year. Who can tell me who they think the Breath Maker could have been?

From this sacred fire, all household fires will be rekindled anew. The next five days of the festival were spent playing games and dancing. On the last day of the festival, a respected speaker of the tribe told the people to keep the ancient rites and reminded them that they were bound together because they shared the same sacred fire. Another important ceremony was the burial ceremony. There's evidence that Indians had a form of religion. They would bury their dead with ornaments and personal possessions. They were careful in the treatment of their dead implying emotions of strong affections.

Ceremonies were an important part of Indian life. Significant dates and events in the lives of Indian people were times that tribes came together to celebrate. They believed that these ceremonies could affect the outcome of certain events.

One ceremony that held great importance in the Southern tribes was the Green Corn Ceremony. This ceremony could be said to be similar to Thanksgiving.

Ceremonial Objects - Besides ceremonies, our Indian ancestors considered several things sacred. The items were of great importance to the tribe and the people who were the keepers of the items were also of importance. Some of the items considered to be scared were tobacco, pipe, eagle feathers, and many of the items used in ceremonies. Usually the keeper was the only one who ever touched the sacred item. It was considered to be disrespectful to touch another person's property, or an item that was in their possession without their permission. Also, in Celtic culture, it was disrespectful to touch another person's belongings without their permission.

LESSON 8– CEREMONIAL ACTIVITIES

Ceremonial pipes were among the most sacred possessions of a tribe. Depending on the person who made the pipe, it usually had things on it to represent the earth, water, and air. Some of the things used were fur from an animal, a feather from a bird, a shell from a river, and a crystal from the earth.

The bowl of the pipe was carved from stone and decorated with animals or human figures. The stem of the pipe was usually made out of red (meaning war) and white (meaning peace) wood of the eastern red cedar. It was then adorned with feathers or other materials. The ceremonial pipe was passed around the council and each member took a puff before handing the pipe to the person on his left. The pipe came to be referred to as a peace pipe because it was smoked with former enemies as a peace treaty.

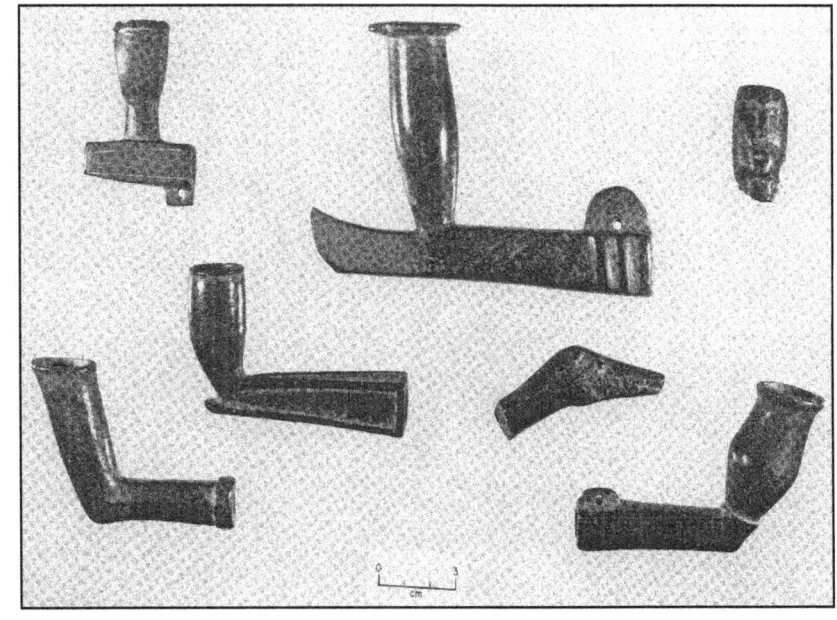

Cherokee Pipes and Pipe Fragments *(Tellco Archaeology)*

Review Questions
1. What was the most important musical instrument to the Cherokee Indians?
2. What was a game the Cherokee's played?
3. What were the girls dolls made from?
4. What were mask made from?
5. What were rattles made from?
6. What did our early Cherokee wear as a symbol while they were dancing during a ceremony?
7. Usually, who was the only person that touched the sacred items?
8. Why did the Cherokee wear masks while hunting?
9. How did music make our ancestors feel?
10. What two colors was the stem of the pipe?
11. What was the most sacred possession of a tribe?
12. What two items were use to play guessing games?
13. Why were gourds and rattles used during ceremonies?
14. What did our ancestors use to bet during a game of stickball?
15. What was the name of the ceremony like our Thanksgiving?
16. During the game of stickball, everyone awaits signal from who to start the game?
17. What did the ceremonial pipe become known as?

LESSON 8– CEREMONIAL ACTIVITIES

18. Why did Indians have a Green Corn Ceremony?
19. Who taught the boys how to fish and hunt?
20. Which direction was the ceremonial pipe passed around the council?
21. What did they bury with their dead?
22. What is another name for stickball?
23. What did the Cherokee dancers carry around as a part of their dress?
24. What did our Indian ancestors believe the beat of the drum would do?
25. Name several things that could have been carved in their pipes:

LESSON 9 – TENNESSEE RIVER

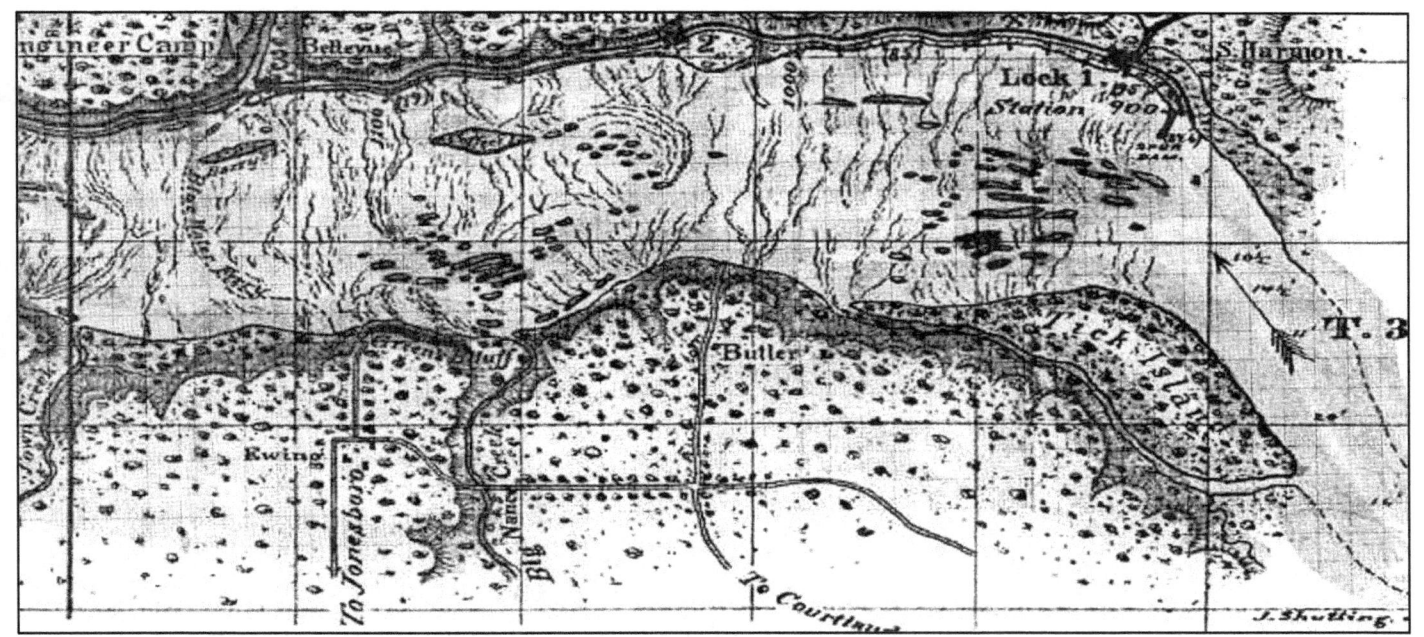

"Big Muscle Shoals"

Tennessee River - We are going to talk about how our Cherokee Indian ancestors used the Tennessee River. The Tennessee River was first named the Hogohegee (Ho'Go'He'Gee') River of the Cherokees. The Tennessee River is the largest river that flows through North Alabama. It begins in Tennessee, comes into Alabama in the northeast, and goes out in the northwest. The Tennessee River is a small part of the state line between Alabama and Mississippi.

How many of you have ever enjoyed visiting or swimming in the Tennessee River? Some of you may have and just don't know it. If you have ever crossed the Decatur Bridge or visited the Boat Harbor then you have been at the Tennessee River. Also, some other places you may recognize which are located on the Tennessee River are Spring Creek, Mallard Creek, McFarland Park and O'Neal Bridge in Florence, Joe Wheeler Park, Wheeler Dam, Wilson Dam, Champion Park, and Ditto Landing in Huntsville.

Have you ever wondered about how we know so much about how Indian people used to live? Most of what we know about the pre-historic Indians came from shell mounds beside the Tennessee River. Shell mounds, as you have studied earlier, are huge mounds of mussel shells (which are shells of freshwater mussels) found along the banks of the rivers. The Archaic Indians sometimes buried their dead in the mussel shells. The reason so many mussels were found in the North Alabama portion of the Tennessee River is because of the Great Muscle Shoals. Elk River Shoals and Big Muscle Shoals lay along the northern border of Lawrence County. In addition, Little Muscle Shoals and Colbert Shoals complete the four shoals that make up the Great Mussel Shoals of North Alabama. Two other lesser Shoals

LESSON 9 – TENNESSEE RIVER

were the Bee Tree Shoals and Waterloo Shoals. The Shoals were known by the Indian name of "Chake Thlocko", meaning Great Crossing Place or Big Ford.

Our Indian ancestors used the river for many things. Besides the food from the mussels, they used the Tennessee River for drinking water, to bathe in, water to cook with, fish for food, flint rocks from the riverbanks, and shells for making jewelry. They also used the river as a means of transportation.

Chert or commonly called flint was responsible for the Shoals because it does not erode. Who can tell me why flint rocks were important to the Indians? (They used flint rocks to make their tools and weapons). Flint is a type of hard rock, which can be shaped into points like arrowheads.

Much of the early tools of the Indian people were made from flint. There is an abundance of flint located along the Elk River Shoals on the Tennessee River. It was logical for the Indian people to live along the shoals of the river that contained vast amounts of mussels.

Early Cherokee Indian Trading Settlement

Besides providing our prehistoric Indian people stone for tools, the Tennessee River was used as a major transportation route through North Alabama. From the river, early man could obtain a great variety of aquatic plants and animals that were an inexhaustible source of food. Along the banks of the river, early inhabitants could also find wide varieties of

LESSON 9 – TENNESSEE RIVER

terrestrial plant and animal foods, rich soil compatible to farming, and protective caves and bluff shelters to make camp.

The freshwater mussels found in the Shoals were an important food supply for the tribes that settled in this region. The Mussel Shoals extended from present-day Lawrence County through Colbert County and had a fall of 134 feet within a distance of thirty-seven miles creating a vast series of rapids. According to Ortmann (1924), the Mussel Shoals received its name from the immense number of species and individuals of fresh-water mussels, which were found at this locality.

The Tennessee River has played an important role in the habitation of North Alabama because numerous trails crossed the shoals of the river. For example, the Shoals consisted of the Elk River Shoals, Big Muscle Shoals, Little Muscle Shoals, Colbert Shoals, Bee Tree Shoals, and Waterloo Shoals. These shoals were known by Indian people as "Chake Thlocko" which means great crossing place or big ford.

The Elk River Shoals includes that portion of the Tennessee River located in Lawrence County between what is now known as Mallard Creek and Spring Creek. The Big Muscle Shoals started in the area that is now Joe Wheeler State Park and extended into Colbert County which includes Little Muscle Shoals and Colbert Shoals. The present-day Wilson Dam is located at the lower end of the Little Muscle Shoals.

These Shoals had an abundance of aquatic life with the fresh water mussels being very numerous. Our Indian ancestors depended upon these mussels as a seasonal source of meat for their diet. This bountiful supply of mussels caused many Indian tribes to settle in this area along the Tennessee River.

Our Cherokee Indian people called the Tennessee River the Great Bend, the Hogohegee, and River of the Cherokees. The reason was for the shape of the river, which curves into a horseshoe shaped bend through Alabama. From Knoxville, Tennessee it flows to Alabama and winds back into Kentucky and into the Ohio River.

Foot Travel - How did our first Indian ancestors travel on land? Long ago our Indian people did not have cars and trucks to go places like we do today. We can go from place to place very quickly because we have cars and trucks to travel. The only way our Indian ancestors could go from place to place was by foot. They had to walk everywhere they went. It took days and sometimes weeks to get to another place. How long do you think it would take you to walk to school or to town from where you live? It might take you all day, from morning to dusk.

LESSON 9 – TENNESSEE RIVER

We are going to discuss the ways our Indian people traveled. How do you think our first Indian ancestors traveled? Did they have paved roads, cars, or airplanes? No. They were surrounded by woods and streams and had to make a path and travel by foot. So the earliest form of travel was on foot. Traveling by foot was very slow and it took a long time to travel from place to place.

Indian Dugout
(History of Alabama for Junior High Schools)

Dugout Canoe - Our Indian ancestors also had another way to go from place to place. They would build a dugout canoe to travel down streams and rivers. The boat was made from trees. Indians would ride in the dugout canoe sitting on their knees, and use a long pole to paddle with.

Since our Indian folks located their villages along streams and rivers, the dugout was a very necessary vehicle to them. The dugout canoe was a much faster way for them to travel. The dugout was also used by the warriors and could carry as many as 15 to 20 men. A paddle was not used like the ones we use today. The canoe was guided by long poles. Sometimes it was guided by the water's current. The dugout canoe was made from the huge poplar tree. To get the tree down, they would start a fire at the trunk of the tree and mud or clay would be dabbed above the place to be burned to keep the tree from burning up. After the tree was down, the top was burned out and the bark peeled from the tree. Then, came the process of hollowing out the log where the men would sit. The log would burn up if the men were not careful. So, this is what was done. Mud or clay dabbed around the area that was not to be burned. This kept the fire from spreading beyond the area they wanted to hollow out. Slowly and carefully the builders of the canoe took the stone ax and chipped away the charred pieces where the fire had burned until it was hollowed out. This process was continued until the canoe was completed. The size of the dugout canoe sometimes reached 30 or 40 feet long and two feet wide.

Most of you know that the first mode of travel for our Indian ancestors was walking. Well, today, I'm going to tell you about the second way of travel by the Cherokee Indians. This was the dugout canoe, or the tsi-yu' as the Cherokee called it. The dugout was much different from canoes made today.

LESSON 9 – TENNESSEE RIVER

Since the Cherokee located their villages along streams and rivers, the dugout was a very necessary vehicle to them.

Horses - After the first Europeans came to America, the favorite mode of travel became horse. The Spanish were the first to introduce horses into Alabama. The Cherokee eventually loved horses which greatly improved travel.
After the meeting with the first Europeans, our Indian people used horses as another way to travel. The horse was a beautiful animal and our people no longer had to walk long distances and could go a lot faster on land. The first horses in Alabama came from the Spanish explorers led by Desoto in 1540.

Review Questions

1. How did our Indian ancestors travel on water?
2. What shape does the Tennessee River bend look like in Alabama?
3. How many warriors did the dugout canoe carry?
4. What was the canoe guided by?
5. How did our Indian ancestors sit in the canoes?
6. Our early ancestors used what type of material to make their hunting points?
7. Name one thing the Cherokees used the Tennessee River for:
8. What is flint?
9. Name one important food source our ancestors found in the Tennessee River?
10. Where is the Tennessee River located in Alabama?
11. What was the Indian name of the Tennessee River?
12. Where is fresh water mussels found?
13. What is the largest river that flows through Alabama?
14. What year did Desoto and the Spanish explorers bring horses to Alabama?
15. What was the average length of a dugout canoe?
16. The dugout canoe is made from what type of wood?
17. What river was very important to the Cherokee?
18. What rock comes from the Tennessee River?
19. What was another way our ancestors used mussel shells besides food?
20. Chert was commonly called?
21. What does Chake Thlocko mean?
22. Where was there an abundance of flint located?
23. What does Hogohegee mean?
24. What were the three names for the Tennessee River?
25. Name the three states the Tennessee River runs through?
26. Explain why the Tennessee River was also called "The Great Bend" by the Cherokee:

LESSON 9 – TENNESSEE RIVER

27. What did our ancestors use the mussel shells to build?
28. What did the Cherokees call the Shoals?
29. The Tennessee River is a small part of the state line between what two states?
30. What did the Archaic Indian sometimes use the shell mounds for:
31. What state park in Alabama is located on the Tennessee River?

LESSON 10 – EUROPEAN CONTACT

Desoto - Who was Hernando Desoto? (He was a Spanish explorer) Desoto was the first European to move inland to the heart of Alabama Indian Country. Desoto's goal was to conquer the Indians, steal their gold and become a very wealthy man.

In 1540, Desoto entered Alabama and crossed the Tennessee River near Guntersville. He was thought to be the first European to discover the Tennessee River. Desoto's party consisted of about 600 men and in addition numerous Indians who went along as guides, laborers, and bearers of burdens. Desoto obtained food by seizing it from the Indians who had stored up small amounts for their own use. It was Desoto's custom to seize Indian chiefs who were then held hostage to ensure that Desoto got what he wanted. One of these was Chief Tuskaloosa. Tuscaloosa is a Creek Indian word that means "Black Warrior." The lusa or loosa means "black" and tusca or tusica means "warrior".

Meeting of Desoto and Giant Chief Tuscaloosa *(History of Alabama for Junior High Schools)*

When Desoto and his men first came to Alabama, Indian people welcomed the Spaniards. Desoto was cruel to Indians. Chief Tuskaloosa and his warriors fought a battle with Desoto. Since Desoto and his men had guns, the Indians lost the fight. According to Desoto's reports, about 2500 Indians were killed. Tuskaloosa was one of them. There were only 80 of Desoto's men killed. The Spaniards were willing to fight the Indians, because they had armor to protect themselves from the Indian arrows. The greatest of all advantages was the fact that the Spaniards had horses.

Desoto did not find gold in Alabama. After the battle, he led his group further west. Desoto was the first European who discovered the Mississippi River. Desoto was the first European to discover the Tennessee River, the Coosa, the Tallapoosa, the Alabama, the Black Warrior, the Sipsey, the Tombigbee, and many lesser Creeks and streams of Alabama. After he died, his men buried him in the mighty Mississippi River. They did not want our Indian ancestors to know their leader was dead.

After Desoto, other men from Spain came into Alabama. None of them settled down to stay. Although, Desoto never found the gold that he so desperately sought in Alabama, he became one of the most famous explorers anywhere in the world.

LESSON 10 – EUROPEAN CONTACT

Diseases - New world diseases were among the greatest killers of Southeastern Indian people, both intentionally and unintentionally. The devastation of disease helped break the power of Native Americans and left them vulnerable to cultural changes brought by invading Europeans. Our Indian folks had no immunities to these diseases; therefore, the Indian population diminished.

Smallpox was the worst of the new diseases. Other diseases included measles, typhus, tuberculosis, chicken pox, bubonic plague, diphtheria, and influenza. Smallpox would infect almost every individual who became exposed; 30 percent or more would die. For those who did survive, they would have disfiguring pockmarks on their bodies. Some even became blind.

Later, cholera epidemics came about. Cholera was transmitted by water infected by the disease germ. United States troops often transmitted the disease to Native Americans. Another was scarlet fever, which was not identified by the medical profession as a distinct affliction until the 18th century. Other diseases of lesser significance among the Native Americans were whooping cough, malaria, and mumps. There was also diabetes, which still affects American Indian people today.

Lamar Marshall – Proud of his Celtic-Indian Heritage

Celtic Contact - During the 1600s, Celtic people came into the North Alabama area as traders following Indian trails and roads. These Celtic people were Irish, Scotch, Welsh, or Scots-Irish descent. Many Celtic men married these young, beautiful Indian women. In the 1700s, many more Celtic men married Indian maidens and made their home here. The Chickasaws were the first to form communities of mixed ancestry, one known as McIntoshville in northeast Mississippi and another known as Breed Town on the Coosa River in Alabama.

Metis (mixed Native Americans) - Between 1816 and 1840, thousands of the southeastern Indians intermingled by marriage with Celtic (Irish, Scotch, Scots-Irish, Welsh)

Butch Walker – Proud of his Celtic-Indian Heritage

LESSON 10 – EUROPEAN CONTACT

pioneers who rapidly moved into the Indian nations. Many of these mixed-blood Indian people were eventually forced into hiding or denial of their Indian ancestry because of their fear of removal to the west by the United States Government. The newly established southern states, still in their infancy in the early 1800's refused the right of the Cherokee, Creek, or Chickasaw to establish Indian nations within the newly recognized sovereign states of Alabama, Georgia, Mississippi, and Tennessee.

In 1729, James Logan Colbert (Scotch) married three Chickasaw wives who bore him many children. James Colbert was in charge of a large pack train that brought British trade goods to North Alabama. Over the years, mixed-blood settlements separated themselves more and more from primitive full bloods. By the 1800s, the mixed-bloods had taken over management of Chickasaw tribal affairs.

John Melton (Irish) came into Lawrence County in the 1770s with the Cherokee Indians. He married a Cherokee woman. Melton had several children by his Indian wife, most of whom married white people. John Melton lived here in our county until his death in 1815. He founded the Cherokee town known as Melton's Bluff.

Remarkable advancement of the Cherokee as a people came about largely through the influence of Celtic families of mixed ancestry- Irish, Welsh, Scotch, Scots-Irish, and Cornish. During Indian removal, mixed-blood inhabitants remain in North Alabama because they were married to whites or were able to identify themselves with white ancestry. They sometimes called themselves Black Dutch or Black Irish to deny their true Indian blood.

Fearing not only for their personal property but also their lives, the remaining Indian people in North Alabama denied their Indian race, held to white man's ways, and blended their Indian and Celtic culture. The two cultures became assimilated in the general population. As children of mixed ancestry grew older, they were told of their Indian ancestors, but were not allowed to claim their rightful heritage. Since Indian removal, the degree of Indian blood of North Alabama's people has steadily diminished and will continue to do so throughout future generations. With the passage of Section 2 through 7 of the Civil Right Act of 1968, it became legal to be Indian and live in Alabama. Many Indian descendants of mixed ancestry began to seek and reclaim their Indian heritage, but for many it was too late.

Presently, about one-fifth (20%) of Lawrence County's school children are state recognized Indians of mixed Celtic ancestry. The majority of North Alabama 's Indian children have Cherokee, Chickasaw, or Creek, bloodlines. As an Indian person, you have a right to claim your race as Indian and should do so, but never deny any of your other previous ancestors.

LESSON 10 – EUROPEAN CONTACT

European Trade - We are going to be talking about trade with our Indian ancestors. Trade was a very important part of their lives, because they didn't have money to buy things. Can anyone name something that they might have traded?

The whites would trade strings of cheap beads for deerskins. Trade between Indian people and Europeans was based mostly on animal's skins. An Indian could get a rifle for about 30 deerskins.

Trading Party led by Chief Doublehead

Native animals such as whitetail deer, black bear, eastern cougar, timber wolves and eastern elk became depleted throughout the Southeastern United States, because of all the hunting and trading. Trading with the white man changed the way our Indian ancestors lived. Trading wasn't necessarily a good thing for Indian people. The traders found that they could manipulate Indian people. Most of the time, Indians hated them, so the traders usually lived hard and dangerous lives. One of the other items for trade was Indian slaves. The French justified Indian slavery on the grounds that it saved them from cruel deaths at the hands of their enemies. In 1708, the total population of South Carolina was 9,580 including 2,900 blacks and 1,400 Indian slaves. In 1712, an Indian man and woman sold for 18 or 20 pounds.

Doublehead by 1800s was living on the Tennessee River at Brown's Ferry. His old home site is still visible across the river from the Brown's Ferry Nuclear Plant. He requested a keelboat in 1802 for cotton trade to New Orleans. In 1805, he signed the Wafford Settlements, which allowed for Gaines Trace. The Trace allowed cotton trade to Cotton Gin

LESSON 10 – EUROPEAN CONTACT

Port, MS, and East Port, MS. At Doublehead's death on August 9, 1807, he owned 40 slaves.

Jackson – According to the Documents on United States Indian Policy written by Francis P. Prucha, on December 8, 1829, record that President Andrew Jackson said, "The Southern tribes, having mingled much with the whites and made some progress in the arts of civilized life, have lately attempted to erect an independent government within the limits of Georgia and Alabama. These States, claiming to be the only sovereigns within their territories, extended their laws over the Indians, which induced the latter to call upon the United States for protection."

Jackson went on to say, "It seems to me visionary to suppose that in this state of things claims can be allowed on tracts of country on which they have neither dwelt nor make improvements, merely because they have seen them from the mountain or passed them in the chase." Jackson, the great Indian fighter of the Southeast, believed in the spoils system, "To the victor belongs the spoils of the war." After the Turkey Town Treaty in September 1816, Jackson laid claim to the Irish-Cherokee Indian farmland at Melton's Bluff in Lawrence County, Alabama, on November 22, 1816. As he acquired from the local Irish-Indian people at Melton's Bluff prior to the time that any legal land claims could be made, Jackson had no reservations about eliminating all Indian lands east of the Mississippi River after becoming President of the United States.

Denial - During the turbulent times in the early history of the Southeastern United States, Celtic people, who have always been somewhat rebellious freedom seekers, migrated into the Southeastern Indian farmlands, mingled with the native people, and married into their tribes. As the Federal Government forced the removal issue during the 1830's under Jackson's administration, mixed-blood Celtic-Indians began moving from the Cherokee Nation in Alabama, the Carolinas, Georgia, and Tennessee into the Warrior Mountains of northern Alabama. The mountains provided isolation and protection as long as they denied their Indian backgrounds. The Celtic-Indians, who were of dark complexion, would many times claim to be Black Dutch or Black Irish and deny their rightful Indian descent in order to stay in their aboriginal lands.

Intermarriage of Celtic and Indian people, who settled primarily on the poor isolated lands found in the Warrior Mountains as well as other isolated areas of northern Alabama, was common. After looking into their eyes and examining the features of those who make efforts to reclaim links to their Indian past, many common threads appear which not only strengthen but also confirm that the vast majority of these people are truly Celtic-Indians afflicted with over 150 years of denial. Isolationism and intermarriage forced their complexions fairer through the genetic sieve of the Celtic which transcends nearly four

LESSON 10 – EUROPEAN CONTACT

centuries. However, from within their hearts they speak with a straight tongue of their Indian ancestors who survived in the Warrior Mountains of Alabama.

The Trail Of Tears - More than 150 years ago the Southeastern Indians became a conquered people. This did not happen quickly or easily. They had fought to stay and keep their land and had lost. They arrived like ghosts in Oklahoma, their destination. All of them were footsore, sick, and weary of their long journey, which began in October 1838 and ended in March 1839. They had walked more than 800 miles and more than 4,000 died. Many arrived more dead than alive.

Indian Removal Act 1830 - The Cherokee Removal came after years of pressure by white settlers who said they needed the Cherokees' land. And so, they said, the Cherokees must go. President Thomas Jefferson was the first to initiate the removal of some 1,130 Cherokees from our area in the summer of 1808.

On May 28, 1830, congress passed an act authorizing the exchange of lands in the west for those lands east of the Mississippi River held by Indian tribes. President Andrew Jackson was determined to see all Indian people removed from the eastern United States.

Review Questions

1. What did our ancestors trade?
2. Who wanted to steal the Indians gold and become wealthy?
3. Did Desoto and his men have guns?
4. Did Desoto find gold in Alabama?
5. What was the worst of the new world diseases?
6. Who was the first Spanish explorer in Alabama?
7. How many deerskins did our ancestors trade for one rifle?
8. Tuscaloosa is a Creek Indian word meaning what?
9. How many men did Desoto have with him?
10. Was Desoto nice to the Indians?
11. Who was the first white land owner in Lawrence County?
12. Approximately how many people died on the Trail of Tears?
13. Where was Desoto buried at?
14. Who was the first European to discover the Tennessee River?
15. Which disease was transmitted through the water?
16. Which man had three Chickasaw wives?
17. What was Andrew Jackson responsible for?
18. What does Métis mean?
19. What tribe of Indians were the first to form communities of mixed ancestry?
20. What descent are Celtic people?

LESSON 10 – EUROPEAN CONTACT

21. The Celtic-Indians, who were of dark complexion, would many times claim to be?
22. What month did the Trail of Tears begin in?
23. What was it called when Celtic's married Indians?
24. What year did the Trail of Tears begin and end?
25. Approximately how many Cherokees died of the small pox disease?
26. How many miles did our Indian ancestors walk on the Trail of Tears?
27. What act was passed in 1830 that caused the Cherokee to move to Oklahoma also known as the Trail of Tears?
28. What was the destination of the Cherokee people on the Trail of Tears?
29. Where did the Chickasaws first form communities of mixed ancestry?
30. How many of Desoto's men were killed?
31. What race did the Celtic Indians claim to be in order to stay in Alabama?
32. How long did the Trail of Tears last?
33. Who was the Irishman that came into Lawrence County in the 1770's with the Cherokee Indians and founded a Cherokee town known as Melton's Bluff?
34. Why did Doublehead request a keelboat in 1802?

LESSON 11 – FIVE TRIBES OF NORTH ALABAMA

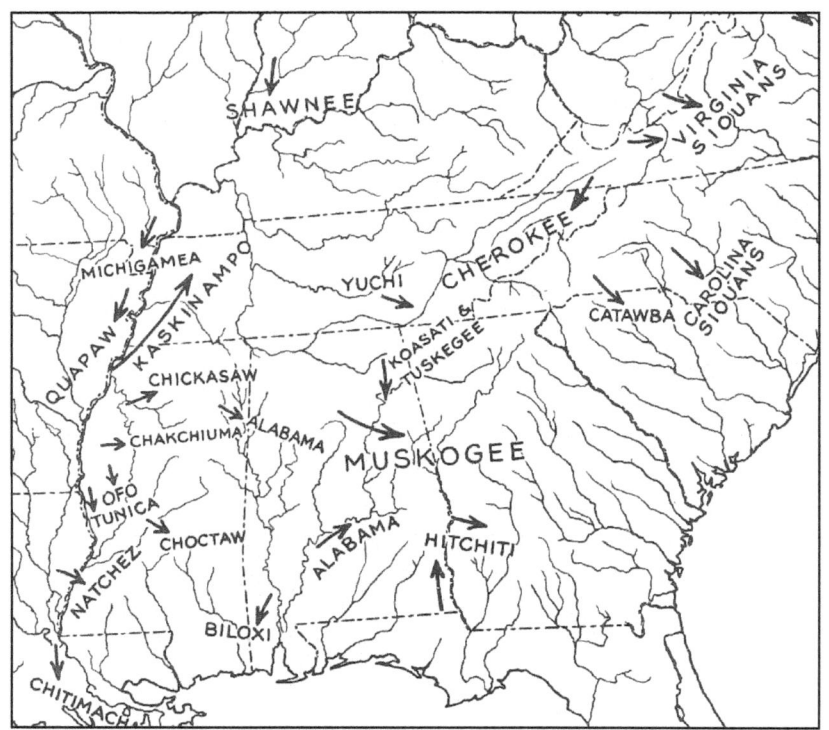

Tribal Movement according to the Tradition and Earliest Records

There were five major Indian tribes of early North Alabama. When the first European settlers came to Alabama, lesser Indian tribes were also found in Alabama. The four major tribes of Alabama: Creek, Choctaw, Chickasaw and Cherokee, along with the Seminoles of Florida, are often referred to as the "five civilized tribes." Their civilization was very advanced according to historic documents about the area and due to the intermarriage with Celtic people and other Europeans.

The five major Indian tribes of North Alabama were Yuchi, Creek, Shawnee, Chickasaw, and Cherokee. These were five groups of historic Indian people known by tribal names instead of by cultures. Most Indian people of the historic period lived in villages near rivers or other waterways. They were both farmers and hunters. They believed the land belonged to all people, and they took care of the part they used. They killed only the animals they needed for food, and then used the skins for clothes or cover.

Andrew Jackson

The four major Alabama tribes occupied most of the southeastern United States, but their territories met in Alabama. Each was in a corner of the state. The Cherokees, Creeks, and Chickasaws lived in North Alabama . The Chickasaw and Cherokee were in the two northern corners. The Cherokees were mainly on the northeast side of Alabama, and the Chickasaws on the northwest. The Choctaws occupied the west and southwest while the Creeks were in the northern side of Alabama, central, and southeastern part of Alabama. Although the four tribes were similar in many ways, they each had their own customs and beliefs. If their differences could have been overcome, perhaps they could have banded

LESSON 11 – FIVE TRIBES OF NORTH ALABAMA

together in the nineteenth century and prevented their removal to western lands by the Federal Government.

Andrew Jackson - Andrew Jackson was the first white landowner in Lawrence County, Alabama, at Melton's Bluff. He purchased the land from a Cherokee, named David Melton, on November 22, 1816. He called the land the Mussel Shoals Plantation and his town, he named Marathon. He sold his Lawrence County land in 1827, probably to the Gilchrist family.

The election of Andrew Jackson as President in 1828 resulted in one of the darkest eras for the American Indians in Alabama. The Alabama Emigrating Company forcefully removed our Indian ancestors from the State of Alabama and surrounding southern states. Thousands of southern Indians died while they were being forced to march on the infamous Trail of Tears.

Yuchi - The Yuchi were here when five Canadians descended down the Tennessee River in 1701. John R. Swanton in his book, The Indians of the Southeastern United States, shows the Yuchi living in this area at the Mussel Shoals in the early 1700's. For some reason, part of the Yuchi migrated to the Hiwassee River in Tennessee and the rest migrated south to the Chattahoochee River on the Alabama-Georgia border. After fighting the Cherokee in Tennessee, these northern Yuchi also migrated south to the Chattahoochee River Valley.

Creek - The Creeks were Muscogee people who lived in the central, eastern and southeastern part of our state. The Creeks were a nation of several small tribes joined together to form the Creek Confederacy. Its capital was Tukabachee, not far from present-day Montgomery.

Creek Indian *(George Catlin)*

Water and fire were sacred to the Creeks and most ceremonies centered on one or the other. The first duty of every Creek each morning was to bathe in the nearby river or stream even in very cold weather. In each village, the sacred fire had to be kept burning day and night. This fire was extinguished only at the time of the Green Corn Festival.

One of the Creek tribes gave us our state's name. Alabama was named for the Alabama River, which was named for the Alibamos Indians. The word "Alabama" comes from the Indian word meaning "thicket clearers."

LESSON 11 – FIVE TRIBES OF NORTH ALABAMA

The Creeks of North Alabama lived from the Tennessee Divide to South. They were the only tribe to live primarily in Alabama. The Creeks' lifestyle was very similar to other Southeastern Indians; therefore, much of the following information in this lesson can be compared to other Indian tribes that occupied much of the state.

The Creeks divided their towns into the red and white. Red was for war and the war chief always came from a red town. Peace talks were always held in a white town, lead by a chief from a white clan. In a white town, in which the buildings were stained white, no man could be killed. But in times of war, reds and whites fought together against the common enemy.

Creek men were fearless warriors, productive farmers, and skilled hunters. Although the warriors gave no quarter in battle, they did offer their captured foes a chance to join the confederacy. The land that they cultivated belonged to the whole town. Men and women worked together to harvest corn, squash, pumpkins, beans, and sweet potatoes. When hunting, the hunter only killed enough food in order for his family to survive. He never took more than he needed.

Apart from farming, men and women engaged in different jobs. The men hunted, built buildings, made war, and governed; and, the women raised children, cooked, and made clothing. From birth, boys were treated differently from girls. The boys were wrapped in cougar furs to take on that animal's fierceness. The girls were dressed in deer or bison skins. The boys spent most of their day wandering in the woods and practicing with their bow and arrows. The girls had less freedom. They usually stayed with the women and learned to tend the garden, keep the fire going, and make pottery, baskets, mats, and clothing.

Shawnee - These Algonquin Indian people migrated into the Tennessee River Valley after it was vacated by the Yuchi. In the early 1700's, the Shawnee came from the Cumberland (Nashville, TN) and Ohio River Valleys and lived in the North Alabama area as a tribe until the middle 1700's. Even though the tribe was forced from the Tennessee River area by a combination of Chickasaw and Cherokee forces, the Shawnee hunting parties continued to forage in the area for years afterward. Tecumseh was the great Shawnee leader who tried to unite the southern tribes against white encroachment. He was supposedly half Creek and half Shawnee. Some Shawnee also intermarried with the Cherokee.

Chickasaw - The Chickasaws were also Muscogee people who lived in Northwestern Alabama and in parts of Mississippi and Tennessee. They are mostly remembered as skilled warriors. Chickasaws usually tried to sneak up on their enemies and surprise them. As a surprise tactic, the group of warriors divided into smaller groups of three or four. They would step in each other's tracks so they would appear to be only one. They kept in touch with the other groups by imitating animal sounds--the owl, wolf, fox, and bird. Often the

LESSON 11 – FIVE TRIBES OF NORTH ALABAMA

Chickasaw warriors were satisfied with just touching the victims with a special stick called a coup. Touching was considered as brave an act as killing.

Cherokee - The Cherokee in Alabama were Iroquoian people who lived in the northeastern part of the state and the Tennessee River Valley. They called themselves "the principal people." One historian says the name "Cherokee" was given to them by other Indians and means "people who speak a different language." Another historian says English traders called them cherk, which means fire. This was because fire was sacred to these Indians.

Cherokee Indian *(George Catlin)*

The Cherokee under the leadership of Doublehead moved into Lawrence County about 1780. Doublehead lived in Doublehead's Village at Brown's Ferry for at least 12 years and possibly much longer. He signed the Cotton Gin Treaty of 1806, which placed a cotton gin in Lawrence County at Melton's Bluff. He was assassinated on August 9, 1807, by Major Ridge, Alex Saunders, and John Rogers. Doublehead is supposedly buried in Butler Cemetery on Blue Water Creek in Lauderdale County, Alabama; however, many believe his grave is located in a small mound of chert stones on a knoll just north of Highway 72 and east of Blue Water Creek overlooking the Blue Water Oldfields, now a polo club.

One famous Cherokee was Sequoyah. He was shown how to write his name in English by Charles Hicks who had equal shares of land with Moses Melton in an early Cherokee Treaty. The Melton's lived in Lawrence County. Sequoyah saw that white men could send news on paper he called "talking leaves." Sequoyah wanted his people to do the same. He spent twelve years creating an alphabet based on the sounds in the Cherokee language. This is called the Cherokee syllabary. The syllabary was finished in 1819. Thousands of Cherokees were taught to read and write. Some Cherokees started a newspaper called the Cherokee Phoenix. It was written in both the English and the Cherokee languages.

Choctaw Indian *(George Catlin)*

Choctaw - The Choctaw tribe did not live in North Alabama; however, they were an important tribe living to the south and west of our area. They lived in southwestern Alabama and in southeastern Mississippi. One of their customs is strange to us. They placed a baby's head against a wooden cradleboard, and then tied it down with leather strips. This pushed the soft bones of the

LESSON 11 – FIVE TRIBES OF NORTH ALABAMA

baby's head, and they became flat like the board. The head stayed flat after it was taken off the board. The Indians thought a flattened head was handsome.

The Choctaws also had an unusual burial custom. The body was covered with skins and bark, and placed on a raised platform near the house. Food, drinks, clothing and personal belongings were placed with the body to ride it on its long journey into the next life. A fire, close by, provided warmth on its journey. The body stayed on the platform until it had decomposed. Then, the "buzzard men" or bone pickers came and picked the remaining flesh from the bones. The bones were then placed in a box or basket and taken to the bone house.

Review Questions

1. How many tribes lived in North Alabama?
2. What work did the Indian people do?
3. What were animal skins used for?
4. Which tribe divided their towns into red & white?
5. What did Andrew Jackson name his town?
6. What tribe gave us our state's name?
7. What tribe was known as "skilled warriors"?
8. What did the two Creek towns stand for?
9. The word "Alabama" comes from the Indian word meaning what?
10. Which tribe was the only tribe to live primarily in Alabama?
11. Who was the famous Cherokee that created the Cherokee alphabet?
12. What tribe placed their baby's head against a wooden cradle board to make it flat?
13. What tribe considered "touching" a very brave act?
14. Who was the Cherokee leader that lived at Brown's Ferry?
15. In a white town, what did it stand for when the buildings were stained white?
16. What did the Cherokee people call themselves?
17. What inspired Sequoyah to invent the Cherokee alphabet?
18. What did the Cherokee call themselves?
19. Name an unusual custom practices by the Choctaw Indians?
20. What tribe did not live in North Alabama?
21. Which tribe lived primarily in Alabama?
22. Where did the Yuchi live in the early 1700s?
23. What was Alabama named for?
24. What tribe divided their town into red and white?
25. What year did Andrew Jackson become president and why did it result in one of the darkest eras for the American Indians in Alabama?
26. What year was the Cotton Gin Treaty signed and who signed it?
27. What were the men called that picked the flesh from the bones of the dead?
28. Name the four major tribes that occupied most of the southeastern U.S. but their territories met in Alabama?

LESSON 11 – FIVE TRIBES OF NORTH ALABAMA

29. What did Sequoyah refer to as "talking leaves"?
30. How long did it take Sequoyah to invent the alphabet?
31. What year was the Cherokee syllabary finished?
32. When was Doublehead assassinated and which three men were responsible?

LESSON 12 – CREEK TRIBE

Since many of our Indian students have Creek blood, we are going to talk about the Creek Indians and their lifestyle. The Creeks of North Alabama lived from the Tennessee Divide to the south. They were the only tribe to live primarily in Alabama. The Creeks' lifestyle was very similar to other Southeastern Indians; therefore, they can be compared to other Indian tribes that occupied much of the state.

Sacred Indian Marker Tree in Indian Tomb Hollows

Creek Towns - The Creeks divided their towns into the red and white. Red was for war and the war chief always came from a red town. Peace talks were always held in a white town, lead by a chief from a white clan. In a white town, in which the buildings were stained white, no man could be killed. But in times of war, reds and whites fought together against the common enemy.

White towns were peace towns. People living in the white towns were very peaceful and did not want to fight. In fact, they only participated in ceremonies not related to war. The Creek Nation's most powerful chief was always from the white town. Red towns were war towns. War ceremonies were carried out in red towns. The people in the red towns organized war parties, led raids, and had religious ceremonies related to war.

Creek Farms - Creek men were fearless warriors, productive farmers, and skilled hunters. Although the warriors gave no quarter in battle, they did offer their captured foes a chance to join the confederacy. The land that they cultivated belonged to the whole town. Men and women worked together to harvest corn, squash, pumpkins, beans, and sweet potatoes. When hunting, the hunter only killed enough food in order for his family to survive. He never took more than he needed.

Apart from farming, men and women engaged in different jobs. The men hunted, built buildings, made war, and governed. The women raised their

LESSON 12 – CREEK TRIBE

children, cooked, and made clothing. From birth, boys were treated differently from girls. The boys were wrapped in cougar furs to take on that animal's fierceness. The girls were dressed in deer or bison skins. The boys spent most of their day wandering in the woods and practicing with their bow and arrows. The girls had less freedom. They usually stayed with the women and learned to tend the garden, keep the fire going, and make pottery, baskets, mats, and clothing.

Creek Religion - Water and fire were sacred to the Creeks and most ceremonies centered on one or the other. The first duty of each Creek every morning was to bathe in the nearby river or stream even in very cold weather. In each village, the sacred fire had to be kept burning day and night. This fire was extinguished only at the time of the Green Corn Festival.

Creek Nation - We are going to talk about the Creek Indians and their lifestyle. Their homes, weapons, clothing, and food are very similar to the Cherokee Indians and other Southeastern tribes because they all lived in the same climate and in the same area. The name Creek was given to these Indians by English traders because they lived on the Ochese Creek in Georgia. Also, Creek tribes were often named for their towns. The southern fourth of Lawrence County, Alabama, was ancestral Creek land and lay from the High Town Path (Tennessee Divide) toward the south and east.

The Creek domain ran from the High Town Path (Tennessee Divide) to the south and east into Georgia. The Creeks of North Alabama, helped Doublehead establish towns along the Tennessee River. Creeks fought the Chickasaws in our county at the Battle of Indian Tomb Hollow. Creeks lost their claim to the land in North Alabama in the 1814 Treaty at Fort Jackson. Andrew Jackson's forces defeated the Creeks at the Battle of Horseshoe Bend. Moulton, Alabama is named after Lt. Michael Moulton, who was killed at Horseshoe Bend.

Creek Indians brought many different tribes together to form a Creek Nation. Some of the tribes which joined with the Creeks were the Alibamos, Koasatis, Apalachees, Yuchies, and the Shawnees. There were more than forty-five Creek towns with a population of 15,000 to 20,000 people. People living in these Creek towns spoke six different languages, had their own customs, and their own chiefs.

The deep, worn, and old route of the High Town Path runs adjacent to the present day Ridge road and along the Continental Divide in Lawrence County

Creek Government - The Upper Creeks lived in about forty towns on the Coosa, Tallapoosa, and Alabama Rivers. The Lower Creeks lived in about twenty towns on the Okmulgee,

LESSON 12 – CREEK TRIBE

Flint, and Chattahoochee Rivers. Each town had its own chief. Then each division, Upper and Lower Creeks had a head chief (called a micco) who had authority over all the other town chiefs. The micco ruled over the tribal council. The chief would sit on a high platform, which raised him above other men.

Creek War - After the Creek-Indian War was over in 1814, the Creek land in North Alabama and areas to the south was declared public land. Land-hungry whites rushed in to claim the Creek land. During the war between the Creek Indians and the white settlers, there were several major battles that may be familiar to you: The Battle of Fort Mims and the Battle of Horseshoe Bend. The fight at Horseshoe Bend was the final battle for the Creeks. The 1,000 mighty Creek warriors could not win against General Jackson and his 3,300 soldiers. After the Battle of Horseshoe Bend, most of the Creek land was taken from them. In 1835 and 1836, with some of their chiefs in chains, some 14,000 Creeks were forced to move to Oklahoma.

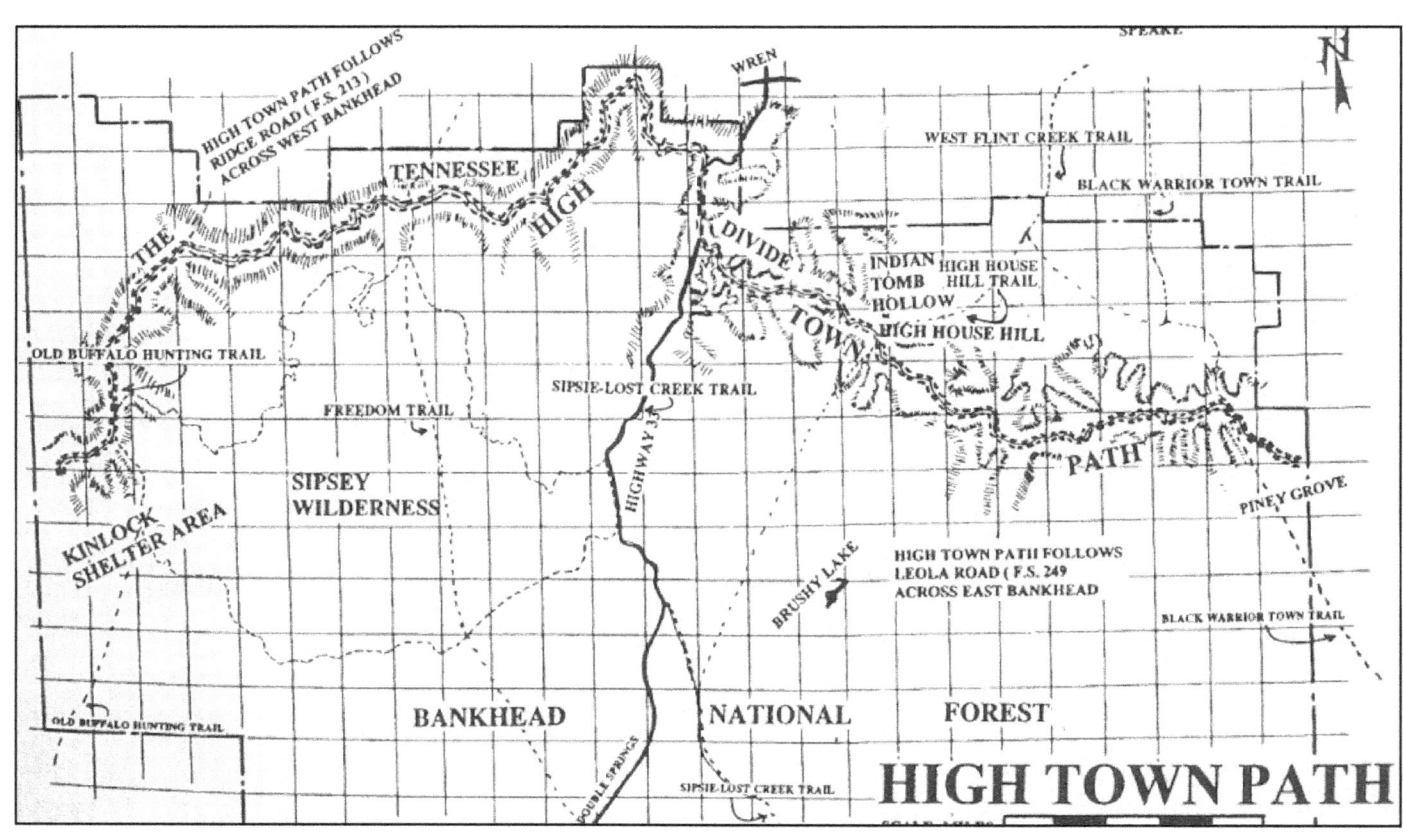

Indian Trails through the Warrior Mountains are shown Crossing the High Town Path

Lawrence County, Alabama - Two groups of Creeks came through Lawrence County during removal. Lawrence County has several things in common with Creek people: (1) Creek land lay from the High Town Path to the south. (2) Moulton is named after Lt. Michael Moulton who was killed during the Battle of Horseshoe Bend. (3) Andrew Jackson who defeated the Creeks became the first white landowner in Lawrence County, Alabama.

LESSON 12 – CREEK TRIBE

(4) The High Town Path, the Creek Nation's northern border, ran across southern Lawrence County. (5) A major Creek trading path, Black Warriors' Path, ran across eastern Lawrence County.

Review Questions

1. What was the first thing the Creeks did each morning?
2. The Creeks divides their towns into what colors?
3. What did men and women grow together in their crops?
4. What were two things sacred to the Creeks?
5. What did the men and women do together?
6. Did the Creek hunter kill more than he needed?
7. What town was the most powerful chief from?
8. How many towns was the Creek tribe divided into?
9. Did the Creek hunter kill more food than they needed?
10. During what ceremony was the fire extinguished?
11. What were Creek men known for?
12. If Creeks divided their towns into red and white, what did the colors stand for?
13. When was the Creek-Indian war over?
14. What did it mean when the buildings were painted white in a Creek town?
15. Which town was the Creek nation's most powerful leader/chief from?
16. What were the Creek women responsible for?
17. Creeks fought the Chickasaws in Lawrence County at what battle?
18. Where was Lt. Michael Moulton killed?
19. How many Creeks fought in the Battle of Horseshoe Bend?
20. The Creeks were often named for their what?
21. What was the final battle for the Creeks?
22. How many Creeks were forced to move to Oklahoma and during what year did this happen?
23. What was a Creek Indian Chief called and why did he sit on a high platform?
24. How many towns did the Upper Creeks live in?
25. Creeks in Alabama Territory lost their claim to their land in the 1814 Treaty of _____.
26. What was the name of the head chief of the upper and lower Creeks, who had authority over all town chiefs?
27. Where did the Creeks primarily live?
28. Who was Moulton named after?
29. Which major trading path ran across eastern Lawrence County?
30. Where was the first battle of the Creek and Indian War?

LESSON 13 – CHICKASAW TRIBE

Chickasaw - Today, we are going to talk about the Chickasaw Indians that lived in North Alabama. The Chickasaw Nation owned most of North Alabama by the Chickasaw Boundary Treaty of January 10, 1786. The Chickasaw tribe claimed a large portion of land covering West Alabama, Northeast Mississippi, Tennessee, Kentucky, and even Ohio.

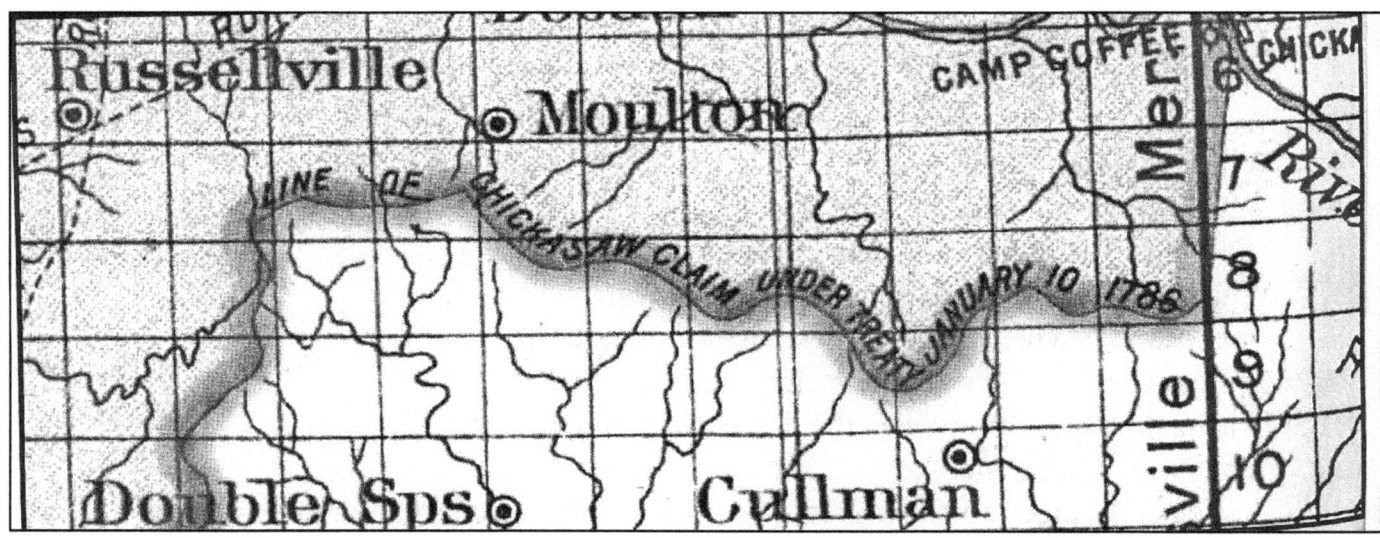

High Town Path – South Boundary of the Chickasaw Nation

George and Levi Colbert were Chickasaw chiefs who were ½ Celtic (Scotch) and ½ Indian (Chickasaw). Colbert County is named after this Indian family.

The Chickasaws were smaller in number than the other Indian tribes in Alabama, yet they claimed a large region of land. Some of the land regions overlapped with the land claims of the Cherokee. The Chickasaws noted for the defense of their land and after the white people came; gained a reputation of being warlike people. They, like the Cherokees and Creeks, intermarried to a large degree with Celtic people.

Chief George Colbert's House at Colbert's Ferry in Colbert County

Warfare was conducted with much ceremony and occurred only in retaliation for attacks made on them. The Chickasaws believed that the success of a raid depended on the prewar ceremonies, which lasted for three days. During this time, the men ate nothing and drank a mixture made from the leaves of a variety of holly called the black

LESSON 13 – CHICKASAW TRIBE

drink. Stories of brave deeds were told by the older men and the young warriors painted their bodies with war paint.

Customs - The Chickasaws were known for being warlike people. That means they often participated in battles against other tribes in order to gain their land and possessions. The Chickasaws shared many of the same customs as the other southeastern tribes. One of these was in marriage. A Chickasaw man was allowed to have more than one wife. This marriage custom was also allowed when the Celtic people came and started intermarrying with the Indian.

Have any of you ever been to a wedding or had someone that you know to get married? The Chickasaws had weddings that were in some ways similar to the weddings we have today. The boyfriend would send his girlfriend a gift. If she accepted the gift that meant they would get married soon. When the time would come for them to be married, the man and woman would exchange gifts before other people. The man would select a nice ear of corn, divide it in half, give the woman one half and keep the other for himself. He also gave her a deer's foot as a sign that she should be ready to serve him, and in return she would give him some cakes of bread.

Who is responsible for taking care of you in your family? Your mother or daddy? Well, the mother was responsible for the children in the Chickasaw family. One interesting custom practiced by the Chickasaws was the flattening of the infants (baby's) forehead. The mother would place a block of wood covered with buckskin or a bag of sand fastened to the head. They thought this made the child look pretty. Later, over the years, they stopped doing this.

Chief George Colbert *(William L. McDonald – Lore of the River)*

In the family, the girls were disciplined by the mother. The boys were disciplined by the oldest uncle of the mother's family. Women were responsible for the up bringing of the girls, and the elders (older people in the tribe) took responsibility for the care and instruction of the boys.

Colbert - A well-known Celtic man to the Chickasaws was James Logan Colbert. He had three Chickasaw wives who had sons, which became important men in Chickasaw history. One of these sons was George Colbert, George married two of the Cherokee Chief Doublehead's daughters-Tuskiahooto and Saleechie. He was head chief of the Chickasaws for 12 years and became the wealthiest man in the Chickasaw Nation. Levi Colbert also became Chief of the Chickasaw Nation and is buried in Colbert County west of Cherokee, Alabama.

LESSON 13 – CHICKASAW TRIBE

Many of the Colbert family went west with the Chickasaw tribe during the removal, however; Colbert County in northwest Alabama was the home of this family and bears their name. Today many Chickasaw descendants still call northwest Alabama home. The houses of the Chickasaws in the North Alabama area were cabins built very much like those of the white people. George Colbert lived in a large two-story house that burned in 1927.

Review Questions

1. Who raised the Chickasaw children?
2. Were the Chickasaws warlike people?
3. Did the Chickasaws own Lawrence County?
4. What ceremony did they have that we still have today?
5. Name the two things the man would give the woman during their wedding ceremony?
6. What kind of houses did the Chickasaws build in North Alabama?
7. Name two brothers that were Chickasaw chiefs:
8. The mother's brother was responsible for what?
9. Who became the wealthiest man in the Chickasaw nation?
10. Were the Chickasaw men allowed to have more than one wife?
11. Who was the well-known Celtic man that had three Chickasaw wives?
12. What Alabama County is named after a Chickasaw chief?
13. What objects were used by the Chickasaws to flatten the baby's forehead?
14. What Chickasaw married Cherokee Chief Doublehead's daughters Tuskiahooto and Saleechie?
15. What Ceremony did they practice that we still practice today?
16. What kind of house did George Colbert live in?
17. Who was a well-known Celtic man to the Chickasaws that had three wives?
18. Who took responsibility for the care and instruction of the boys?
19. When did Gorge Colbert's house burn?
20. What county is named after George and Levi Colbert?
21. Who owned most of North Alabama by the Boundary Treaty of January 10, 1786?
22. What tribe was smaller in number than any other tribe in Alabama?
23. Like the Cherokees and Creeks, the Chickasaw intermarried to a large degree with what people?
24. What tribe claimed a large region of land despite their small number?

LESSON 14 – CHEROKEE TRIBE

Cherokee Nation - Our state and others together, make up what we call the United States. (look at U.S. map) Long ago, this map did not look this way. Most of the land we live on now belonged to our Indian ancestors.

The Cherokee people lived in mostly three states. (look at state map again) Most of the Cherokee Nation lay in Georgia, Tennessee, and Alabama. The northern part of Georgia was known as Cherokee County and made up half of the Cherokee Nation in the 1800's. The other half lay approximately between east Tennessee and North Alabama. In 1832, the State of Georgia made it illegal for Cherokees to assemble as a group at their capitol at New Echota; therefore, they moved their capitol from New Echota, Georgia to Red Clay, Tennessee. In 1838, most of the Cherokees east of the Mississippi were removed to Oklahoma by President Andrew Jackson.

North Alabama was Cherokee and Chickasaw country until the Turkey Town Treaty of 1816. Our Cherokee people lived in the North Alabama area from the Tennessee River on the north and the Warrior Mountains to the south.

Cherokee Legends - We are going to talk about Indian stories and legends. Legends and myths were an important part of Cherokee life. The mind of the Cherokee storyteller or myth-keeper was a storehouse of Indian traditions. Much of what we know today of our ancient Cherokees, we have learned from their myths and legends. Since our people had no written language, only word of mouth kept alive the traditions of their history, ceremonies, rituals, and their beliefs. The Cherokee stories were handed down from generation to generation. They told stories about animals, famous people, and creation.

A young boy was taken by a storyteller and taught how to tell a legend and be a good storyteller. As the child grew, he was not allowed to do the things other children did. He was given one primary goal in life which was to learn every myth or legend of his people and to eventually pass them on to someone else. A storyteller was a highly respected member of his tribe. No tribal function was considered complete without the presence and assistance of the storyteller. He took pride in his people and strived to preserve their heritage.

Today, many of our older Cherokee descendants (our grandparents and great grandparents) carry on the traditions of storytelling. You need to listen very closely to the stories your grandparents tell and show respect to your elders. Each family usually has one member that is a storyteller who passes down family history.

North Alabama Cherokees - The Cherokee lived in North Alabama from about 1770, under the leadership of Doublehead. The Chickasaws actually owned the land by the Chickasaw

LESSON 14 – CHEROKEE TRIBE
Cherokee Council House Museum at Oakville

Boundary Treaty of January 10, 1786, but the Cherokees lived here. Doublehead's two oldest daughters, Tuskiahooto and Saleechie, married Chickasaw Chief George Colbert. He allowed the Cherokees to live in North Alabama because they were the people of his wives. Today, we have descendants of Doublehead and George Colbert still living in North Alabama.

All Cherokee towns usually had a community building known as a council house where the local government was run by the people of the village.

The Cherokee council house had seven sides representing each of the seven matrilineal clans and the seven directions of the world. The seven directions are east, north, west, south, up, down, and inside yourself because you are always the center of your universe. Seven was a sacred number to our Indian people.

The Cherokee Tribe has seven clans. Who can tell me what a clan is? A clan is like a family of close relatives and the tribe is made up of all these seven different clans who are distantly related to each other. The seven clans are Bird, Deer, Long Hair, Paint, Wolf, Wild Potato, and BLUE, which you are a member of.

Cherokee Stickball - Although Indian people worked very hard to do their chores in the village, they also took time out to play. One of the first games they played was called "stickball" or "ballplay." Stickball or the ballplay is one Cherokee sport that has lived on throughout the years. Even though today it has been changed to erase some of its dangers, everyone still loves the ball game. The Cherokee in Cherokee, N.C. still play stickball at their Fall festival.

LESSON 14 – CHEROKEE TRIBE

The day before the ball game is played is a day spent in preparation. Special sequences of events are followed to prepare participants for the game. The ball dance, going to water (dipped themselves seven times), and scratching are carefully done to bring strength, speed, courage, endurance, and purification to your team and to weaken your opponents. Sometimes players will draw a cross or a semicircle with a dot in it on their upper body as a sign of good luck. Slippery elm is chewed and the spit was rubbed on their bodies to make themselves slippery.

In the ball game, there are two teams. One village or clan plays against another village or clan. They play in a large field with a goal at each end for each of the teams. The equipment needed to play consists of two ball sticks for each player and a game ball made from soft animal skins, about the size of a walnut.

Cherokee Stickball

The object of the game is to be the first team to score twenty points. You score one point each time the ball crosses your goal post. You can only move the ball with your ball sticks. Sometimes it takes all day long for a team to win. Today, the points have been cut back and twelve points wins the game.

Everyone anxiously awaits the signal from the Medicine Man that he has finished the rites and is coming up from the water. One team yells three short calls that are repeated by the opposing team. They are ready to get onto the field. The Medicine Man begins the game by tossing the ball into the air and then the players try to get to the ball, by using their sticks, to score points for their team.

Many would go home with broken arms or legs, cuts, or bruises. Sometimes, players even died in their eagerness to prove their clan was the most skilled. Today, rules are given to help prevent the players from getting hurt.

Before the game began, everyone would bring their possessions to bet with. Ladies would put on all of their clothing and wager skirt against skirt, blouse against blouse with the opposing team's women. Men would wager weapons, animals, whatever they had.

State Recognized Cherokee Tribes - There are nine Indian tribes in the State of Alabama that have enrolled several thousand Indians. These represent about 13% of the 165,416 persons in Alabama who disclosed that they were of Indian ancestry in the Federal Census of 1980. Most of those with Indian ancestry in Alabama are descendants of the Cherokee, Choctaw, and Creek tribes who were the aboriginal inhabitants of the State. While the majority of the members of these tribes were removed to Indian Territory in the 1830s, a

LESSON 14 – CHEROKEE TRIBE

significant Indian minority remained in the State, including Cherokees in North Alabama, Creeks in South Alabama, as well as a sizeable community of Choctaws in Southwest Alabama (Alabama Indian Affairs Commission, 1988). Today, four state recognized tribes represent the aboriginal Cherokee people who claimed Alabama as their home. These tribes are the Echota Cherokee Tribe of Alabama, Cherokees of Northeast Alabama, Cher-o-Creek Intra Tribal Indians, and United Cherokee AniyunWiya Nation.

Review Questions

1. What was the Cherokees favorite game?
2. The Cherokee people lived mostly in how many states?
3. What is a storyteller?
4. What clan are you a part of?
5. Where is the Cherokee capitol located?
6. How many sides does a Cherokee Council House have?
7. Name four of the seven directions:
8. What was the Cherokee's sacred number?
9. No tribal function was considered complete without the presence and assistance of what person?
10. Explain the importance of a storyteller?
11. Name the three states the Cherokee people lived in:
12. Where was the local government held?
13. The Cherokee capitol was moved from where to where?
14. How have the Cherokee people kept alive their traditions of their history, ceremonies, rituals, and their beliefs?
15. What games did the Cherokee love to play?
16. Name the seven clans of the Cherokee? Where was the Cherokee capitol in Georgia?
17. Since our ancestors had no written language how was their past kept alive?
18. The stories or myths our ancient Cherokee ancestors told were also known as what?
19. Who was the Chickasaw chief that allowed the Cherokees to live in North Alabama?
20. All Cherokee towns had a community building where local government was run known as what?
21. What type of Indians lived mostly in Alabama, Georgia, and Tennessee?
22. Our Indian ancestors kept their past alive by word of mouth, this is also known as what?
23. Who was the leader of the Cherokees'?
24. The people of the Cherokee Nation lived in mostly what three states?
25. The Cherokees' stories usually told about what?
26. Why was storytelling important to the Cherokees?
27. Whose leadership was the Cherokee's under while living in North Alabama?

LESSON 14 – CHEROKEE TRIBE

28. What president removed most of the Cherokees living east of Mississippi to Oklahoma?
29. The Cherokee people used a council house for what purpose?

LESSON 15 – SEVEN CLANS OF THE CHEROKEE

Our Cherokee ancestors regarded seven as their sacred number. Cherokee had seven directions. Can anyone name these directions? You should know four of them at least? (east/red, west/black, north/blue, south/white--the other directions were up/yellow, down/green, and center/brown). The center would be the direction pointing toward you. Because you were considered the center of your universe and you must walk your own direction in life.

"Seven" was a very significant and sacred number to the Cherokee people. In addition to the seven counselors and seven women, there were seven Cherokee clans, seven mother towns to serve as clan headquarters, and a seven-sided council house with a section of seats for representatives from each clan. The council house held approximately five hundred people.

Clan membership was inherited from one's mother and retained for life. Each person had a close relationship with four of the seven clans: the mother's clan (of which he was a member), the father's clan, the paternal grandfather's clan, and the maternal grandfather's clan. A person was expected to marry into one of the latter two of these four clans. Marriages took place in the council house with a priest officiating. In any single town, all of the clans were represented, and all members of any one clan considered themselves to be brothers and sisters. Clan membership was indicated by the color of feathers one wore.

The civil or peace government conducted the religious ceremonies of the tribe and acted in both a judicial and legislative capacity, holding court and making laws. Murder and inter-clan marriage were both punishable by death. Most criminal acts were avenged by members of the wronged family and were seldom left up to the government.

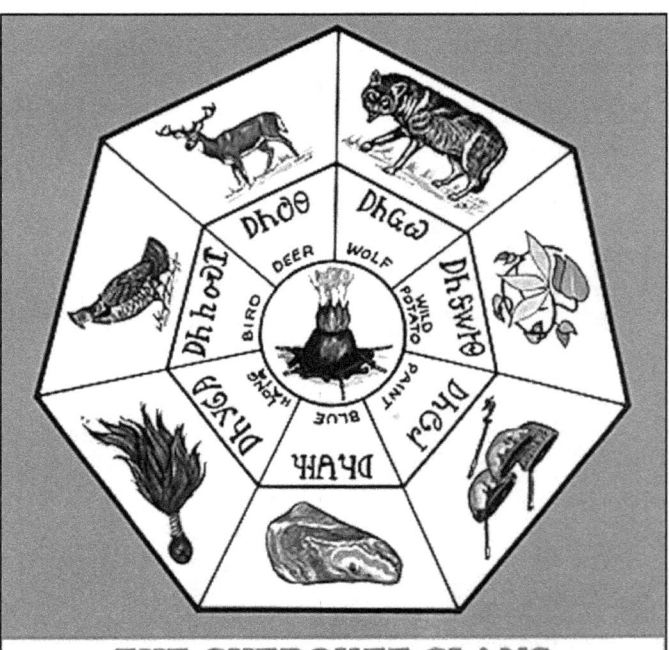

THE CHEROKEE CLANS
The above design symbolizes the seven clans of the Cherokee. The seven-clan system was a relational, social, religious and political structure brought forward from ancient times to have its remnant effect on the Cherokee people today. The number seven was sacred.

One's clan was derived from the mother and his/her only kinsmen were those who could be traced through her. One could not marry within his/her clan and his role in society and his political alignment was determined by his clan. Today the Cherokee communities closely resemble the old clans and representation in the Cherokee council is based on them.

SEVEN CLANS:
LONG HAIR (A NI GI LO HI)
BIRD (A NI TSI S KWA)   WILD POTATO (A NI GA TO GE WI)
BLUE (A NI SA HO NI)   WOLF (A NI WA YAH)
PAINT (A NI WO DI)   DEER (A NI KA WI)

In times of war a war chief, Kalanu, and his organization replaced the civil-peace organization. The war organization always wore red. The peace chief, though installed in yellow, customarily wore white.

LESSON 15 – SEVEN CLANS OF THE CHEROKEE

This design is the symbol of the seven clans of the Cherokees and the seven sided council house, which was the center of their governmental and ceremonial life. In the center, burns the sacred fire, kindled with seven kinds of wood. Around this fire, the struggles, victories, and agonies of the Cherokee empire were discussed and many momentous decisions of their history made.

A. Clans-   THE SEVEN CLANS
- Wild Potato A NI GA TO GE WI
- Bird............. A NI TSI S KWA
- Long Hair .... A NI GI LO HI
- Blue .... A NI SA HO NI
- Paint..................... A NI WO DI
- Deer..................... A NI KA WI
- Wolf................. A NI WA YAH

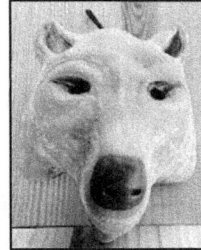

The Aniwayah, or **Wolf Clan**, in ancient days hunted like wolves, running after game and attacking in packs. They were fond of wolves and raised them in captivity, training wolf pups just as dogs were trained. It was considered bad luck to kill a wolf, although there is mention of a professional wolf killer who used magic to avoid the bad-luck consequences. Wolf Town is named after the Wolf Clan.

The Anikawi, or **Deer Clan**, members were once like the deer in swiftness. They kept deer in captivity and through special training became skilled in hunting and killing deer. They used prayer formulas and rituals to ward off divine retribution for any mistakes made in following their profession. A portion of Paint Town was once called Deer Place.

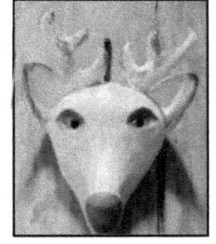

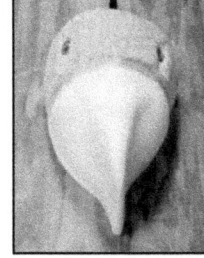

The Anitsiskwa, or **Bird Clan**, was fond of birds, and often had captive crows and chicken hawks. Members of the Bird Clan were renowned for their use of snares and blowguns in hunting. Bird Town is named after this clan.

The Aniwodi, or **Red Paint Clan**, members were noted for their skill in ritually employing red iron-oxide paint to attract lovers and gain protection from witches and other harm. They were known as great conjurers in those matters.

LESSON 15 – SEVEN CLANS OF THE CHEROKEE

The Anisahoni, or **Blue Clan**, was named after a bluish plant that was gathered from swamps and used for food and medicine. The plant was called sakoni or sahoni and was a kind of narrow-leafed grass that produced berries that looked like young cucumbers. The roots of the plant were used to protect children from diseases, and it was customary to bathe the children at the appearance of each new moon in a liquid made from the plant's boiled roots.

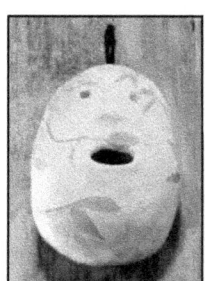
The Anigatogewi, or **Wild Potato Clan**, were gatherers of wild potatoes. These grew in swampy places along the rivers and were like sweet potatoes, except that they were round.

The Anigilohi, or Twisters Clan (**Long Hair**), obtained its name in one of two ways. One version has it that the name evolved through the word gagiloha, "one who twists," later changed to ugilaha, "one born twisted" --referring to the fact that they once were a proud people who strutted when they walked and twisted their shoulders in a haughty manner. A second version maintains that the name was derived from ugilohi, or "long hair," referring to the clan's love of personal adornment and elaborate hairstyles.

Seven Festivals -There are other ways that seven is significant to the Cherokee. This includes the seven festivals of the Cherokee.

SEVEN FESTIVALS OF THE CHEROKEE YEAR
    First New Moon of Spring .... March
    Solutsunigistisi.................Green Corn Ceremony .... August
    Donagohuni ....Ripe Corn Ceremony .... September
    Nuwatiegwa................ Great New Moon Ceremony..................... October
    Atohuna .... Friendship Ceremony.... October or November
    Elawatalegi ....Bouncing Bush Feast .... September
    Uku Dance .... The Chief Dance....................Every 7th year

Instruments used for music during the festivals and dances were: the drum, gourd rattles, turtle shell rattles, and flutes. The "Square," on a flat ground by the river and near the Council House, was an area designated and prepared for the ceremonies and dances. Green branches tied to high poles provided shade in the dance area, and the river close by provided the water for cold ceremonial plunges.

LESSON 15 – SEVEN CLANS OF THE CHEROKEE

Things sacred to the Cherokees - Eagle, Eagle Feathers, Rattlesnake, Fire, Smoke, Sun, Moon, Corn, "Seven", Quartz Crystals, The Ark.

Review Questions

1. How many directions are there?
2. What color is produced when you use blood root?
3. What ceremony was like our Thanksgiving?
4. What color represents north?
5. When was the Green Corn Ceremony?
6. Name two things sacred to the Cherokee?
7. Name three of seven Cherokee clans?
8. During the Cherokees'' Green Corn Ceremony, thanks were given for what?
9. What color represents the south?
10. Where did marriages take place?
11. What were some of the instruments used during the festival and dances?
12. How was a clan membership obtained?
13. What color did the peace chief customarily wear?
14. What was the most important instrument to the Cherokee?
15. The color of one's feathers indicated what?
16. What is placed in the center of the council house that kindles seven kinds of wood?
17. What type of potato is similar to the potatoes the Wild Potato clan gathered?
18. What clan was known as the twister clan?
19. What color did the war chief always wear?
20. What shape was the area close to the council house where ceremonies took place?
21. Name two reasons the Wolf clan obtained its name:
22. What were the two crimes punishable by death?
23. Name some things that were sacred to the Cherokee.
24. What was the flat ground by the river and the council house designated for ceremonies called?
25. How was clan membership indicated?
26. What served as the clan headquarters?
27. The Chief Dance was celebrated how often?
28. How did the Deer clan obtain its name?
29. How did the Bird clan obtain its name?
30. What clan were noted for their skill in employing red-oxide paint to attract lovers and gain protection from harm?

LESSON 16 – INDIAN TRAILS AND PATHS

Early Travel - Our Indian ancestors considered the land sacred; therefore, it could not be bought or sold. They believed that the earth was their mother and the sun was their father. They wanted to honor the land, as you are to honor your mother. They believed that the sun watched them with its great blazing eyes and, as long as it was on them, everything was all right. If the sun's eye was not shining on them, they were doomed. As they walked the trails across the land under the sun, they felt the precious land under their feet.

Our Cherokee Indian people traveled long ago by foot and dugout. These were the most common ways. Later on, the Cherokee used horses that were brought from overseas by the Europeans. At that period of time, they did not have the use of wheels, motors, and gasoline. Our Cherokee people were not a nomadic (roam from place to place) tribe and travel was limited to certain areas.

Early Trails - In order for our people to travel from neighbor to neighbor, or village to village, a system of trails was developed for easier traveling. Most of these trails and paths could be followed on foot or horseback but were not suitable for coaches or wagons. These Indian paths became important to white settlements and white development of the North Alabama area.

Some of these trails extended all the way across Alabama. There were a great many short trails and hunting trails, but there were fewer long trails. These trails were determined by the lay of the land. Many of today's highways and railroad lines follow these early trails.

We are going to discuss some important Indian trails that came through North Alabama . The early trails and paths later became some of the roads we travel today. Why do you think the trails were important to the Indian and white settlers during the 1700's and 1800's?

Many important Indian trails or roads ran through North Alabama. Trappers and Indian traders came down the Tennessee River by flatboat to the head of Elk River Shoals at Melton's Bluff. These early white intruders on Indian lands were allowed to remain because most of these Celtic traders had married into and were accepted in the Creek, Chickasaw, and Cherokee Nations.

From Melton's Bluff, two early Indian roads ran south through the Warrior Mountains. Gaines' Trace (Black Warriors' Path) went through the west and was established by a treaty negotiated by Doublehead in 1805. Mitchell Trace went Southeast through the Warrior Mountains and was named from Fort Mitchell in Russell County, Alabama. Mitchell Trace ran from Ft. Mitchell to Ft. Hampton in Limestone County, Alabama. Many other Indian trails traversed the dividing ridges of the Warrior Mountains creating a north-south network from the Warrior River Valley to the Tennessee River Valley. Doublehead's Trace followed

LESSON 16 – INDIAN TRAILS AND PATHS
1839 Map of Indian Roads

the approximate route of Highway 101 through Lauderdale and Lawrence Counties. Brown's Ferry Road ran from Huntsville to Courtland and crossed the Tennessee River by ferry as early as 1813 while still Indian land.

The High Town Path was an example of a long Indian trail that passed through North Alabama. This trail was named for the Creek village of High Town in present-day Rome, GA. The High Town Path extended from the site of Charles Town, South Carolina by Atlanta, Georgia, westward through the Cherokee Nation south of Sand Mountain, through the Creek Nation, and into the Chickasaw Nation. The trail passed through the present counties of Lawrence, Franklin, and Marion in Alabama prior to entering Mississippi. The trail ran in an east-west direction along the mountain ridges avoiding lowlands and creek crossings. The Leola Road and Ridge Road in Lawrence County represent the most accurate route of the High Town Path.

Another major Indian route into the Warrior Mountains was by way of the High Town Path also known as The Path or Ridge Path. The Path ran along the Continental Divide and followed portions of the Old Corn Road, Leola Road, Cheatham Road, Ridge Road, and Byler Road.

The High Town Path was probably most heavily used as an Indian foot path in prehistoric times and was free of creek crossings and wet weather or water barriers. Major portions of the High Town Path followed high lands, which appear to be the general route of early Indian trails. The trail ran from Charles Town or Charleston, South Carolina, to Chickasaw Bluffs at the junction of the Wolf River and the mighty Mississippi at what is today known as Memphis, Tennessee.

LESSON 16 – INDIAN TRAILS AND PATHS

According to the Annals of Northwest Alabama, "before the coming of the white man, the ridge generally separated the lands of the Chickasaws on the west from those of the Creeks to the east and the lands of the Cherokees on the north from the Creeks to the south. During the late 1700's and early 1800's, the ridge top path and the Continental Divide were referred to in treaties with the Chickasaw and Cherokee Indians. Later, The Path was used to divide early counties in the Mississippi Territory.

The High Town Path in addition to an Indian trail became the line of the Chickasaw land claims under the Treaty of January 10, 1786. According to a map of Chickasaw boundaries, the Chickasaw claims line followed the Continental Divide through Lawrence and Cullman Counties and turned north and east of the Chickasaw Oldfields on the Tennessee River near Huntsville.

The High Town Path was one of the most famous Indian trails in the Southeastern United States. The Path traversed across the Continental Divide portion of William B. Bankhead National Forest. The Indian trail completely crossed the southeastern United States in an east-west direction and traveled through Alabama along the dividing watersheds of the Tennessee River to the north and the waters that drain into Mobile Bay to the south. The long Indian trail was some 1000 miles in length with the Indian village of High Town (Rome, GA) located somewhat near the middle of the route.

Indian people, including metis Indian people of mixed Celtic ancestry, and early settlers moving into North Alabama from east Tennessee and north Georgia, came in contact with the High Town Path and probably followed along its course. The Indian trail crossed Georgia just north of Atlanta and another fork traversed diagonally across Tennessee toward the southwest from the Knoxville area and through the area east of Chattanooga. Portions of the trail crossed Lookout Mountain and Sand Mountain as it proceeded toward the dividing ridges of Bankhead National Forest in the southern portion of Lawrence County.

High Town, which was near present-day Rome, Georgia, and Turkey Town, which was near present-day Gadsden, Alabama, were important Indian towns along the eastern portion of the route. It was by this route that numerous settlers of the Warrior Mountains can trace the western movement of their ancestors.

According to the Annals of Northwest Alabama, The High Town Path was an Indian trail that extended from near the present site of Atlanta, Georgia, westward through the Cherokee Nation south of Sand Mountain, through the Creek Nation, and into the Chickasaw Nation and the present counties of Lawrence, Franklin, and Marion in Alabama prior to entering Mississippi. Settlers from North Georgia and South Carolina could migrate to Winston along this route having good roads until they turned southward to cross the mountains. After

LESSON 16 – INDIAN TRAILS AND PATHS

the building of the Cheatham Road and Byler's Road, they could have fair roads all the way."(Elliott, 1972:20) It should be noted that the High Town Path probably entered only the northwest corner of Winston County. Settlers traveled from The Path along present-day Highway 41 (Jasper Road), the Cheatham Road (Sipsie Trail) which is present-day Highway 33, and the Byler Road to get into Winston County.

The following is two descriptions of the High Town Path as reported in The Story of Alabama, "High Town Path, from High Shoals on the Apalachee River to High Town in the fork of the Oostenalla and Etowa Rivers, the site of the modern Rome Georgia, thence to Turkey Town of the Cherokee Country, to Coosa, thence to Flat Rock in the northwestern part of the state, thence to Copper Town of the Chickasaw Nation. Two great trails from the east united at Flat Rock in Franklin County, Alabama, and thence-continued west to the Chickasaw Nation. One of these trails comes from the Chattahoochie to Little Okfuskee thence to Flat Rock. The other, the High Town Trail, started from Tellico in Monroe County, East Tennessee, thence southwest to Coosa Town, and from it to Flat Rock."(Owens, 149:240, 244)

The book Alabama History for Schools describes the trail in the following, "One example of a long Indian trail was the High Town Path. This was named for the Creek Indian village of High Town in present-day Etowah County. This trail ran all the way across Alabama from the land of the Chickasaws in the west, through the Creek Country to Turkey Town. From Turkey Town, it ran through the Cherokee Country and across the Chattahoochee River into Georgia." (Summersell, 1981:187)

According to the book, History of Alabama, "The Creeks had numerous paths radiating from eastern Georgia into Alabama, along which Carolina and Georgia traders, and later settlers, penetrated the interior of the state. The most notable of these were the 'High Town Path' and the 'Southern Trail'. The former crossed the Chattahoochee at Shallow Ford, just north of the present city of Atlanta and extended by way of High Town (Etowah), Turkey Town, and other villages along the Cherokee border to the Chickasaw Country." (Moore 1951: 292)

According to the Sesquicentennial Edition 1819-1969 of the Franklin County Times, "Indian trail was first County road: The first account in history of a traveled pathway through Franklin County is of an Indian trail that came from the east and intersected another trail from the north at "Flat Rock" in Franklin County.

From Brown's Village, the High Town Path followed the Continental Divide through Marshall and Cullman Counties along the "Old Corn Road". The Old Corn Road traversed along the Continental Divide crossing present day Highway 31 at Vinemont and crossed present day Highway 157 at Battleground Mountain in Cullman County.

LESSON 16 – INDIAN TRAILS AND PATHS

From Battleground, The Path continued west to an Indian crossroads, which became known as Basham's Gap. Basham's Gap was located near the present-day site of Piney Grove in the southeast corner of Lawrence County. At Basham's Gap, the High Town Path intersected the north-south Indian path, known as Black Warriors' path, from the Tennessee River at Melton's Bluff to Elyton (Birmingham) and on south. The Jasper Road also intersected The Path at Basham Gap and traversed from the Tennessee River (Decatur), to Jasper, then to Tuscaloosa.

From Basham's Gap, the High Town Path traversed westerly along the Leola Road portion of the Continental Divide to the Wren Mountain area where it intersected another southerly divide which was an Indian path, Sipsie Trail. The Sipsie Trail from Mussel Shoals, on the Tennessee River, through the Bankhead Forest to Tuscaloosa became the Cheatham Road.

From the Wren Mountain area, The Path continued on westerly along the Ridge Road portion of the Continental Divide to Kinlock. Near Kinlock, the Path intersected an Indian trail known as Doublehead's Trace or the Old Buffalo Trail from the French Lick (Nashville). Doublehead's Trace or the Old Buffalo Trail later became the Byler Road along the mountain ridge in Lawrence and Winston Counties.

It should be noted that another diamond pattern of the High Town Path may begin at The Path's junction with the Old Buffalo Trail. Some think one fork turned northwest along the Old Beulah Motorway with the other fork traversing southwest by Haleyville, Alabama along the Continental Divide between Bear Creek and the upper Tombigbee River system. To continue west along the Old Beulah route would require at least one stream crossing on the western portion of the Bear Creek system. Some early maps do indicate a Flat Rock on Little Bear Creek. It appears that both routes were used and probably rejoined at a point on the divide southwest of Bear Creek. From that point, evidence exists both in text and maps that one trail led to Copper Town and one to Chickasaw Bluffs.

In addition to traders and early settlers, the High Town Path was not only a geographic boundary but also used as a tribal boundary and a political boundary. The ridge was a prominent feature or landmark through North Alabama noted in early history as the Continental Divide of the waters draining south into Mobile Bay and the waters draining north into the Tennessee River. According to a report of the Alabama History Commission, "the true Cherokee southern boundary, after following the ridge separating the waters of the Tennessee and Black Warrior to the headwaters of Caney Creek, ran thence down said creek to the Tennessee River."

In identifying the Cherokees' southern boundary the <u>Manual for Writing Alabama State History</u> states, "Consequently we may conclude in a general way that from the lower end of Ten Islands the line followed the most prominent dividing ridge butting on the river in that vicinity, around the headwaters of Canoe Creek, until it reached the height of Blount

LESSON 16 – INDIAN TRAILS AND PATHS

Mountain, thence northward with said mountain along the ridge dividing the waters of the Coosa from those of the Black Warrior to the top of Raccoon or Sand Mountain near the Town of Boaz in Marshall County. From this point westward to the Chickasaw boundary, wherever that lay, it is quite clear that the line was the ridge dividing the waters of the Tennessee from those of the Black Warrior. Gov. Blount in 1794, writing to the chiefs and headmen of the Creeks said: "In the original division of land amongst the red people, it is well known that the Creek lands were bounded on the north by the ridge which divides the waters of the Mobile and the Tennessee." Judge Haywood, criticizing a Mr. Barnard for some erroneous statements the latter had made to the Governor of Georgia in 1793, says, "And he (Barnard) ought to have known that the Creek claim to lands was bounded by the ridge which divides the waters of the Tennessee and Mobile."

In the Turkey Town Treaty of 1816, which ceded land from both the Chickasaws and Cherokees, the Ridge Path (High Town Path) was used as the southern boundary for the land cession of both Indian nations including Franklin, Lawrence, and Morgan Counties (Jones, 1972:2). Article 2 of the treaty with the Cherokee, 1816, states, "The Cherokee Nation acknowledge the following as their western boundary: South of the Tennessee River, commencing at Camp Coffee, on the south side of the Tennessee River, which is opposite the Chickasaw Island, running from thence a south course to the top of the Dividing Ridge between the waters of the Tennessee and Tombigbee Rivers, thence eastwardly along said ridge, leaving the head waters of the Black Warrior to the right hand, until opposed by the West branch of Well's Creek down the east bank of said creek to the Coosa River, and down said river."(Kappler, 1904:133)

According to the book <u>Myths of the Cherokee</u>, "failing in this, pressure was at once begun to bring about a cession in Alabama, with the result that on September 14 of the same year, a treaty was concluded at the Chickasaw council-house, and afterward ratified in general council at Turkey Town on the Coosa, by which the Cherokee ceded all their claims in that state south of the Tennessee River and west of an irregular line running from Chickasaw Island in that stream, below the entrance of Flint River, to the junction of Wills Creek with the Coosa, at the present Gadsden."(Mooney, 1982:98) It should be noted that the irregular line to the west was on the High Town Path along the ridge top and followed the Chickasaw claims of January 10, 1786. The line ran south from Chickasaw Island to the Continental Divide then west along the dividing Ridge Path.

Several references indicate the Continental Divide through North Alabama was not only a geographic boundary between major watersheds but also an important political boundary in separating the counties of Blount and Shelby in the Mississippi Territory. The county to the north included what is now the Tennessee Valley portion of North Alabama. According to the <u>Journal of Muscle Shoals History</u> (1977) the following statement is given, "All that tract country lying south of the Tennessee River, east of the Chickasaw boundary line, north of

LESSON 16 – INDIAN TRAILS AND PATHS

the highlands that divide the waters of the Tennessee from the water of the Mobile Bay and west of the Cherokee boundary line shall form one other county to be called and known by the name of Blount, the courts of justice where of will be held at Melton's Bluff." Melton's Bluff is on the south bank of the Tennessee River between Spring and Mallard Creeks in Lawrence County, Alabama.

The Franklin County Times reporting on the history of Franklin County included the following, "It seems from Ramsey's Annals of Tennessee this section was at one time included in the proposed borders of the State of "Franklin" as laid out by Colonel Campbell, the originator of the idea of a state separate and apart from all other states of the union. Colonel Campbell began to agitate for the headwaters of the Tombigbee River, thence east, posed a boundary for the new state to begin at a point on the Holston River and "run west to the shoals of the Ohio, thence south across the Cherokee lands to the headwaters of the Tombigbee River, thence east to the top of the Appalachian mountains, where the waters divide and then north to the beginning."(Times, 1969:8)

It should be noted that the ridge along the top of the Appalachian Mountains is the Continental Divide, which separates the water that drains south into Mobile Bay from the water that drains north into the Tennessee River. Along this dividing ridge, lies the High Town Path, which was a clearly marked geographic division for tribal boundaries, political entities, as well as an east-west route across North Alabama.

Another major route into the Warrior Mountains was by way of the High Town Path also known as the Ridge Path. The path ran along the Continental Divide and followed portions of the Old Corn Road, Leola Road, Cheatham Road, Ridge Road, and Byler Road.

General George Strother Gaines, brother of Captain Edmund P. Gaines.

Gaines' Trace (c1805) was apparently the first federal road beginning in Lawrence County. The Gaines Trace ran from Melton's Bluff north of present-day Courtland, through part of Colbert County, to Russellville in Franklin County, and to Cotton Gin Port at the head of navigation on the Tombigbee River. One fork from Russellville went to Eastport, MS and on to New Orleans, Louisiana.

When reading the early history of Lawrence County, the first existing road mentioned before our county became a county and before our state became a state is the Gaines' Trace. Gaines' Trace authorized by Congress about 1805 was a government road from Melton's Bluff on the Tennessee River, through the Warrior Mountains, to Cotton Gin Port on the

LESSON 16 – INDIAN TRAILS AND PATHS

Tombigbee River. The route divided at Russellville with the northwestern fork going to Eastport, MS. By this route, Doublehead was able to ship his cotton to New Orleans and Mobile. Gaines Trace ran through present-day Lawrence, Franklin, and Marion Counties. It was a connection of the Tennessee River to the Tombigbee River. The route was important for trade among the white and Indian settlers. Gaines Trace was authorized by Article IV of the "Wafford Settlement", a treaty with the Cherokees, which primarily ceded Cherokee lands in central Tennessee and Kentucky. The road was named and laid out by General George Strothers Gaines about 1810. "Gaines' Trace" began approximately eight miles west of Mallard Creek at Melton's Bluff near the head of Elk River Shoals and proceeded southwest where it forked. One route continued west to Eastport, Mississippi, with the other route passing through Russellville to Cotton Gin Port on the Tombigbee River. This trace was laid by Captain Edmund P. Gaines in December 1807, and passed through the Warrior Mountains in the western portion of Lawrence County.

Captain Edmund P. Gaines noted on January 14, 1808 that he had already made one survey in 1802. "Gaines' Trace" began approximately eight miles west of Mallard Creek at Melton's Bluff near the head of Elk River Shoals and proceeded southwest where it forked. One route continued west to Eastport, Mississippi, and the other fork to Cotton Gin Port, Mississippi. The earlier route, surveyed in 1802, was approximately the same period as Natchez Trace was established.

The Gaines route was described by Captain Edmund Pendleton Gaines in a letter to the Secretary of War on January 29, 1808. As requested by the Secretary of War on July 31, 1807, Captain Gaines surveyed and marked a way for a road from the head of Muscle Shoals (Melton's Bluff) to Cotton Gin Port on the Tombigbee River.

> Gaines said in his letter, "I have also explored the route,…From the head of the shoals (Brown's Ferry) to the northeast sources of Bear Creek, distance 35 miles, is as nearly level as could be wished, either for making a good road for carriages by going near a straight course; but by waving the course in conformity of the slopes of the ridges all will be crossed without ascent or decent of more than 13 ½ degrees… The route for the greater part of this distance, is on the dividing ridges, between the waters of the Tennessee and Mobile…Several Cherokees have designated different places, where they promised to settle in the course of the present year, along the way as far as Bear Creek Ridge, which they call their South boundary…"

As given in the Territorial Papers of the United States compiled and edited by Clarence Carter, one description describes the dividing ridge south of Mt. Hope in western Lawrence County between the Bear Creek drainage, which flows to the Tennessee River, and the Sipsey River drainage, which flows to Mobile. The High Town Path, which was the

LESSON 16 – INDIAN TRAILS AND PATHS

Chickasaw's southern boundary, defined by the Treaty of January 10, 1786, also follows the same dividing ridge through this area.

In his letter, Captain Edmund Gaines states that the Cherokee claim the Continental Divide of Bear Creek Ridge as their south boundary. In addition, Edmund Gaines identified two routes from the Shoals that joined on the ridge near the headwaters of Bear Creek; however, the 1808 route runs basically 45° southwest of north through the Tennessee Valley from Melton's Bluff. The two other routes could be previous surveys.

It is thought that one of the other two routes run the dividing ridge in southwest Lawrence County and also became a small portion of the first legislative road in Alabama – the Byler Road. In addition, the closest route of 35 miles, from Melton's Bluff at the head of the shoals toward the northeast sources of Bear Creek, would be just south of Mt. Hope approximately some four miles. Since the headwaters of Bear Creek and the headwaters of Sipsey River lie in southwestern Lawrence County, a small portion of one of the Gaines routes probably lay along the portion of mountain ridges of the watershed divide that became the Byler Road by Act of Alabama Legislature on December 15, 1819.

Natchez Trace - In October 1801, a treaty between the U. S. and the Chickasaws gave permission to cut and open a wagon road between Nashville, Tennessee and Natchez, Mississippi. The road known as the Natchez Trace, passed through Colbert and Lauderdale Counties in North Alabama.

Colbert's ferry at the crossing of the Natchez Trace on the Tennessee River

Black Warriors' Path was a trail that ran from Melton's Bluff, through the eastern portion of Lawrence County, toward Ft. Mitchell on the Chattahoochee River in Russell County, Alabama.

LESSON 16 – INDIAN TRAILS AND PATHS

The Indian trail known as the Black Warriors' Path or Mitchell Trace led from Melton's Bluff toward the Mulberry and Sipsey Forks of the Black Warrior River, and then traversed southeast to Fort Mitchell on the Chattahoochee River in present-day Russell County, Alabama. The route continued from Cusseta near Ft. Mitchell to the Atlantic Coast at St. Augustine. The route became known as the Mitchell Trace, and connected Fort Hampton in Limestone County to Fort Mitchell in Russell County, Alabama.

The 1818 John Melish Map shows the Black Warriors' Path through Lawrence County beginning at Marathon (Melton's Bluff), proceeding east of Courtland several miles, following closely to the present-day Hillsboro Road to Fairfield Church, crossing Elam Creek and the Fish Dam Ford on the West Fork of Flint Creek passing through the Oakville Indian Mounds Park near the ceremonial mound, into Beaty Hollow south of Speake, through Poplar Log Cove, and exiting the county near Basham's Gap at Piney Grove.

The Black Warriors' Path led south through Lawrence County and passed the area of Oakville. Just north of Oakville, the trail crossed the West Fork of Flint Creek and appears to have proceeded adjacent to the large ceremonial Indian mound at the Oakville Indian Mounds Park. Remnants of the very old road are still visible on the west side of the mound.

According to William Lindsey McDonald's article on Melton's Bluff, "The renowned pioneer and soldier, David Crockett, remembered two occasions when his military unit crossed at Melton's Bluff. The first instance was in November 1813. Actually according to Crockett, he crossed the Tennessee River twice on this first occasion in order to maneuver around the local Indians. After crossing at Huntsville, they moved westward to cross the river again at Melton's Bluff. Crockett described the river at this point as being about two miles wide. The rocky bottom of the river was rough and dangerous. While fording the river, several of the horses became stuck in the rocky crevices and had to be left there while the military command moved onto their destination. Crockett's second crossing at Melton's Bluff was in October 1814. Payroll and muster records reveal that he was a third sergeant in Captain John Cowan's company at the time." According to McDonald, the above information was obtained from the book A Narrative of the Life of David Crockett.

In 1813, David Crockett helped General John Coffee's forces burn the large Creek Indian village known as Black Warrior Town after finding it deserted. Crockett and General Coffee's forces traveled along the Black Warriors' Path through present day Lawrence County to destroy the Creek town. James Richard Gillespie from Indian Tomb Hollow also served with David Crockett. Gillespie served under Captain Cowan in 1813 during the same period of time as David Crockett. Gillespie attended the muster rolls in Blount County, Tennessee on January 1, 1814.

LESSON 16 – INDIAN TRAILS AND PATHS

Lawrence County's forgotten Indian trail or road, the Black Warriors' Path, from Melton's Bluff at the head of Elk River Shoals, across the Warrior Mountains, to the center of the Creek Indian Nation near the Little and Big Oakfuskee Towns, preceded Gaines' Trace. The trail or road was last known as the Mitchell Trace. Mitchell Trace probably received the name after the building of Fort Mitchell in 1811 on the Chattahoochee River in present-day Russell County, Alabama. Mitchell Trace became a post route which connected Fort Hampton, a Cherokee Indian outpost located near the forks of Elk River and the Tennessee River in present-day Limestone County, to Fort Mitchell, a Creek Indian outpost. Fort Mitchell was named after David Brady Mitchell, who was listed as Indian Agent or Governor.

Black Warriors' Path just west of the crossing on the Mulberry Fork of the Warrior River near old Baltimore

The relationship of the Gaines and Mitchell Traces does not end with a common beginning point at Melton's Bluff the trails were connected on their southern ends by a trading route from Fort Mitchell to St. Stephens; therefore, an early Indian trading triangle was established in the area that became the State of Alabama.

Along the western edge of the ceremonial mound are remnants of the Black Warriors' Path or Mitchell Trace. This trail was a major trading route utilized by Indian people. The path connected Fort Hampton near the Tennessee River crossing at Elk (Chuwalee) River Shoals to Fort Mitchell near the Chattahoochee River in present day Russell County, Alabama. The Black Warriors' Path is clearly shown on the 1814 and 1818 Melish maps and shows it crossing both the West Fork of Flint Creek and Elam Creek. These crossings are still clearly visible just one mile north of the burial mound at Oakville. Remnants of the very old road are still visible on the west side of the ceremonial Indian mound at Oakville. In addition, just south of Lindsey Cemetery at the edge of the mountains, the old road bed is clearly visible as it crosses U.S. Forest Service property into Beaty Hollow and on into Poplar Log Cove. The trail crossed the Southeastern United States from Nashville, TN, to Columbus, GA, and onto St. Augustine, FL on the Atlantic Coast.

Fort Mitchell, marked a southern point along the Mitchell Trace (Black Warriors' Path) and played a vital role in the final days of the Creek Indian removal during the 1830's. By 1835, many Creeks had been removed west. A detachment of 511 Creeks passed through the Oakville Indian Mounds Park along the Mitchell Trace on December 19, 1835.

LESSON 16 – INDIAN TRAILS AND PATHS

The Old Mitchell Trace crosses the West Fork of Flint Creek approximately one mile north of the Oakville Indian Mounds Park. After crossing the Fish Dam Ford on West Flint, an old wagon road between Flint and Elam Creeks known as the Chickasaw Trail runs west toward Moulton. Both Black Warriors' Path and the Old Chickasaw Trail that runs from Chickasaw Island (Huntsville) to Cotton Gin Port cross Elam Creek in the same place. The Creeks arrived in Moulton on December 19, 1835. An 1813 map of Indian country in the area that became Lawrence County shows two roads beginning at Melton's Bluff which is located at the head of Elk River Shoals. Of course, the two roads shown on the map are the Gaines and Mitchell Traces. The date of the map was three years before these Indian lands were given up by the Turkey Town Treaty of 1816.

The Indian trail or road known as the Black Warriors' Path, from Melton's Bluff near the head of Elk River Shoals, across the Warrior Mountains, to the center of the Creek Indian Nation near the Little and Big Oakfuskee Towns, probably preceded Gaines Trace. The trail or road was last known as the Mitchell Trace. Mitchell Trace probably received the name after the building of Fort Mitchell in 1811 on the Chattahoochee River in present-day Russell County, Alabama. Mitchell Trace became a post route which connected Fort Hampton a Cherokee Indian outpost located near the forks of Elk River and the Tennessee River in present-day Limestone County, to Fort Mitchell, a Creek Indian outpost. Fort Mitchell was named after David Brady Mitchell, who was listed as Indian Agent or Governor.

Beginning near the eastern end of Elk River Shoals on the Tennessee River at Melton's Bluff in Lawrence County, the old Black Warriors' Path lead south into the foothills of Bankhead Forest, through the forest, and into the Black Warrior River Valley. The Black Warriors' Path crossed the Warrior River just northeast of the junction of the Mulberry and Sipsey forks where it intersected another trail coming from the Tennessee River at Ditto's Landing near present-day Huntsville called Black Warrior Road. The trails joined and a few miles southwest of the road junctions and river crossing was the Indian village of Black Warrior Town. The Creek Indian town was destroyed by the military forces commanded by General Coffee and David Crockett.

Since General Coffee and Davy Crockett crossed the Tennessee River at Melton's Bluff twice during 1813, it is highly probable that Crockett and Coffee traveled the Black Warriors' Path (Mitchell Trace) to Black Warrior Town. In a letter from John Coffee to General Jackson, dated October 22, 1813, and belonging to Mr. Richard C. Sheridan, the following describes the crossing: "...I proceed to cross the river at the upper end of the Shoals, all my efforts failed to procure a pilot. I took with me one of John Melton's sons who said he knew not the road, he showed me a path that had been reputed the ***Black Warriors' Path***..."

LESSON 16 – INDIAN TRAILS AND PATHS

To confirm the existence of the Black Warriors' Path, one can just look at old maps showing the area known as Melton's Bluff in Lawrence County. The Black Warriors' Path or Mitchell Trace is clearly shown on the following maps listed by date: 1813, 1818, 1823, 1825, 1831, and 1842. Since the road is not shown after the 1850's, the route probably became a part of the vast Wheeler Plantation and the Town of Marathon became one of the dead towns of North Alabama. After the railroad around the Shoals was completed in 1834, Marathon at the head of Elk River Shoals died.

It does not appear accidental that the trail connected areas of cultural importance to the Indian people of the Tennessee River Valley, the Black Warrior River Valley, and the Chattahoochee River Valley. An Indian trail also ran from Ft. Mitchell to St. Stephens on the Tombigbee, thus completing a trading triangle.

Doublehead's Trace (Old Buffalo Trail) was formerly a Chickasaw trail. It ran the general route at Highway 101 and crossed the Tennessee River from Blue Water Creek to Lawrence County between Big Nance and Town Creek and went to Tuscaloosa.

Along the western edge of the present-day Black Warrior Wildlife Management Area, a trail running the Tennessee Divide was the Old Buffalo Trail, Doublehead's Trace, and later, the Byler Road. The portion of this early route that runs the divide, identified by old timers as Doublehead's Trace or the Old Buffalo Trail, ran portions of the Byler Road and High Town Path. The route followed a ridge between Bear Creek and Sipsey River for some five miles in the southwestern corner of Lawrence County.

The trail was used by Creeks and Choctaws traveling north toward the French Lick (Nashville, Tennessee area) in search of buffalo and later as a trade route by the Cherokees. Doublehead's Trace or Buffalo Trail ran from the French Lick (Nashville, TN) to Duck River, to Shoal Town (Blue Water-Town Creek Villages), to Town Creek, to Hatton, Old Town Creek Church, McClung Gap, then followed what is now the Byler Road to Haleyville, then to Tuscaloosa. Doublehead's Trace or the Old Buffalo Trail probably crossed the Tennessee River at Blue Water Creek near Wheeler Dam to Path Killer's Creek (Big Nance), and followed close to the route now known as State Highway 101. At one time, the route was a Chickasaw trail.

Along the western edge of the present-day Black Warrior Wildlife Management Area, a portion of the Byler Road runs the divide that was recorded by Captain Edmund Pendleton Gaines on January 29, 1808. According to the Territorial Papers, he described a route from the head of the Shoals toward Bear Creek Ridge, then south toward Cotton Gin Port. The portion from the Ridge Road to Haleyville (Flat Rock) of the early route has been identified by old timers as the Old Buffalo Trail or Doublehead's Trace. Doublehead's Trace or Old Buffalo Trail ran portions of the Byler Road and High Town Path along the ridge dividing

LESSON 16 – INDIAN TRAILS AND PATHS

Bear Creek and Sipsey River for some five miles in the southwestern corner of Lawrence County, then turned south toward Tuscaloosa.

Doublehead's Trace or Buffalo Trail came from the French Lick (Nashville), to Duck River, to the mouth of Blue Water Creek to Town Creek, to Hatton, Old Town Creek Church, McClung Gap, then to Byler Road, to Haleyville, and then Tuscaloosa. The trail was used by Creeks and Choctaws traveling north toward the French Lick (Nashville, Tennessee area) in search of buffalo. Buffalo were known to be abundant in middle Tennessee around the Duck River and Buffalo River Valleys. It later became a trade route used by the Cherokees. Eventually, part of the approximate route of Doublehead's Trace or Buffalo Trail became portions of the Byler Road. Doublehead's Trace or Old Buffalo Trail crossed the Big Mussel Shoals on the Tennessee River near Wheeler Dam from the east mouth of Blue Water Creek to the area between Town Creek and Big Nance Creek (Path Killer's Creek) in Lawrence County.

Coosa Path between Moulton and Oakville

Coosa Path - Just past the entrance of Oakville Indian Mounds Park, some 100 yards north, the Coosa Path turns west and crosses West Flint Creek toward Moulton. By December 19, 1835, this was the major road from Moulton to Somerville by way of Oakville. During this time, the Coosa Path (also known as the Moulton to Sommerville Road via Irwin's Mill) had the only known bridge across Flint Creek from Moulton to the Black Warriors' Path at Oakville; therefore, the Creek removal followed Black Warriors' Path to this old crossing then turned west to Moulton along the major road - Moulton to Somerville via Irwin's Mill (Coosa Path was also known as the Muscle Shoals Path).

Brown's Ferry Road - Trappers and Indian traders came down the Tennessee River by flatboat to the head of Elk River Shoals at Brown's Ferry. As early as 1813, travelers could travel southwest by way of one of the best Indian roads in Lawrence County which is known as Brown's Ferry Road. At this time, Brown's Ferry Road ran from Huntsville to Courtland and crossed the river at the Brown's Ferry which was the location of Doublehead's Town.

These early white intruders on Indian lands were allowed to remain because most had married into and were accepted in the Cherokee Nation. Ann Royall gave an account of one such individual in a letter dated January 12, 1818. Ms. Royall called the white guide Rhea and explained that he had married one of John Melton's half blood Cherokee daughters. John Melton, who was an Irishman by birth, had a large plantation in Lawrence County at

LESSON 16 – INDIAN TRAILS AND PATHS

the head of Elk River Shoals. Rhea had lived among the Cherokees for 15 years (1803) and John Melton had established his plantation around 1790.

Braziel Creek Trail - According to local folklore, this trail was originally an Indian path which ran from the Elk River Shoals south toward Tuscaloosa along the creek and river bottoms. In The Warrior Mountains, the trail followed Braziel Creek to Borden Creek, to Sipsey River, and to parts south. Portions of the trail of which I write may represent the escape route of some Cherokees during removal, as well as other Southern Indians and black slaves and appears untouched by white man. According to Jim Manasco, the trail was a secret route, which now runs through Bankhead Forest's Sipsey Wilderness Area in Lawrence County, Alabama.

The trail was strategically located between the Byler Road to the west, and the Cheatham Road to the east both of which traverse the Warrior Mountains in north-south directions. Isolated from military movements and traffic along the two major Bankhead roads and passing through the forest on a north-south course, the trail offered protection from detection over its long course from the south to its junction with the High Town or Ridge Path on the northern border of the forest.

According to folklore and Indian legend passed through some 130 years of time, arbor glyphs of snakes were drawn on beech trees along the trail by Indian people around the time of removal. According to Jim Manasco, his Indian ancestors passed through the area along the trail to settle on the Rocky Plains.

Sipsie Trail - According to early historical information concerning the Indian inhabitants of the Warrior Mountains, most of the major dividing ridges of the forest served as trails, paths, and primitive roads from one part of the country to another. The dividing ridge which separates the watersheds of Brushy Creek and Sipsey River was no different and was known in local folklore as the Sipsie Trail.

Archaeological evidence in bluff shelters near the Sipsie Trail indicates the route was used as early as the prehistoric Woodland period. One such bluff site, the McDougal shelter and mortar rock, was located not far from the dividing ridge. The McDougal Shelter lay close to the divide route and had numerous artifacts dating back to prehistoric times.

The High Town Path ran a portion of the Sipsie Trail from near the junction of the Leola Road to the Ridge Road. Local folklore indicates the north-south dividing ridge was one of many routes utilized primarily by Creek Indians in the early historic period and most likely by Creek people during late prehistoric times just prior to Desoto.

LESSON 16 – INDIAN TRAILS AND PATHS

The Sipsie Trail junction with the High Town Path was on top of Wren Mountain some five miles south of Moulton. The route crossed Sipsey River in Winston County, proceed south to Lost Creek, and then paralleled Wolf Creek toward the Black Warrior River Basin near Tuscaloosa. In all probability, the route was utilized by southern Indians hunting buffalo in the Cumberland River basin during the prehistoric and historic periods. Creek and Choctaw hunters used the trail when heading north from the Warrior River Basin toward the French Lick in search of buffalo.

According to an 1830's map of the Cherokee Nation, the route ran the dividing ridge of Brushy and Sipsey to the Sipsey crossing about one mile southeast of the Sipsey and Caney Creek junction. Another 1850's map shows the route running from Pulaski, Tennessee, to the Rogersville crossing of the lower Elk River Shoals of the Tennessee River at Lamb's Ferry, then through Courtland, Moulton, and Wren in Lawrence County, to Double Springs, and then to Rocky Plains in Winston County and on to Tuscaloosa. According to local folklore, Rocky Plains was an Indian stronghold even after the 1838 removal known as the "Trail of Tears."

Review Questions

1. How did our early Indian ancestors travel on land?
2. Name three ways the early Indians travel?
3. What was the longest Indian trail/path in Lawrence County?
4. What road was known as the wagon road?
5. How did our Indian ancestors travel on water?
6. In order for our people to travel from place to place, what was developed for easier traveling?
7. What were these paths used for?
8. What was the name of the first federal road in Lawrence County?
9. Gaines' Trace was also known as what?
10. Doublehead's Trace or Old Buffalo Trail was formerly what type of Indian trail?
11. Along with the High town Path, what trail was on top of Wren Mountains some five miles south of Moulton?
12. What two Indian trails crossed at Oakville?
13. What do we have today that follows early Indian trails?
14. Were the Cherokees nomadic?
15. What Indian village was located near present-day Brown's Ferry?
16. What path was also known as the Moulton to Sommerville Road via Irwin's Mill?
17. The High Town Path was also known as:
18. How would you confirm the existence of an old road, path, or trail?
19. Where was Black Warriors' Path located?
20. The Natchez Trace road passed through what two counties in North Alabama?

LESSON 16 – INDIAN TRAILS AND PATHS

21. Doublehead's Trace or the Old Buffalo Trail crosses Big Mussel Shoals of the Tennessee River near what two creeks?
22. What two roads represent the most accurate route of the High Town Path through Lawrence County?
23. What path was used to divide early counties in the Mississippi Territory?
24. In 1813, who helped John Coffee burn the large Creek Indian village known as Black Warrior Town?
25. What trail, according to the legend, was marked with arbor glyphs on beech trees at the time of removal?
26. How early, according to archaeological evidence in bluff shelters near the Sipsie Trail, indicate that the route was used?
27. What trail was formerly a Chickasaw Trail?
28. According to local folklore, what was an Indian stronghold even after the 1838 removal known as the Trial of Tears?
29. What path was not only a geographic boundary but also used as a tribal and political boundary to traders and early settlers?
30. Which path crosses west Flint Creek toward Moulton?
31. Which trail was known as the dividing ridge that separates the watersheds of Brushy Creek and Sipsey River?
32. What path became the line of the Chickasaw land claims under the Treaty of January 10, 1786?
33. The High Town Path was not only a geographic boundary, but what other type of boundary?

LESSON 17 – INDIAN VILLAGES

Today, we are learning about the different kinds of Indian mounds located in North Alabama which was the focus of early Cherokee villages. Raise your hand if you know what the answer is. What is an Indian mound? There were different kinds of Indian mounds such as burial, ceremonial, and shell. Many things were found in the mounds that tell us about the past. Some of the things found in a burial mound were skeletons, jewelry, pottery, weapons, and tools. Burial mounds were places where Indian people buried their dead. When a person died, they would bury them by covering with a layer of dirt. The next person to die would be buried on top until a huge mound was formed. Burial mounds could be found in the shapes of circles, ovals and pyramids. Burial mounds were found throughout the Tennessee River Valley. The ceremonial mounds were used for weddings, celebrations, and religious purposes of different kinds. The most important ceremony was the Green Corn Ceremony. The festival was like our Thanksgiving and New Year rolled into one. It was a time to give thanks for a successful harvest, to settle differences, and to begin a New Year. The Cherokee's of North Alabama lived in houses from log cabins to two-story plank houses. Many owned slaves and had plantations of cotton, corn, sugar cane, and other crops. The large Indian farms usually had lots of livestock—cattle, horses, mules, hogs, sheep, goats, and chickens.

Cherokee towns of Lawrence County

1. Mouse Town was, also known as Monee Town, located at the mouth of Fox Creek on the Tennessee River.
2. Doublehead's Town or Brown's Ferry was the location of Cherokee Chief Doublehead's home from c1790 to 1802.
3. Melton's Bluff (known later as Marathon) was owned by General Andrew Jackson from November 1816 until 1827.
4. Gourd's Settlement was located at Courtland and was named after a Cherokee soldier who fought at Horseshoe Bend under Andrew Jackson. Gourd also had an island in Elk River Shoals named after him which was called Gourd's Island.
5. Cuttyatoy's Village was located near Courtland on an Island in the Tennessee River.
6. Shoal Town (known as Town Creek-Blue Water Town) was Doublehead's home from c1802 until his death, August 9, 1807.
7. Oakville was Cherokee village located at the forks of Black Warriors' Path and Coosa Path (Old Indian Trace or Muscle Shoals Path).

Moneetown or Mousetown – Some three miles easterly, from the head of Elk River Shoals at the junction of Fox Creek and Tennessee River was the Cherokee Indian town of Moneetown or Mousetown. This was the first Cherokee town beginning on the east edge of

LESSON 17 – INDIAN VILLAGES

present-day Lawrence County and was our county's most upstream Cherokee town on the south side of the Tennessee River. The Indian village was located between Courtland and Decatur on Fox Creek on the north side of Trinity Mountain.

According to a letter from Waco, Texas, May 9, 1882, and printed in <u>The Moulton Advertiser</u> on May 25, 1882, page 2, column 4, *"Lawrence was the banner County in Alabama in furnishing soldiers in the Texan struggle. Had not Dr. Shackleford and the Red Rovers been captured near Goliad, just after the fall of the Alamo, there would, doubtless, be many a veteran of that gallant band now living...Lawrence County still has her representatives in that band of patriots. I noticed...Aaron Burleson. The latter will be remembered by the old people who lived between Courtland and Decatur in the year 1817. If any such are now living. He was a brother of Gen. Ed Burleson of Texan Revolutionary fame. He was engaged in the killing of some Indians at **Mousetown** on Foxe's Creek, east of Courtland in 1817, for which he fled the country, went to Missouri, thence to Texas. He has made many greasers as well as red skin bite the dust...He now lives in Bastrop, County."*

In another account, the Indian village is called Moneetown. *"James Burleson settled with his family on the north side of the mountain on Fox Creek. Here near an Indian village called **Moneetown**, the family became involved in a feud following an altercation between a son-in-law, Martin, and the Cherokees. After three of the Indians were slain, James Burleson and his son, Edward, fled to Missouri"* (Gentry, 1962).

In personal communication on December 18, 2003, Mr. Paul Ausbon and Mr. Bill Sams, whose ancestors lived on the river at Brown's Ferry, reported that Mousetown was located at the junction of Fox Creek and the Tennessee River. Mr. Ausbon told me that he was born in 1925 and had known all his life of the Indian town that was called Mousetown by his grandparent and parents. Both men told that the Mousetown area was a favorite fishing location of their families. For years, the story of Mousetown was passed down to Mr. Paul Ausbon. According to his grandparents, an Indian fight occurred at the old town site. They said the town was on the present-day Lawrence and Morgan County line, north of Trinity Mountain some two miles from Highway 20.

Rayford Hyatt (1993) gives the best description of the altercation between Burleson and the Cherokees as follows: *"The last Indian and white battle in present Lawrence County, of which we have found and record, occurred near Meltons Bluff (Mousetown) in 1816. This indicates that some whites had already come into the area and were leasing farms from the Cherokee Indians.*

James Saunders, in 'Early Settlers,' writing many years later from oral tradition, says the fight occurred on Foxes Creek near a village called Moneetown when James Burleson and

LESSON 17 – INDIAN VILLAGES

family killed three Cherokees and fled to Missouri. The 1820 census shows Burleson still in Lawrence County. This is the related Burlesons of later Texas fame.

In the 'National Intelligencer,' Washington, D.C., September 5, 1816, is given editorially the substance of a letter, dated August 13, 1816, to Col. Winston from James Burleson. It states in effect 'that he, Burleson, and others who had settled near Meltons Bluff (Mousetown), on the south side of the Tennessee River to the number of eight men were attacked by a party of Cherokees armed with guns and warclubs, the number not known, on the night of the 11th inst. The whites resisted and three Indians were killed and one wounded. The fear of the Indians caused consternation among the settlers, and many moved away leaving promising crops.'

The 'Intelligenser' of September 10, 1816, from information at Huntsville dated August 17, 1816, enters further into details concerning the disturbance. "'t seems that a Mr. Taylor had rented a field from some Cherokees. In his absence they offered some insult to Mrs. Taylor, who escaped to the home of her father, James Burleson. Burleson, Taylor and others went to the Indian settlement, where they found a number collected. They demanded an explanation. The Indians raised a yell and said fight. An attempt was made by the whites to cut them off from their arms. This produced a conflict.'"

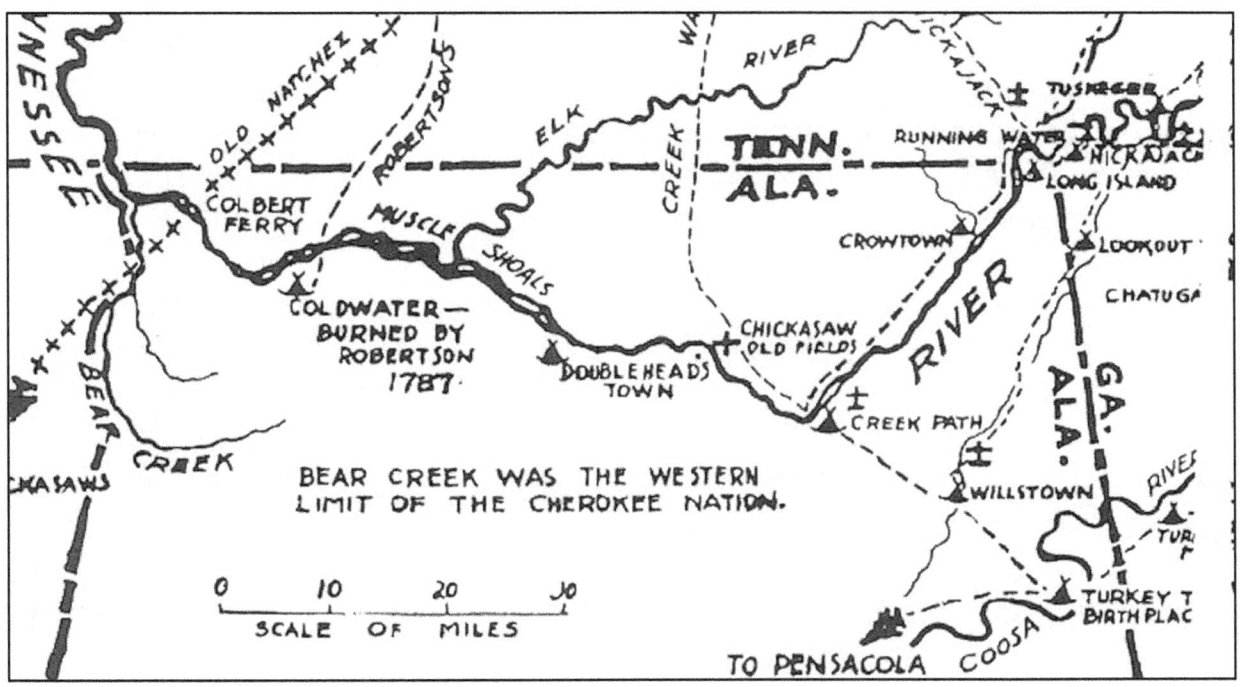

Map of Doublehead's Town at Browns Ferry

Doublehead's Town – Doublehead's Town was located at Brown's Ferry near the head of Elk River Shoals. *"Yet, Doublehead was without influence or position until about the year 1790, when he established a town on the Tennessee River at the head of the Muscle Shoals. An early map of the Cherokee country shows this village at a site near the sough bank of*

LESSON 17 – INDIAN VILLAGES

Brown's Ferry below Athens. He later in 1802 moved it to the north bank of the river near the mouth of Blue Water Creek in Lauderdale County, Alabama…Inhabitants of Doublehead's Town, originally about 40 in number, were mostly cast-offs from other Cherokee and Creek villages. This motley bunch became infamous in Tennessee history as The Ravagers of the Cumberlands" (McDonald, 1989).

Historical records indicate that Doublehead lived in his Cherokee Indian town at Brown's Ferry from 1790 through December 1801. According to History of Alabama by Albert James Pickett (1851), *"Dec. 1801: Emigrants flocked to the Mississippi Territory…constructing flat-boats at Knoxville, they floated down the river to the head of the Muscle Shoals, where they disembarked at the house of Double-Head, a Cherokee Chief…placing their effects upon the horses, which had been brought down by land from Knoxville, they departed on foot for the Bigby settlements."* Based on his historical note, Doublehead was still living at Brown's Ferry until 1802. The route immigrants utilized for bringing their horses to Brown's Ferry was no doubt portions of the South River Road.

In 1803, Patick Wilson traveled along the southern side to the Tennessee River and followed the same route as the South River Road. The following excerpt describes the route along the South River Road, *"The expedition continued on the Natchez Trace to present-day Alabama, here Wilson observed land controlled by the Chickamauga Cherokee, who,…were highly resistant to territorial encroachment in the Tennessee Valley… At the Muscle Shoals…the expedition left the Natchez Trace to follow the south bank of the Tennessee River. Here the party rested in a Chickamauga Cherokee town (Doublehead's Village at Brown's Ferry) administered by Tal Tsuska (Doublehead), a controversial and historically significant chief who controlled transportation routes…continuing in Cherokee territory, Wilson's party traveled north, passing through "Watts or Wills Town"… Wilson's narrative ends in Hiwasee, a Cherokee town no longer in existence"* (Hathorn and Sabino, 2001). By the time of Wilson's expedition in 1803, Doublehead had already moved from Brown's Ferry to the Shoal Town area on the north side of the river near Blue Water Creek.

Doublehead's Town at Brown's Ferry was also known for a brief period as Cox's Ferry. A man by the name of Cox, who was supposedly the son of Zecharaiah Cox, had apparently married one of the Brown Cherokee girls and briefly called the area Cox's Ferry. Some two miles west of the Indian village, the Brown's Ferry Road intersected Black Warriors' path and the South River Road.

Doublehead's Town was on the south bank of the Tennessee River at river miles 293 and 294. The town site lay between present-day Mallard Creek Campground and the old Brown's Ferry Road. Doublehead's home was thought to be on a point just downstream from the ferry location but within sight of the old river crossing. Doublehead ran a house of entertainment that catered to all kinds of needs of travelers. It is said that he was very

LESSON 17 – INDIAN VILLAGES

generous to allow two older ladies, both of whom had a bunch of girls, to live in his house. Many have speculated that Doublehead's entertainment probably included many types of mischief. Doublehead had learned very rapidly about making money from his mixed-blood friends. One such business partner was Captain John D. Chisolm.

Butch Walker and Charles Borden walking the Brown's Ferry Road at Doublehead's Town

Today, you can walk over the fields along the old river bank and find plenty of evidence of a large, extensive, and historic dwelling site. Old nails are in abundance along with pieces of glassware, historic pottery, slave made bricks, and even a large area of garlic, buttercups, and other plants that indicate historic occupation. In particular, the garlic grows on a small knoll just a few hundred yards from the ferry site. We refer to this knoll as Doublehead's homesite and the plants as Doublehead's garlic. His garlic has been transplanted to the Oakville Indian Mounds Park. Remains of chert projectile points indicate prehistoric Indian occupation as early as the Archaic Period; therefore, Doublehead's village site was used for thousands of years by native people.

Melton's Bluff - The next downstream Indian village was Melton's Bluff approximately seven miles west of Brown's Ferry. The site was also a prehistoric town located on the west side of Jack's Slough, at Tennessee River mile 288.5. The site contains a large ceremonial Indian mound covering over one acre in size and stands some 15 to 20 feet high. In addition, approximately 100 feet from the Tennessee River, a small snail mound is located between the large mound and the present river bank. During historic occupation by the Cherokee Indians, the site from the mounds west for about one mile became known as Melton's Bluff, named after an Irishman, John Melton. Melton's Bluff was a historic Cherokee Town that was purchased by General Andrew Jackson from half blood Cherokee David Melton on November 22, 1816 (McDonald, William Lindsey, 1989). At Melton's Bluff, located between Tennessee River miles 287 to 288.5, the South River Road continued west while Black Warriors' Path turned north, crossed the river, and passed Ft. Hampton, Bridgewater, Elkton, and on to the French Lick.

In <u>Letters from Alabama</u> 1817-1822 by Anne Newport Royall is a description of a route to Melton's Bluff from Florence as follows, *"Melton's Bluff, January 8th, 1818... I was three days on the road to this place. Melton's Bluff is at the head of Mussel Shoals...I went direct to the foot of the Shoals, 70 miles from Huntsville, crossed the river, and come upon the*

LESSON 17 – INDIAN VILLAGES

south side of Tennessee River...three miles in width! the largest body of water that I ever saw. It was at this time very high and muddy; and the noise produced by the water washing over the rocks was tremendous... we saw a boat hung on a rock, about the middle of the stream...I took a guide, one of the pilots, and crossed the river next morning, in a ferry boat...upon leaving the ferry... I was to pass by several Indian farms... About ten o'clock we came in sight of the first Indian farm... you cross Town Creek in a canoe and swim your horses; this will cost you one dollar...I, with my horses, were safely on the other side... Rhea (my guide's name) said I had two more creeks to pass... however, these were easily forded...Rhea... had piloted boats through the Muscle Shoals, fifteen years; sometimes four at a time, at ten dollars each. He sails down one day, and walks back to the next... this land is so clear of undergrowth that you may drive a wagon any where through the woods...we passed many Indian houses in the day, and some beautiful springs. Melton's Bluff is a town, and takes its name from...John Melton...Irishman by birth...attached himself to the Cherokee Indians... Melton's Bluff... a very large plantation of cotton and maize, worked by about sixty slaves and owned by General Jackson, who bought the interest of old Melton."

This first hand account in January 1818 of Ms. Royall confirms the existence of a road along the south bank at the Tennessee River which still has Indian houses standing. The Cherokee and Chickasaw Indians had given up the land in September 1816 approximately 15 months prior to Ms. Royall's visit to Melton's Bluff. The route of the South River Road was clearly established and had been in existence for some time.

The following portion of a story on Melton's Bluff by Rayford Hyatt (1993) gives details on the Indian village. *"The place was named for a white man, Melton, who settled there probably as a trader, married a Cherokee woman, thereby becoming a member of the Cherokee Nation. James Saunders in "Early Settlers" says his name was James Melton. Anne Royall in "Letters From Alabama" says he was John. A Cherokee Treaty of 1806 ceding lands north of the Tennessee River exempted a tract 2 by 3 miles to Moses Melton and Charles Hicks in equal shares. Oliver D. Street in a paper on "The Indians of Marshall County" says that Meltonsville of Marshall County was named for Charles Melton, an old man of Herculean frame who once lived at Meltons Bluff. Whichever he was, the others were probably his sons.*

Meltons Bluff was located at the head of the Muscle Shoals in the SE 1/4 - SE 1/4 Sec 25 T3S R7W. Most of the buildings were in a line on top of the bluff. Anne Royall in "Letters From Alabama" who stayed at the Bluff for a long period in 1818-19 says Melton got started by robbing flat boats coming down the river. It is more likely that Indians did the robbing and he traded for the slaves and goods. He also for many years furnished river pilots to boats through the Muscle Shoals for a fee with the pilots walking back to the Bluff from Florence.

LESSON 17 – INDIAN VILLAGES

In 1774, a settlement party of 15 whites and 21 slaves from South Carolina led by William Scott, were descending the Tennessee by flat boat to Natchez when they were attacked at the head of Muscle Shoals by a number of Cherokees under the Bowle. All of the white people were killed, and the slaves and goods taken. The Cherokee tribe disavowed the act of The Bowle and his followers who, fearing capture and punishment, fled to the west and located on the Arkansas River and with subsequent additions to their settlement they remained there many years.

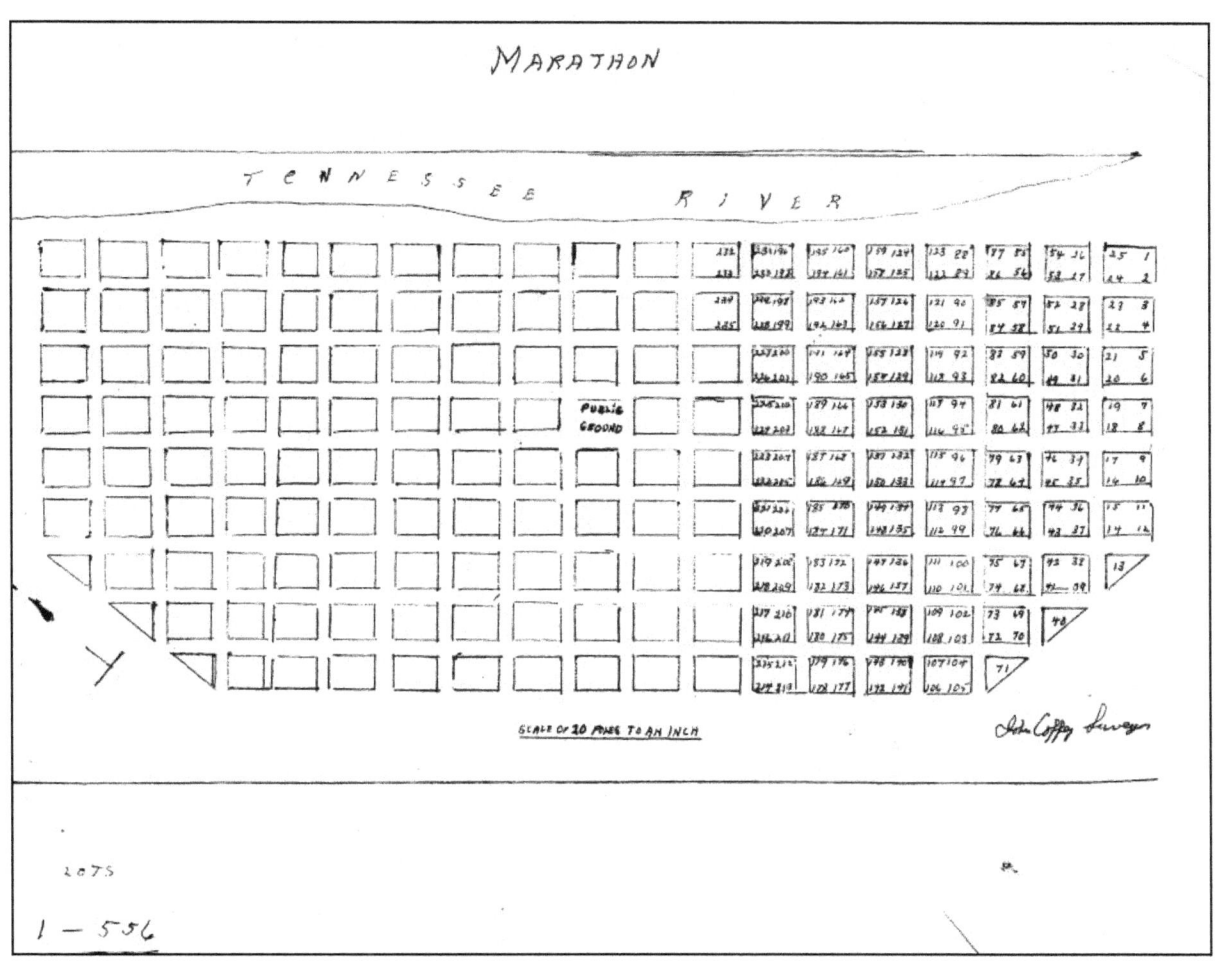

Marathon

In later years, Melton seemed to operate in a profitable legal manner. Besides houses of entertainment and boating activities at the Bluff, he owned large cotton and corn plantations on both sides of the river. There were numerous travelers down the river. Goods came down by flatboat from the Watauga settlement bound for New Orleans. Settlers from Virginia and Carolina crossed the mountains and descended by boat, some bound for the lower Mississippi and others for the lower Tombigbee. Those bound for the latter stopped at the bluff, traveled by horseback to Cotton Gin Port, built more boats and descended. Those going on downstream sometimes had to lay over a long time at the Bluff waiting for a rise in the river to get over the Shoals.

LESSON 17 – INDIAN VILLAGES

In "Letters From Alabama", Anne Royal states that Melton had removed across the river in present Limestone County and died there about 1815 in old age. General Andrew Jackson leased his Melton Bluff plantation. It consisted of cotton lands, about 60 slaves and an overseer who lived in Melton's old log house of two stories, located a short distance from the village. General Jackson had trouble with his overseers and fugitive slaves, and was an anxious absentee landlord.

In 1818, the village stretched along the top of the bluff, consisted of two large houses of entertainment, several doctors, one hatters shop, one warehouse, and several mechanics. Living there were ten permanent families. There were a lot of travelers there at this time looking at lands and waiting for the coming land sales.

Melton's Bluff village died out soon after the land sales in the fall of 1818. All lands in present Lawrence County became the property of the United States and had to be purchased from it. The first event that then occurred at Melton's Bluff was a failed attempt to set up the city of Marathon, apparently by General Andrew Jackson, General John Coffee, and other speculators. The town which was surveyed into blocks and lots by Coffey, who was then surveyor general, was almost a mile square and located at and west of Melton's bluff. A few of the 556 lots were sold with a down payment, but all were relinquished, and there is no evidence any buildings went up.

A block in the center of Marathon was set aside as a public square, so there may have been hope that it would be selected as county seat. Moulton was selected, and it and Courtland built quickly into towns, and this may have caused the downfall of Marathon. The former site of Melton's Bluff is now TVA property, and Marathon is a part of the Wheeler Plantation."

The following lesson is a shortened and edited version of "Melton's Bluff" by William Lindsey McDonald. Melton's Bluff was the site of a Cherokee Indian village established about 1770 on the Tennessee River in Lawrence County. The site is between Spring Creek and Mallard Creek.

John Melton, according to lore and legend, was a fearsome pirate at the Muscle Shoals from the early 1790s until about 1806. He made a sizable fortune preying upon often times luckless adventurers who came down the Tennessee River in their flatboats or keelboats while North Alabama was the home of the Cherokee and Chickasaw Indians.

Melton's Bluff is located across from the mouth of Elk River, a few miles upstream from Rogersville; this site is north of Wheeler Station in Lawrence County. Some of the land that was once owned by Melton is now a part of the vast General Joe Wheeler Estate. Completely isolated, it affords one of the most scenic sites along the Tennessee River.

LESSON 17 – INDIAN VILLAGES

It has been said that Melton was an Irishman who for some reason harbored a deep grudge against the early white settlers. He attached himself to the Cherokees and soon had his own followers. He took for himself a Cherokee wife and built a large log house on the bluff that bears his name.

In the Articles of Agreement made that year between Henry Dearborn, Secretary of War, and the chiefs and headmen of the Cherokee Nation, Moses Melton was granted an interest in a tract of land described in part as follows: "... and the other reserved tract, on which Moses Melton now lives, is to be considered the property of said Melton, and of Charles Hicks in equal shares."

John Melton's notorious days as a pirate came to an end following the Cherokee Treaty of 1806. It is believed, however, that Melton's final decision to quit his pirating came about when Fort Hampton was established around 1810, near the mouth of Elk River. Although federal troops were sent to the Muscle Shoals to expel the early white settlers from Doublehead's Reserve, it is probably not without coincidence that Fort Hampton was located near the north bank of the Tennessee River.

Following his earlier years of high crime on the Tennessee, Melton opened an inn or tavern at this house on the bluff. By then a much-traveled wilderness road, known as Gaines Trace, had been established. This road was part of an effort to save from extinction the American settlements on the Tombigbee River in South Alabama. In 1805, the Secretary of War appointed George S. Gaines to negotiate a treaty with the Chickasaws for the right to build this road so as to connect the Tennessee and Tombigbee Rivers. The Chickasaws resisted, but finally agreed to a horse path which was to become known as the Gaines Trace. The language in Gaines' original survey specified that this road began "at the house of Mr. Melton, on a bluff, left (or south) bank of the Tennessee River, near the head of the Muscle Shoals." This early Wilderness Road terminated at Cotton Gin Port on the Tombigbee River in Mississippi. After the establishment of Gaines Trace on the south side of the river and the building of Fort Hampton and the early roads on the north side of the river, Melton's Bluff became a much-used river crossing point. Hence, John Melton's Inn did a prosperous business until about 1816.

Early documents show a number of military crossings at Melton's Bluff during the Creek War. General John Coffee, in his report dated October 22, 1813, described one event as follows: "... I proceeded to cross the river at the upper end of the Shoals, all my efforts failed to procure a pilot. I took with me one of John Melton's sons, who said he knew not the road, he showed me a path that had been reputed the ***Black Warriors' Path***..."

LESSON 17 – INDIAN VILLAGES

The renowned pioneer and soldier, David Crockett, remembered two occasions when his military unit crossed at Melton's Bluff. The first instance was in November 1813. Actually, according to Crockett, they crossed the Tennessee River twice on this first occasion in order to maneuver around the local Indians. After crossing at Huntsville, they moved westward to cross the river again at Melton's Bluff. Crockett described the river at this point as being about two miles wide. The rocky bottom of the river was rough and dangerous. While fording the river several of the horses became stuck in the rocky crevices and had to be left there while the military command moved on to their destination. Crockett's second crossing at Melton Bluff was in October 1814. Payroll and muster records reveal that he was a third sergeant in Captain John Cowan's company at the time.

Early letters show that Melton gave excellent service at his inn where the travelers could find plenty of meat, coffee, tea, and the best of liquors. A gentleman who had been a guest for a week remarked to a fellow traveler that he had never fared better in any part of the country.

The most colorful accounts of Melton's Bluff can be found in Anne Royall's letters. She described Melton's house as a large mansion built probably between the years 1788 and 1793. There was an impressive courtyard that fronted the house, and a road that ran to the river. She said that one could see upriver to Brown's Ferry, about eight miles away, and about the same distance down the river from the house.

John Melton and his Cherokee wife had a number of children. One son, James, made quite a reputation for himself as a pilot or guide. This involved meeting the boats at the upper end of the Muscle Shoals and piloting them through the dangerous and often deadly passage over that part of the river. There were a number of these pilots who operated from Melton's Bluff. They would ride downriver to Colbert's Ferry where they would disembark and walk back to Melton's Bluff. James became identified with the bluff that was named for his father. In fact, a number of early historians refer to James as the Indian for whom Melton's Bluff was named.

James Melton, half blood Cherokee, worked mainly for Malcolm Gilchrist to pilot flatboats over the Muscle Shoals. Gilchrist, whose ancestors were from Scotland, settled near Melton's Bluff before Alabama became a state. He became the "Commodore Vanderbilt" of the lower Tennessee River. He owned a fleet of flatboats that plied the river from Muscle Shoals to New Orleans and made for himself quite a fortune. In fact, his earnings from boating and land speculation became so enormous that his descendants enjoyed the prestige and power of their inherited wealth for many years after his death.

One of John Melton's daughters married a white man by the name of Rhea. He was the pilot who guided Anne Royall at the Muscle Shoals:

LESSON 17 – INDIAN VILLAGES

> "I learned he was from Rockbridge County, Virginia; had piloted boats through the Muscle Shoals, fifteen years; (since 1803) sometimes four at a time, at ten dollars each. He sails down one day, and walks back the next. He never met, in all that time, with an accident! There are several of these pilots."

General Andrew Jackson in partnership with his wife's nephew, Colonel John Hutchings, purchased Melton's Bluff from a David Melton in 1816. It is believed that David was a son of the old pirate, John Melton. This deed, signed November 22, 1816, described the property as follows:

> "I David Melton of the Cherokee Nation do by these presents bargain and sell ... unto General Andrew Jackson and Captain John Hutchings all my right title and interest to the tract of land where I now live, and agree to give them possession of all the improvements laying north and east of the spring, including said spring, on said tract where I live and adjoining where I live, and the houses and ... land southeast of the spring. Possession to be given of as many Negro houses as will house the Negroes of the said Andrew and the said John ... and possession of the other houses on or before the first day of February ... For which I acknowledge to have received the consideration of sixty dollars in cash and in full of the above sale."

Jackson and Hutchings were owners of Melton Bluff at the time Anne Royall wrote her interesting letters from there in 1818. She wrote:

> "Here is a very large plantation of cotton and maize, worked by about sixty slaves, and owned by General Jackson, who bought the interest of old Melton."

In another letter written two days later she described a visit by Jackson to his Melton's Bluff plantation:

> "... I was devouring Phillip's Speeches ... in a corner, when a loud cry, 'General Jackson, General Jackson comes!' and, running to my window, I saw him walking slowly up the hill, between two gentlemen, his aids."

There is no accounting for the number of trips Jackson made to his Alabama plantation over the period of ownership from 1816 until 1827. However, as many as they may have been, these infrequent inspections of his holdings were not enough to insure stability in matters of management. One noted historian concluded that Old Hickory "... had trouble with over seers and fugitive slaves and was a rather anxious absentee landlord."

LESSON 17 – INDIAN VILLAGES

A biographer, Marquis James, listed a number of the General's trips to Alabama. One such journey occurred following the emptying of Jackson's cotton warehouses at his Hermitage plantation and his Melton's Bluff plantation in March of 1822. This occasion came about following the swelling of the Cumberland and Tennessee Rivers which allowed his boats, loaded with cotton, to commence their journeys to New Orleans. Three months later, General Jackson rode his horse from Nashville to Alabama to inspect his plantation. This same biographer, in relating the events of the 1824 national presidential election, wrote:

> "During the last weeks before the balloting began, General Jackson visited Melton's Bluff to make arrangements for the marketing of his Alabama cotton - an important detail, as the winter in Washington had been costly and the absentee planter was pressed for funds."

Jackson's political life seems to have been the major cause for his extended absences from the affairs of his cotton kingdom. By 1827 he was in financial trouble. A biographer noted:

> "The General's cotton seemed to have suffered from inattention, however, the 1827 crop being no better than average in quality. A plague decimated the stables leaving Jackson without a team to take him to Alabama to straighten out an overseer tangle."

The General and his partner soon afterwards sold their Melton Bluff plantation. Jackson was convinced that one cotton farm was enough for a busy politician to handle. It is believed that one of his mismanagement problems stemmed from the old soldier's extreme loyalty to his servants and former comrades. As an example, the General placed one of his beloved slaves, David Hutchings Smith, who had been his camp man during the Indian campaigns, as overseer of the Melton's Bluff plantation. "Old Pap" as Smith was called was as devoted to his master as his master was to him. Yet, from all indications, Old Pap was not the man for the job. After the General disposed of his Melton's Bluff Cotton farm, he tenderly placed Old Pap in the care of his ward Andrew Jackson Hutchings. David Hutchings Smith lived a long and eventful life that amounted to 108 years. His last days were at Ardoyne plantation near Florence where he is buried. A number of tales were handed down through the Coffee family about Old Pap's remembrances of the time he was overseer of "Marsa Jackson's plantation" at Melton's Bluff.

In 1818, soon after Jackson and Hutchings purchased the property of Melton, they opened up and promoted a town on that part of the plantation on the bluff facing the river. They named it for the ancient Greek city, Marathon, which we affiliate with foot races. This selection probably had something to do with Jackson's love for the racetrack. Marathon was located adjacent to John Melton's log house, later Melton's Inn.

LESSON 17 – INDIAN VILLAGES

The first mention of plans for the town was in a letter from Josiah Meigs to John Coffee, dated May 26, 1818. Jackson had employed his friend and kinsman, General John Coffee, to plan and survey his new town. Coffee laid out 658 lots.

Marathon served as the seat of justice for Lawrence County while Alabama was a territory; for a number of years it was the first and largest town in the county. People rapidly moved in from Virginia and North and South Carolina. They built their homes facing the river on the main residential road that stretched for more than a mile along the bluff.

Marathon soon became a ghost town when the county seat was moved to Moulton in 1820. The town site was included in the large tract of land purchased by Colonel Richard Jones in 1829, to become one of the largest ante-bellum plantations in the Tennessee Valley. Jones built his home not far from Melton's Bluff. Here was born his daughter Daniella Ellen, who in 1866 became the wife of the famed Confederate Cavalry General "Fighting Joe" Wheeler.

A large monument adjacent to Melton's Bluff identifies the site as the place where General Wheeler crossed the Tennessee River on October 9, 1863, following his raid down the Sequatchie Valley after the Battle of Chickamauga. Nearby is an abandoned watering hole that still bears the name "Dora Belle's Well." Not far away is a decaying log house. Down the lane, they say, is where the beloved ex-slave, Sweet Peter, and his wife once lived. The old bluff, anchored in antediluvian limestone formed near the dawn of time, is strangely silent now. Only the refreshing winds across Wheeler Lake can be heard through the overhanging limbs of old, gnarled trees. The likes of John Melton and his marauding pirates are but fading memories to the wanderer of the Twentieth Century. Yet the story of Melton's Bluff ever remains history's flamboyant account of a place on the Tennessee River called the Muscle Shoals.

Goard's (Gourd's) Settlement - The fifth downstream Indian town was a Cherokee village called Goard's Settlement which was at the present-day town of Courtland. On December 28, 1807, Captain Edmund Pendleton Gaines made this note on his survey from Melton's Bluff to Cotton Gin Port, "8th mile…. At 119 chs. Cross the path which leads from the Shoal Town, eastwardly, to the *Goard's Settlement, about 3 miles distance"* (Stone, James H., 1971). Based on Gaines measurements of some 8.7 miles westerly from Melton's Bluff, then easterly for three miles, Goard's settlement was in the center of present-day Courtland, Alabama. Eventually, three Indian roads intersected at Goard's settlement which were Gaines' Trace, South River Road, and Sipsie Trail which later became the Cheatham Road or portions of present day Highway 33.

Goard's Settlement was obviously named after a Cherokee Indian man called Goard. According to Letters from Alabama 1817-1822 written by Anne Royall on January 12, 1818, page 131, is the following, *"Guide says Goard was very kind; he knew him for fifteen years.*

LESSON 17 – INDIAN VILLAGES

He helped subdue the Creeks, and made an excellent soldier." Anne Royall described Goard's log house as being on the west side of Town Creek which was ten years after Gaines location; however, she wrote her letter after the fact and might have been wrong on the exact location; furthermore, Gaines was a surveyor and made precise measurements and locations.

Goard's Town was at the junction of the South River Road and the Sipsie Trail, an early Indian route from Tuscaloosa to the French Lick (Nashville, TN). Also, a prehistoric village containing an Indian mound was located at the site on the banks of Path Killer Creek which later became known as Big Nance. According to Captain Edmund Pendleton Gaines on December 27, 1807, *"we proceeded, same course...6th mile...At 116 [chaines] (west of Melton's Bluff) Path Killer's Creek, 3 chains wide from tops of banks"* (Stone, James H., 1971). In 1807, when Captain Gaines identified Path Killer Creek(named after Cherokee Chief Path Killer), he was traveling portions of the South River Road but was intent on surveying a line from Melton's Bluff on the Tennessee River to Cotton Gin Port on the Tombigbee River; therefore, he basically followed the Old Chickasaw Trail to the heart of the Chickasaw Nation.

According to a February, 1829 Lawrence County court record, *" a road from Gourd landing on the Tennessee River to intersect the road from Courtland to Lamb's Ferry at or near Gordon's fence the nearest and best way...Order, 1829, Jury of Review of a road from Courtland to Gourds."* This road either crossed or followed portions of both the Sipsie Trail and Gaines' Trace.

Cuttyatoy's Village - The fourth downstream Indian town connected by the South River Road was Cuttyatoy's Village. The village was actually on Gilchrist Island at the western end of Elk River Shoals near the south bank of the Tennessee River. According to the American Whig Review, Volume 15, Issue 87, March 1852, page 247, *"Colonel (Joseph) Brown...a participant in the battle of Talledega (November 9, 1813)...met Charles Butler... and learned from him that...Chief Cuttyatoy, was still alive...he was then living on an island in the Tennessee River, near the mouth of Elle (Elk) River, and that he had with him several Negroes ... taken by him at Nickajack on the 9th of May, 1788... with ten picked men, Brown proceeded to the island, went to the head man's (Cuttyatoy) lodge and exhibited to him General (Andrew) Jackson's order, and demanded that Cutty-a-toy's Negroes be immediately sent over to Fort Hampton...In crossing the river, Colonel Brown and his men took up the Negroes, and Cutty-a-toy's wife behind them, to carry them over the water while the Indian men crossed on a raft (Brown's Ferry) higher up (stream)."* Cuttyatoy and his men utilized the South River Road to reach Brown's Ferry. Colonel Joseph Brown and his men reached Fort Hampton that morning while Cuttyatoy and his men arrived in the afternoon.

LESSON 17 – INDIAN VILLAGES

Today, Cuttyatoy's Village is under the backwaters created by Wheeler Dam. The old Indian town site lies buried below the surface of Wheeler Lake, as most of the river villages that were located on islands of Elk River Shoals. Between the mouth of Spring Creek on the south side and Elk River on the north side of the Tennessee River, the islands of Elk River Shoals are under some twenty feet or more of water. It was between these islands of Elk River Shoals that General Joe Wheeler's cavalry crossed the Tennessee River on October 9, 1863.

Shoal Town - The final Lawrence County Indian town connected by the South River Road was the Cherokee village of Shoal Town located between Blue Water Creek and Town Creek on the Tennessee River. Shoal Town was the home of Talohuskee Benge, the half brother to Sequoyah. Later, Talohuskee's great uncle Doublehead moved to the Shoal Town area about 1802. Shoal Town was located some six miles from the eastern end of Big Muscle Shoals at the junction of Doublehead's Trace and the South River Road. Again, during Captain Edmund Pendleton Gaines survey on December 28, 1807, he notes the following, *"8th mile... at 119 chs. Cross the path (South River Road) which leads from **Shoal-Town**, eastwardly, to the Goards Settlement (Courtland), about 3 miles distance"* (Stone, James H., 1971)

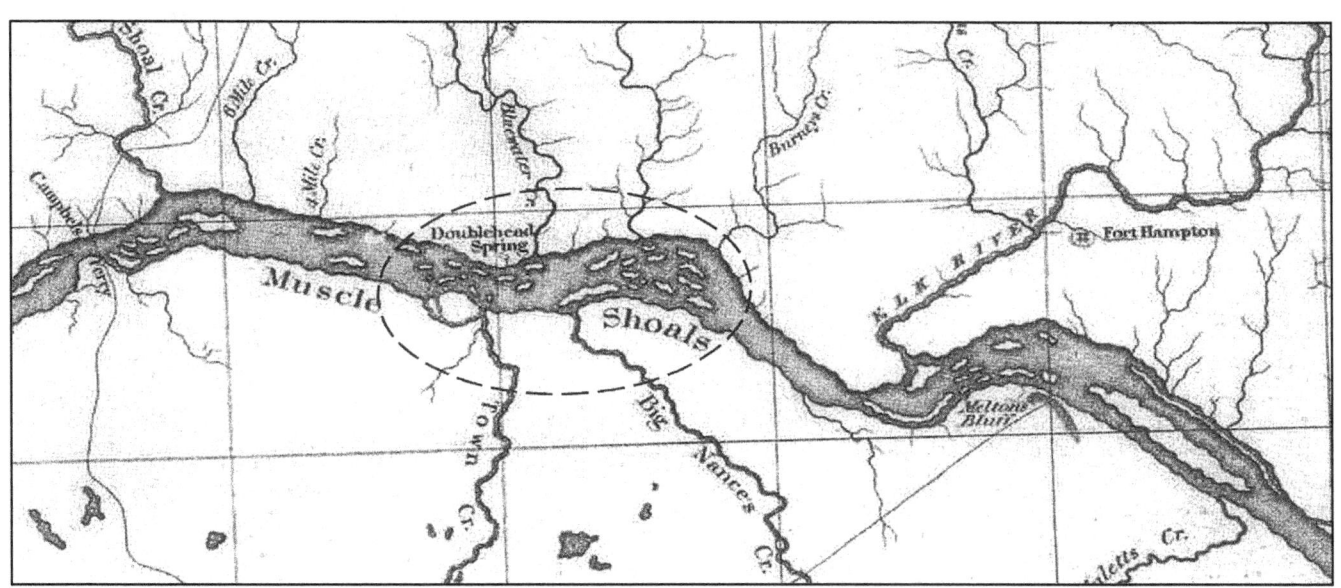

Circle shows location of Shoal Town – Doublehead Spring

Shoal Town was considered the largest Cherokee Indian village in the Big Bend of the Tennessee River. At the location, the Blue Water Ferry crossed the river from the eastern side of the mouth of Blue Water Creek to the western side of the mouth of Path Killer's Creek. Talohuskee Benge, son of Doublehead's niece, Wurteh Watts and trader John Benge, and Doublehead lived at Shoal Town and probably operated the ferry which was common practice at large Cherokee River Towns.

LESSON 17 – INDIAN VILLAGES

*"Both the French and the English contended for the Indian trade along the western waters; the French planted a post at Muscle Shoals before 1715. Because of the increasing importance of trade with the whites the Cherokees planted villages near the Muscle Shoals area in the last quarter of the eighteenth century. There was Doublehead's village on the Tennessee and **a large settlement (Shoal Town) at the mouth of Town Creek, extending a mile along the river and far up the creek**"*. (Leftwich, Nina, 1935) The Cherokee village described above is Shoal Town which was located on Big Muscle Shoals of the Tennessee River between Big Nance (Path Killer's) Creek, Town Creek, and Blue Water Creek.

While living at Shoal Town, Doublehead requested help from the U.S. Government; however, he was no stranger to the government when asking for help, money, or handouts. This particular incident is recorded in Henry T. Malone's (1956) book <u>Cherokees of the Old South</u>:

"A scarcity of corn caused by a drought in the Cherokee Nation during the year 1804 was a crisis which Meigs faced in his typical fashion. The first request for food came from **Doublehead** *and other Cherokees in the Muscle Shoals area on the Lower Tennessee River. The Agent immediately sent them three hundred bushels of corn, for which the Indians paid $110. Meigs, however, requested and received permission from the War Department to return the money; he thought it his duty "to give the necessary relief — believing that humanity and interest combine to make it proper especially when interesting negotiations with them are now soon to be opened." Meigs' policy pleased his government. Henry Dearborn sent him the President's congratulations, urging Meigs to continue helping needy Indians: "You will embrace so favorable an opportunity for impressing the minds of the Cherokees with the fatherly concern and attention of the President to the distresses of his red children."*

Today, Doublehead's Resort is located in Lawrence County, Alabama, at the site of Shoal Town. The resort is a modern facility catering to thousands of people each year and is located on the east bank of Town Creek near where it empties into the Tennessee River. The resort area extends up the river toward Big Nance Creek and has became a popular tourist site. Along the bank of Town Creek are numerous two-story cabins which can accommodate entire families. Each cabin has a water-front dock which provides boating facilities for resort visitors. The resort also boasts a lodge, swimming facilities, horseback riding, and many other accommodations that make for a pleasurable stay. If Doublehead were alive today, he would have to be proud of the facility at his old homesite that bears his name; therefore, the legends of Doublehead live on at this beautiful recreational facility in the county his descendants still call home.

Oakville - Do you know of any mounds in Lawrence County? (There are burial and ceremonial mounds found in Oakville). Do you know where Oakville is located? (Oakville

LESSON 17 – INDIAN VILLAGES

is in Lawrence County east of Moulton). Maybe you can visit there sometime. Do you know why a mound would be called a shell mound? (shell mounds were found along the Tennessee River where our early Indian ancestors had piled up huge mounds of mussel shells)

Indian villages were located near natural springs with lots of water. Mussels were a main source of food. (show mussel shell) When they ate the mussels, the shells would be thrown down and they would pile up and form a shell mound. Also found in the shell mounds were animal bones, stones, pebbles, flint chips, and broken objects. The shells were used for jewelry and tools.

Our story begins over 12,000 years ago when our Indian ancestors first entered the beautiful Tennessee Valley and settled in Oakville which is one of the most beautiful places in North Alabama. Oakville is located between the Warrior Mountains to the south and the Tennessee River to the north. For thousands of years, our ancestors lived, died, and worshipped in our area primarily because of the bountiful nurturing elements of life.

Our Indian people in Lawrence County have long sought to have a more active role in retaining the remnants of our Indian heritage, traditions, customs, and history. Today, we have the opportunity and ability through our Indian program to provide the areas and facilities where glimpses of our rich pre-historic and historic Indian past can be seen at the Oakville Indian Mounds Education Center.

The Oakville Indian Mounds have long been a site in Lawrence County deserving of protection and utilization as an educational area. Since, Lawrence County Schools' Indian Education Program was established, the Oakville Indian site has been seen as an area which would compliment and enhance our county's rich Indian heritage. Today, the Indian education program is headquartered at the Oakville site.

The Oakville site has been written about for over 100 years with historic settler burials occurring some 175 years ago on the burial mound. The burial mound was the site of Copena Indian burials some 2,000 years ago. The large ceremonial mound is estimated to have been built during the Woodland Period, which covers a time span from 1,000 BC to 1,000 AD. The Oakville area was considered a religious center and social complex of the middle woodland Indian people with outlying villages and farms. Additional Copena mounds located nearby supports the complex social center theory.

During historic times, the area was the site of an early Cherokee town located at the junctions of the Coosa Path and Black Warriors' Path. Oakville became a settler town on the southeastern frontier of Lawrence County, Alabama. Early 1800 maps show Oakville being one of only four towns located in Lawrence County with the others being Courtland,

LESSON 17 – INDIAN VILLAGES

Marathon (no longer exists), and Moulton. The Town of Oakville appeared near its peak during the middle 1800's just prior to the Civil War.

In 1817, the first government surveys of the Oakville area identified a good stream of fresh water flowing from a huge spring. The stream ran about 1/2 mile before running into a limestone crevasse and going underground. Eventually hogs stopped up the sink, which caused the area to flood. In addition to flooding, a disease called the "bloody flux" led to the death of many Oakville residents. The Town of Oakville was abandoned around 1855.

In 1924, a Smithsonian archaeological team, who were part of pre-impoundment survey for Wilson Dam and Lake, visited the site. During the Oakville site visit, Smithsonian archaeologists identified five Indian mounds in the area. Three of the mounds were in the process of being plowed down. At that time, some three miles upstream on West Flint Creek, the Smithsonian crew excavated the Alexander Mound, which was smaller, but similar to the Oakville burial mound. Some 106 skeletons along with numerous artifacts were removed from the Alexander Mound.

Ceremonial Mound at Oakville

Oakville is located in Lawrence County near the Jesse Owens Monument at Speake. Oakville was the birthplace of Jesse Owens, but also an important part of Indian history. Long before it was ever called Oakville; it was the site of a large Woodland Indian village. Later, tradition has it that the Cherokees had a large village at the site. There are two mounds still intact in the Oakville area. One mound is a ceremonial mound is about 1.8 acres in size and stands about 27 feet high. It is believed that a temple may have been on top at one time. Archaeologists survey from places in the same area, date the mounds around 2,000 years old. For this reason, it is considered a Woodland mound. It is the largest Woodland mound in Alabama and the second largest mound in the state by volume. Two Indian trails crossed near the big Oakville mound-Black Warriors' Path and Old Indian Trace (Coosa Path).

The other mound is a burial mound. It is conical in shape and believed to hold Indian burials. These two mounds have not been excavated so no one is certain. The Indian people have been trying to protect the mounds and preserve them for some time. At one time there were at least five mounds in the area.

On top of the Indian burial mound are several false stone crypts where early settlers were buried. Some say they considered it a sacred place because the Indian burials were already

LESSON 17 – INDIAN VILLAGES

there. There are black slaves in unmarked graves believed to be buried on the large ceremonial mound at Oakville.

Evidence gathered from surrounding areas indicates the Indian people here worked with copper and galena metals. Therefore, they were called Copena Indians. As time progressed, the fate of these people is unknown as to where they went. Mixed-blood marriages, warfare, and trade probably scattered the tribe throughout the Southeast.

Years later, the Town of Oakville was established in the same area as the mounds. This was a thriving town with a hotel, saloon, post office, blacksmith shop, and a few stores. It is uncertain exactly what became of the Town of Oakville. Most likely, the people living there died after an epidemic called the bloody flux contaminated the area in the 1850's. Many of the graves date in the 1850's. In 1830, Oakville was one of only four towns in Lawrence County and was incorporated in 1833. Another reason for its demise may have been the depression or crash of 1837. The merchants became broke and almost every building rotted down.

Regardless of exactly what happened, the Town of Oakville ceased to exist. The early settlers' graves have been vandalized over the years. Several of the local Indian education students worked on a summer youth project to repair these. This cemetery is called the Indian Mound Cemetery.

Review Questions

1. What ceremony is the most important to the Indians?
2. Where was Melton's Bluff located?
3. Whose village was located at Brown's Ferry?
4. What is a burial mound?
5. What is a ceremonial mound?
6. Where is the Indian mounds cemetery located?
7. Where is the largest ceremonial mound in Lawrence County made by Woodland people?
8. Name three types of Indian mounds?
9. Who was the Irishman that Melton's Bluff is named after?
10. Where is Shoal Town located?
11. What is another name for Melton's Bluff?
12. How did our ancestors form a shell mound?
13. Melton's Bluff was owned by whom and was later known as what?
14. Which Indian town was a Cherokee village located at present-day Town of Courtland?
15. Who lived at Shoal Town from 1802 until his death on August 9, 1807?

LESSON 17 – INDIAN VILLAGES

16. Why was the Green corn Ceremony celebrated?
17. Where was Mouse Town/Moneetown located?
18. Who was a fearsome pirate at the Muscle Shoals from the early 1790's until about 1806?
19. What early town was flooded and abandoned after a disease called "bloody flux"?
20. Oakville was a Cherokee village located at the forks of which two paths?
21. What town served as the county seat before it was moved to Moulton in 1820?
22. Where was Cuttyatoy's Village located?
23. What early town is presently buried below the surface of Wheeler Lake?
24. Shoal Town was the home of whom?
25. Which town was three miles east of Elk River Shoals and was the first Cherokee town beginning on the east edge of Lawrence County?
26. About what year did Doublehead establish his village on the Tennessee River?
27. Which Indian town was connected by the South River Road?
28. Where was Doublehead's Town located?
29. Name a renowned pioneer and soldier:
30. Name the seven Cherokee towns of Lawrence County?

LESSON 18 – LOCAL INDIAN LEADERS

Sequoyah - Sequoyah, George Gist, was born about 1776, near Fort Loudoun, Tennessee in the village of Tuskegee. His mother, Wurteh Watts, who was a daughter to the sister of Doublehead, a full-blood Cherokee, and John Watts (Scotch). Sequoyah's father probably was Nathaniel Gist, the famous scout and soldier. Nathaniel Gist was thought to be German or Irish.

Doublehead's older sister married a Celtic man (Scotch) named John Watts. They had two famous children, John Watts, Jr. who became Chief of the Cherokee Nation and Wurteh Watts, the mother of Sequoyah.

Although Sequoyah's father was white and his mother was only half Cherokee, he had a traditional Cherokee childhood. When Sequoyah was a small boy, his mother moved them to Alabama to an Indian settlement near Willstown. Here, Sequoyah spent most of his early life, learning to trace honey bees, to shoot the bow and arrow, and to look after his mother's small farm. Sequoyah's great uncle, Doublehead and his half brothers lived in and around North Alabama.

Sequoyah Teaching His Alphabet

Army records show that Sequoyah fought in the Creek War of 1812 with a group of Cherokee volunteers. He, along with Junaluska, another famous Cherokee, fought with Andrew Jackson in the Battle of Horseshoe Bend. Early in life, Sequoyah was a silversmith. He wanted to sign his silver work and got Charles Hicks to show him how to write his name. This stimulated his early interest in writing an alphabet for his Cherokee people.

There are many stories about when and how Sequoyah started working and thinking about his alphabet. One of these stories is that he and some of his friends fell into a discussion about writing, after having heard the Bible translated at a white man's house. His friends said that writing was a most wonderful thing, to be able to put all the wisdom down on the talking leaves so that they would not be forgotten. Sequoyah, hearing this remark, said, "I could do this thing that the white man does." His friends laughed and said, "You are foolish, you could not even begin to do this wonderful thing. This has taken many long winters for the white man to do. It is his gift. The Great One has not given us this gift.

LESSON 18 – LOCAL INDIAN LEADERS

It would be foolish for us even to try such a task." But Sequoyah did not hear their last remark. He was already turning over in his mind how he was going to put his own talk down on the talking leaves.

He first drew a picture or symbol to represent each word, but there were so many that he realized this was impossible. Then he tried to figure out a way to make a symbol for a sentence. But this too, he saw would not do because there were so many ways to make a sentence. Eventually, he began to listen for the different sounds that the Cherokee language had. These, he would record with a mark that he thought would be easy to remember. Soon, he ran out of ideas for new marks; his signs began to all look alike. For a long time, he did not know what to do. Then, while walking one day, he found a piece of old newspaper that he discovered was full of symbols, which he had never even thought of making. Thus, Sequoyah not knowing one English letter from another used a great many of our own crooked marks to represent sounds in the Cherokee language. Sequoyah encountered many

LESSON 18 – LOCAL INDIAN LEADERS

problems before he completed his project. He neglected his family responsibilities and once, his angry wife burned two years of his work. Since many Indians believed that Sequoyah's strange marks meant he was in league with the devil, they burned his cabin while he was away.

In 1821, his work was completed. He had 86 characters to represent each syllable in the Cherokee language. Thus, a three-syllable word needed only three characters to write. Within a few years, almost all the young and middle-age men in the Cherokee Nation could read and write the Cherokee syllabary.

With the interest to learn to read and write in their own language, Bibles, pamphlets, and other materials were printed using Sequoyah's syllabaries. The first Indian newspaper, the Cherokee Phoenix, was published. This paper printed news in both English and Cherokee.

Sequoyah was a famous member of the Cherokee tribe. His mother, Wurteh Watts, was ½ Cherokee and ½ Celtic (Scotch). Her father was John Watts and her brother, John Watts, Jr., became chief of the Cherokee Nation. Sequoyah's father was a white man, Nathaniel Gist; but, Sequoyah, also known as George Gist, always considered himself as an Indian. Doublehead was Sequoyah's great uncle. Sequoyah was lame in one leg, probably from polio. Young Sequoyah could not go hunting or on war parties with other Cherokee men; so he became a fine silversmith and artist.

He listened to the Cherokee leaders talk of the white man's treaties. They called the papers with words on them "talking leaves" and felt they were magic. Sequoyah realized that there was no magic that the marks stood for words. Even though the Cherokee leaders laughed and thought him insane, Sequoyah promised that someday, he would be able to write down every word of the Cherokee language.

Sequoyah finally finished his work on the alphabet. Within a few years, almost all of the young Cherokee men could read and write. Newspapers, pamphlets, Bibles were printed using Sequoyah's alphabet.

Two of Sequoyah's half brothers, Robert (Bob) Benge (The Bench) and Tahlontoiskee (Talohuskee) Benge, for a while lived in or near Lawrence County. Bob Benge and Talohuskee Benge were the sons of trader John Benge (Scotch) and Wurteh Watts; therefore, Bob Benge was ¼ Cherokee and ¾ Celtic and was the most feared warrior in the Appalachian Frontier. Charles Hicks, half-Cherokee, first showed Sequoyah how to write his name in English. David Melton deeded the land in Lawrence County between Mallard and Spring Creeks at Melton Bluff to General Andrew Jackson on November 22, 1816.

LESSON 18 – LOCAL INDIAN LEADERS

John Melton – John Melton was one of the early Irish people in Lawrence County who came during the 1780's with the Cherokee Indians. Melton, an Irishman, married Ocuma, Doublehead's sister and died at a large farm on the north side of the Tennessee River about 1815. Melton owned large farms and a great number of slaves. According to the Cotton Gin Treaty of 1806, the first cotton gin in Lawrence County was placed at Melton's Bluff by the U. S. Government. Cotton became a very important Cherokee product and the use of black slaves in the early 1800s was common among the Cherokee. Melton's Bluff, located near the head of Elk River Shoals on the Tennessee River in Lawrence County, was named after John Melton. Melton had several children by his Indian wife, most married white people. Remarkable advancement of the Cherokee came about largely through the influence of the mixed-blood or metis families. Many Celtic people coming into North Alabama in the 1700s, made friends with the Indians and married their young women. During Indian removal, mixed-blood inhabitants were allowed to remain in North Alabama because they were married to whites or were able to identify themselves with white ancestry. Due to Indian removal and intermarriage, North Alabama's Indian people became thoroughly absorbed into the general population.

Doublehead - another important Cherokee man. Doublehead, (c1744-1807), aka Dsugweladegi or Chuqualatague, was the son of Great Eagle (Willenawah) and grandson of Moytoy. Among his siblings were Pumpkin Boy, Old Tassel, and unnamed grandmother of Sequoyah. After his sister's son, John Watts Jr. was elected chief over him, Doublehead moved into Lawrence County becoming a powerful Cherokee leader. Living at Browns Ferry, the head of Elk River Shoals (c1790-c1802), Doublehead terrorized settlers on the Appalachian frontier until his 1794 meeting with George Washington. By the treaty on January 10, 1786, most of Lawrence County became Chickasaw land. Doublehead was permitted to stay because of his daughters, Tuskiahooto and Saleechie, marriages to Chickasaw Chief George Colbert. Learning of the wealth in cotton, Doublehead in 1802 petitioned the government for a keelboat, signed the 1805 treaty authorizing Gaines Trace, and negotiated the 1806 Cotton Gin Treaty. This treaty placed a cotton gin at Melton's Bluff and gave him a 99-year lease on Doublehead's Reserve between Elk River and Cypress Creek. In partnership with John D. Chisholm, they leased this reserve to settlers. On 9 Aug 1807, Major Ridge, Alex Saunders and John Rogers killed Doublehead, either for control of the cotton trade or for his ceding of Indian lands.

Doublehead or "Talo Tiske"-meaning two heads. What do you think that means? (two personalities)

Doublehead was from a prominent family of the Cherokee. His brothers were Old Tassel, a principal chief of the Cherokee Nation, and Pumpkin Boy. Doublehead's older sister married a Fort Loudoun soldier, John Watts. Their son, John Watts, Jr. became chief of the Cherokee Nation. They had, "Wurteh" who was the mother of Sequoyah. Wurteh Watts was ½ Celtic

LESSON 18 – LOCAL INDIAN LEADERS

(Scotch) and ½ Cherokee. Sequoyah's father was Nathaniel Gist (Guess), who was of uncertain European lineage, but was thought to be Irish. Who knows who Sequoyah was? What did he do that was important to the Cherokee? (Cherokee alphabet) Nathan Gist and Wurteh Watts became the parents of the most famous Cherokee of all, the notable Sequoyah. Wurteh Watts had earlier married trader John Benge (Scotch) and had Robert Benge, Talohuskee Benge, and Utana Benge.

In 1790, Doublehead established his first town on the Tennessee River at the head of Mussel Shoals. Now, I'm talking about Shoals as being the river and not the city. The town was located in Lawrence County at Brown's Ferry just east of the mouth of Mallard Creek. The town was known as Doublehead's Town or Brown's Ferry.

After moving from the area that became Lawrence County in 1802, Doublehead settled on Blue Water Creek in Lauderdale County. Today, the Blue Water Polo Club on Highway 72 is located on the Cherokee Blue Water Old Fields. The main Cherokee Town near Doublehead's home was called Shoal Town located between Blue Water Creek and Town Creek on the Tennessee River.

In the beginning, Doublehead was a village chief. After the death of Old Tassel in 1788, Doublehead became a powerful chief over the lower Tennessee River in our area. He moved into the Chickasaw Country because his nephew John Watts, Jr. (½ Celtic – ½ Cherokee) was elected Chief of the Chickamauga over him. Also, Doublehead's oldest two daughters, Tuskiahooto and Saleechie, married Chickasaw Chief George Colbert. Doublehead was assassinated on August 9, 1807, and is supposedly buried on a hill east of Blue Water Creek and on the north side of Highway 72 over looking the Blue Water Oldfields (presently a Polo Club).

After living in Doublehead's Town at Browns Ferry until 1802, Cherokee Chief Doublehead migrated farther west along the Tennessee River into Lauderdale County, Alabama. Historical evidence indicates Doublehead settled for some 12 years at the head of Elk River Shoals at Brown's Ferry. Doublehead helped establish the following villages along the Tennessee River in Lawrence County: Moneetown (Mouse Town), at the mouth of Fox Creek, Doublehead's Village at Brown's Ferry, between Fox and Mallard Creeks; Melton's Bluff between Mallard and Spring Creeks; Gourd's Settlement at Courtland on Path Killer Creek (Big Nance); Shoal Town between Blue Water and Town Creek near present-day Wheeler Dam; and, Oakville located at junction of Old Indian Trace (Coosa Path) and Black Warriors' Path.

From the 1770's Chief Doublehead and the Chickamauga inhabited and controlled the area of the Warrior Mountains and north to the present-day Tennessee State Line. By 1790, Doublehead had settled and lived in Lawrence County at Doublehead's Town at Brown's

LESSON 18 – LOCAL INDIAN LEADERS

Ferry, which was at the head of Muscle Shoals. The following text tells of Doublehead's home and is found on page 62 of Volume V, "The Journal of Muscle Shoals History," and written in a speech by William B. Wood published in 1876 is the following:

> "As early as 1802, a party set out from North Carolina, who, with great difficulty, ascended the Blue Ridge, with their wagons, and descended through its gorges, into the valley of the Tennessee. Constructing flat boats at Knoxville, they floated down the Tennessee River, to the head of Muscle Shoals, where they disembarked at the house of Doublehead, a Cherokee Chief. This party; however, did not remain in this valley, the lands belonging to the Indians, their title having not yet been extinguished."

Sometime around 1802, Doublehead moved down river to the Indian village of Shoal Town between Blue Water and Town Creeks. According to William L. McDonald's "The Lore of Chief Doublehead and His Home at Muscle Shoals" found in Volume IX of the Journal of Muscle Shoals History on page 103 is the following:

> *Yet, Doublehead was without influence or position. That is, until about the year 1790, when he established his first town on the Tennessee River at the head of the Muscle Shoals. An early map of the Cherokee Country shows this village at a site near the south bank of Brown's Ferry below Athens. He later moved it to the north bank of the river near the mouth of Blue Water Creek, in Lauderdale County, Alabama.*

According to this historical information, Doublehead lived at Doublehead's Town at Browns Ferry for some 12 years at the head of Muscle Shoals on the south bank of the Tennessee River in present day Lawrence County. The Cherokee village is also shown on a 1779-1796 map of the proposed "State of Franklin" and was located between Mallard Creek and Fox Creek. Doublehead lived at Browns Ferry prior to moving to his Blue Water home of Shoal Town in present-day Lauderdale County. Doublehead's old two-story log home and tavern was destroyed during the four laning of Highway 72 between Athens and Florence.

Tahlonteskee (Talohuskee Benge) the great nephew of Doublehead, had his settlement of Shoal Town at the mouths of Town Creek in Lawrence County and Blue Water Creek in Lauderdale County on the banks of the Hogohegee (Tennessee) River, known as the "River of the Cherokees". The village actually lay on both sides of the river about six miles from the eastern upstream end of the Big Mussel Shoals. Actually at this point, the Blue Water Ferry crossed the river from the eastern point of Blue Water Creek to the area halfway between Town Creek and Big Nance Creek in present day Lawrence County. According to Nina Leftwich's book <u>Two Hundred Years at Muscle Shoals</u>, the Cherokees had a large

LESSON 18 – LOCAL INDIAN LEADERS

settlement at the mouth of Town Creek, which extended a mile along the river and far up the creek.

Doublehead was the feared war chief of the Big Bend of lower Tennessee River Cherokees known as Chickamaugans. Tahlonteskee, Talohuskee Benge, was Doublehead's nephew. The Shoal Town, (Blue Water-Town Creek Village), was the final Alabama home of both men. Doublehead is supposedly buried on Blue Water Creek in Lauderdale County, Alabama. Some say he is buried on the east side of Blue Water Creek and just north of Highway 72 on a knoll overlooking the Blue Water Old Fields now known as Blue Water Polo Club.

In 1806, Cherokee Chief Doublehead, Tahlonteskee, and other Cherokees signed the Cotton Gin Treaty, which gave up Cherokee Claims to land north of the Tennessee River except from Doublehead's Reserve. The reserve lay between Elk River (Chuwalee) and Cypress Creek (TeKeetanoeh) in present day Lauderdale County.

The signing of the Cotton Gin Treaty brought the wrath of other Cherokee leaders upon the individuals who signed the treaty giving up Cherokee Lands. Major Ridge, a powerful Cherokee leader, made known that Doublehead and others would pay with their lives for relinquishing Cherokee lands. At a meeting of Cherokee headmen in Tennessee, Doublehead paid with his life at the hand of Ridge, Alex Saunders, John Rogers, and their accomplices. Alex Saunders and John Rogers had ties to Lawrence County and probably profited from the assassination of Doublehead.

Doublehead's town site, near Center Star, was located where his nephew, Tahlonteskee (Talohuskee) Benge, had lived before moving to Arkansas in 1809. This location had the advantage of about a square mile of bottomlands that Tahlonteskee's people had cleared and made ready for farming. These "Old Fields" at the mouth of Blue Water Creek were very fertile and appealed to the very first white settlers, and, subsequently, became the enticement that made this community the first to be settled in the county.

Inhabitants of Shoal Town where Doublehead lived, originally about forty in number, were mostly cast-offs from other Cherokee and Creek villages. This motley bunch became infamous in Tennessee history as "the ravagers of the Cumberland's." However, as years passed, other and more respectable Indians, mostly Cherokees, moved in, and by the time of the arrival of the first whites, they were of the genial sort and, according to some diaries, made "mighty good neighbors."

The Shoal Town site was in the disputed reserve that was called the "Chickasaw Hunting Grounds." For over two hundred years, the Creeks, Chickasaws, and the Cherokees claimed these lands as their own. Thus, the settlement at the Muscle Shoals was cause for concern

LESSON 18 – LOCAL INDIAN LEADERS

by the Federal Government, and especially General James Robertson, the protector of the Cumberland's. However, the Cherokee Agent, Colonel Return Jonathon Meigs, thought Doublehead's settlement was an attempt by the Cherokees to test their title to that portion of the disputed Chickasaw Hunting Grounds. Robertson was finally calmed by the assurance from Chickasaw Chief George Colbert, who operated a ferry across the Tennessee at the nearby Natchez Trace that Doublehead was at the Muscle Shoals by his permission.

George Colbert was a double son-in-law of Doublehead. Colbert, according to one traveling preacher, "indulged in more than one marital adventure simultaneously." Two of his wives, observed Methodist historian John B. M'Ferrin, were daughters of Chief Doublehead. The principal wife, Tuskiahooto, presided over the household. She raised a few eyebrows when she attended a formal dinner with her husband at the White House, dressed in the latest Washington fashion and barefooted. Old families of Colbert County remembered how this princess by birth, and principal "first lady" in marriage by her extremely good looks, refused to ride in the elegant carriage provided by her husband. Instead, she followed the carriage and driver, astride her favorite pony seated on a colorful blanket, and, as usual barefooted. The other wife was Saleechie, or sometimes "Shullechie." She was a successful businesswoman and operated an inn on the Natchez Trace near Tupelo, Mississippi. Edwin C. Thomas stayed at their inn during the year 1836 and wrote: "She was a woman well fixed up, had a good house, and gave a good fare."

Old Tassel, head chief of the Cherokees, was a well-known friend of the whites. In the year 1788, he was invited, along with his son and two others, to the headquarters of Mayor James Hubbert under a flag of truce. Hubbert quartered the unarmed Cherokee party in a vacant house. Here, while he guarded the door, they were murdered by a young man with a tomahawk, who it seems had recently lost his parents in like manner to a party of Cherokee raiders. He demanded revenge, and was handed a tomahawk by Hubbert, who even set up the scenario for the blood bath. Doublehead, upon hearing this tragic report of his brother's death, sought and found revenge against the white man.

He went on the warpath, and took his followers from Shoal Town with him. The very name of Doublehead and his raiding party brought fear and trembling to the white settlements between Muscle Shoals and Nashville, and especially in the Cumberland Mountain area between Nashville and Knoxville.

Doublehead's first "hunting party" of record was in the fall of 1791. He had with him a group of 28 men plus women and children. Together they made a horrendous "scalping excursion" up the Cumberland. General Robertson sent an expedition to "get Doublehead" on January 16, 1792. This noble crusade, however, resulted in the death of five of Tennessee's finest young men. Doublehead killed the three sons of Colonel Valentine Sevier, the noted brother of General John Sevier, and two of their friends.

LESSON 18 – LOCAL INDIAN LEADERS

The murder of Captain William Overall and a man named Burnett in 1793, at Dripping Springs, was gruesome and gory. Doublehead, it has been recorded, dishonored Overall's body by cutting away and eating the flesh from his bones, and dancing with his scalp in the Indian villages at Lookout Mountain, Willstown, and Turnip Mountain. In May of that same year, while meeting with a delegation of Chickasaws, he apparently alluded to this act of cannibalism when he said: "We, the Cherokees, had eaten a great quantity of the white men's flesh, but have had so much of it we are tired of it, and think it too salty."

Doublehead was accompanied on many raids by his great nephew "Bench" (also known as Robert Benge), and his brother, "Pumpkin Boy." Bench was a wild sort of fellow himself. Yet, on at least one occasion he tried to hold back his Uncle Doublehead in an unmerciful crime against women and children. Pumpkin boy was a handsome warrior, well equipped with trinkets and a pair of expensive silver mounted pistols. When Pumpkin Boy was killed by Sevier's men, his brother Doublehead, fierce and sullen by nature, proposed that every settler's cabin be burned.

The saga of Doublehead's warpath covers some six years, beginning in 1788, and ending, rather abruptly, in June of 1794. Always ambitious, the eager chief had managed an appointment of importance and prestige. He became the leading delegate of a party of Cherokee chiefs visiting Philadelphia, where they met the first President of the United States, George Washington. It is said that Doublehead was the center of attention and that he was dressed in his most elaborate costume that was embroidered with a silver eagle design. Later, following what must have been a long and drawn out negotiation with Secretary of War Henry Knox, Doublehead and the other chiefs in the party of Cherokee chiefs came away with their personal annuities increased from $1,500 to $5,000 annually. This enabled the crusty old warrior to go home and live in style. Loaded with presents, he came back to Alabama by way of Charleston, and reached Doublehead's Town at Brown's Ferry in October, 1794. A lot had happened while the chiefs were in Philadelphia. On the way home he wrote Governor Blount a long letter concerning his meeting with the President. Two parts of this rather lengthy letter say something about the "new personality" of Chief Doublehead that emerges in history.

Determined now to copy the whites rather than to destroy their possessions and take their lives, he built what was then considered to be a pretentious story and a half log house in the wilderness about 1802. This structure, which later became a stagecoach inn, was nestled on the side of a hill that overlooked his expanding village in the Blue Water Creek valley below. Here he lived at peace with man, and became a well-known figure in various treaties between Indian Nations and the Federal Government.

LESSON 18 – LOCAL INDIAN LEADERS

At a meeting of head men near Hiwassee, real trouble began almost immediately afterwards when Doublehead was accosted by a fellow chief by the name of Bone Polisher. He denounced Doublehead as a traitor, referring to Doublehead's trip to Washington on January 7, 1806, with Chief Vann, Chief Taluntuskee, and Colonel Return J. Meigs. At that time, the Cherokee delegation ceded all the area between the Tennessee and Duck Rivers, except for Doublehead's Reserve. Most of this land actually belonged to the Chickasaws by the January 10, 1786 treaty.

This episode with the trader, John Rodgers, gave the others time to act. Someone managed to extinguish the tavern light and instantly a pistol shot rang out from a dark corner. When the light was restored, Rodgers, Ridge and Saunders had fled and Doublehead lay motionless on the floor. The ball had shattered his lower jaw and lodged in the nape of his neck.

Friends pulled the mortally wounded chief from the building, and across a field, and hid him in the loft of the schoolmaster at Hiwassee. But they left a trail of blood and it was easily followed by Major Ridge, Alex Saunders and two clansmen of Bone Polisher. When they arrived the dying warrior was lying on the attic floor in a pool of blood. Showing no mercy, not even to the dying both Major Ridge and Alex Saunders drew their pistols with the intent to finish off their adversary. But the hand of fate that had been so busy that night again intervened, causing their pistols to misfire.

This seemed to be a cue in this dialogue of death for old Doublehead suddenly sprang to life and physically attacked Major Ridge with almost super human strength. Sam Dale wrote that he would have overpowered Ridge had Ridge's partner, Alex Saunders, not shot Doublehead again - this time through the hips and then jumped him with his tomahawk swinging! But Doublehead wrenched free and leaped again upon Major Ridge. This gave Saunders time to grab another tomahawk and drive it full force into the skull of the dying Doublehead. As he fell to the floor again, one of Bone Polisher's tribesmen crushed the old warrior's head with a sharp spade.

At last, Doublehead was dead! He was no ordinary man, and his was no ordinary death. He died as he had lived, and it took a room full of enemies to bring it about. Ironically, Major Ridge, who played a key role in this execution, came by a similar fate some thirty years later in Oklahoma.

Cotterill, the historian, states that Colonel Meigs drove the Cherokees out of the Shoal Town (Blue Water Creek village) following Doublehead's death and that he burned the home of the old chief.

Both the lore of the land at the Muscle Shoals is filled with its own version of stories. Legends have been passed from generation to generation. One legend tells us that the

LESSON 18 – LOCAL INDIAN LEADERS

friends of the old chief carefully brought his battered and lacerated body back to Blue Water Creek where they gave him a white man's burial.

Two graves have been pointed to as the possible sites of his resting place. One is at the top of the hill behind where his log house stood. The other grave is in the bottomland about where Doublehead's village once stood. Kit Butler, an ex-slave who met the stagecoaches and tended to the horses at Wayside Inn, remembered the "awesomeness of that Indian's grave upon the hill behind the house." Old Doublehead's spirit he said, "would rant and rave on that hill, especially on dark and stormy nights."

Cuttyatoy - Another important Cherokee Indian living in Lawrence County by 1813 was Chief Cuttyatoy. Cuttyatoy lived near the mouth of Spring Creek with his main home located on an island in the area. He had earlier stolen the slaves of Joseph Brown's father. In 1813, Joseph Brown was fighting at the Battle of Talledega when he learned where Cuttyatoy had his father's slaves. With Andrew Jackson's permission, Joseph Brown and 10 of Jackson's best men came to Lawrence County and took back his family's slaves. Brown became a big landowner between Columbia and Pulaski, TN. His slaves eventually killed him.

Dragging Canoe - While a young boy, this future Cherokee Chief wanted to accompany his father, Attakullakulla, and a Cherokee war party going to battle the Shawnee. Attakullakulla flatly refused the young boy permission to go, but he slipped away from home ahead of the war party and hid in a dugout canoe he knew the warriors must use. When the warriors arrived at the portage and discovered the determined lad, there was much teasing. Attakullakulla told his son that if he could carry the canoe across the portage he could go along, so the young boy grabbed one end of the canoe and started dragging it through the sand. The excited warriors shouted encouragement, saying "he is dragging the canoe," and Dragging Canoe was his name from then on.

Dragging Canoe became a leader of a group hostile Indians to the Americans and American settlements during and after the Revolutionary War. He was unusually tall for a Southeast Indian, standing well over six feet, was very broad-shouldered and excellently proportioned. His most striking feature was a pockmarked face due to a case of smallpox. Nevertheless, he was rated as one of the handsomest and strongest in the Nation. He was a great warrior, had been wounded in battle, and hated the Americans implacably. He was always dressed for battle, wearing only a breechcloth and a necklace of long bear claws.

After being driven south by white forces, Dragging Canoe and his warriors established what came to be known as the Five Lower Towns of Dragging Canoe in the east portion of the Great Bend in the Tennessee River. Two of these, Long Island Town and Crow Town, were located in Jackson County, Alabama. These towns formed a natural fortress ringed with

LESSON 18 – LOCAL INDIAN LEADERS

cliffs and mountains, and on the west side had a great cave, roofed at the entrance with great horizontal layers of solid rock. Protecting this stronghold was a series of guard posts manned by fleet runners. Thus barricaded, Dragging Canoe and his braves successfully resisted the advance of white settlement on the Tennessee for a quarter of a century.

At the same time, his south flank was open, so that he could receive food, munitions, and trade goods from the English and occasional reinforcements from the friendly Creeks. Thus it was said that under his blanket, Dragging Canoe's tomahawk laughed at the white man. He died in 1792, but his stronghold continued to be effective until well into the next century.

Red Eagle - One of the most picturesque and courageous scenes of the whole war took place here in the appearance and surrender of Chief "Red Eagle", William Weatherford, who had led the Battle of Fort Mims, Calebee, and Holy Ground. "Red Eagle" had come alone, accompanied by neither warriors nor soldiers. I am sure General Jackson was greatly surprised. According to Pickett, General Jackson upon seeing "Red Eagle" ran from his marquee and exclaimed, "How dare you, sir, to ride up to my tent, after having murdered the women and children at Fort Mims?"

Charles Weatherford, Son of Red Eagle

Weatherford replied, "General Jackson, I am not afraid of you. I fear no man, for I am a Creek Warrior. I have nothing to request in behalf of myself; you can kill me, if you desire. But I come to beg you to send for the women and children of the war party, who are now starving in the woods. Their fields and cribs have been destroyed by your people, who have driven them to the woods without an ear of corn. I hope that you will send out parties, who will safely conduct them here, in order that they may be fed. I exerted myself in vain to prevent the massacre of the women and children at Fort Mims. I am now done fighting. The "Red Sticks" are nearly all killed. If I could fight you any longer, I would most heartily do so. Send for the women and children, they never did you any harm. But kill me, if the white people want it done."

At this point, many persons present cried out, "Kill Him! Kill Him! Kill Him! But General Jackson commanded silence, and in an emphatic manner, said, "Any man who would kill as brave a man as this would rob the dead!" Thus his life was spared and Chief "Red Eagle"

LESSON 18 – LOCAL INDIAN LEADERS

took no more part in the war except to encourage his warriors to surrender. He became a resident of Monroe County where he operated a farm and gained the respect of his neighbors.

Pickett reports that some 5000 of the Indian women and children for whom "Red Eagle" pled for were fed at the various American Posts. Jackson later dictated peace terms to the Creek, who gave up 23 million acres of land in present-day Georgia and Alabama.

Talohuskee Benge (Tahlonteskee) - After the assassination of Chief Doublehead by his own people, due to the circumstances of the Cotton Gin Treaty of 1806, several Cherokees living in the North Alabama area moved west to avoid the same fate. The following is from The Cherokees by Grace Steele Woodard published in 1963 and found on page 131:

> *"However, in 1808, the Compact 1802 was not needed to effect the removal of some 1,130 Chickamaugans to lands west of the Mississippi (today Dardanelle, Arkansas, in Pope County). Jefferson had merely to suggest to Tahlonteskee and other Chickamaugans that if they did not care to remain in the same country with their enemy countrymen; they could remove to Dardanelle Rock. Thus, in the Spring of 1808, Tahlonteskee-fearing assassination-notified President Jefferson that his people were ready to migrate. Following their migration, Tahlonteskee's band of Cherokees called themselves "Cherokees West" or "Old Settlers."*

Since Tahlonteskee (Talohuskee) signed the 1806 Cotton Gin Treaty and feared the same punishment that Doublehead received for giving up land north of the Tennessee River, Tahlonteskee and his Cherokee followers agreed to move from the Shoal Town Village at the Big Muscle Shoals of the Tennessee River to the west. It is believed by some that Sequoyah, George Guess, went west after the 1816 Turkey Town Treaty in search of his half-brother, Tahlonteskee or Talohuskee Benge.

Even though some Cherokees in the Warrior Mountains area left with Tahlonteskee's (Talohuskee) group in 1809, many Cherokee people still lived in the Tennessee Valley from the river to the High Town Path in North Alabama. Within the great valley of the Tennessee, cotton became the agricultural "king" for making money. With the new government cotton gin at Melton's Bluff and black slaves for farm labor, both the Chickasaws and Cherokees, who shared ownership of the river valley, became wealthy; however, the government and settlers wanted the cotton wealth of the Tennessee Valley, which was controlled by the Indians.

In 1816, with several more years of pressure, the Chickasaws and Cherokees finally relinquished their claim to the remainder of Warrior Mountains. Therefore, due to the

LESSON 18 – LOCAL INDIAN LEADERS

circumstances of the Turkey Town Treaty of September 16 and 18, 1816, another contingent of Chickasaws and Cherokees moved west, from the land of the Warrior Mountains in North Alabama.

Tahlonteskee (Talohuskee Benge) was the great nephew of Doublehead. Talohuskee's half-brother was Sequoyah and his full brothers were Robert (Bob) Benge, and Utana (The Tail) Benge. His settlement was located at the mouths of Town Creek in Lawrence County and Blue Water Creek in Lauderdale County on the banks of the Hogohegee (Tennessee) River, known as the "River of the Cherokees". The Shoal Town village actually lay on both sides of the river about six miles from the eastern upstream end of the Big Mussel Shoals. Actually at this point, the Blue Water Ferry crossed the river from the eastern point of Blue Water Creek to the area west of the mouth of Path Killer on Big Nance Creek in present day Lawrence County. According to Nina Leftwich's book Two Hundred Years at Muscle Shoals, the Cherokees had a large settlement at the mouth of Town Creek, which extended a mile along the river and far up the creek.

In 1806, Cherokee Chief Doublehead, Tahlonteskee, and other Cherokees signed the Cotton Gin Treaty, which gave up Cherokee claims to land north of the Tennessee River except from Doublehead's Reserve. The reserve lay between Elk River (Chuwalee) and Cypress Creek (TeKeetanoeh) in present-day Lauderdale County. The Treaty placed a Cotton Gin at Melton's Bluff in present-day Lawrence County and a blacksmith by the name of Sameul Hall to be paid one shilling of silver each day by the government.

Black Fox- (Inali, Enoli, or Eunolee), the Principal Chief of the Cherokee Nation, lived in Lawrence County, Alabama during the latter portion of his illustrious life. Fox's Creek in the northeastern corner of this county still bears his name. Black Fox was chosen by the Cherokee Nation to be chief of his people in 1801.

Black Fox was associated with many important Indian people and leaders in this area during his reign as chief: Doublehead; Doublehead's daughters who married George Colbert-Tuskiahooto and Saleechie; James Colbert's half blood Chickasaw sons-George Colbert-Tooteemastubbe (Ferryman) and Levi Colbert-Itawamba Mingo (Wooden Bench Chief); John Benge's sons who were half brothers to Sequoyah-Talohuskee (Tahlonteskee) Benge and Robert (Bob) Benge-The Bench; John Melton's half blood Cherokee sons-Charles, David, James, and Lewis-the father of Moses; Cuttyatoy; Pathkiller; Charles Hicks; John Brown; Richard Brown, and others had their names associated with the area of northwest Alabama. However, after the Turkey Town Treaty of September 1816, the historical records of Indian people became somewhat clouded for this area. Nevertheless, very influential Indian people made their reputations, homes, and lifestyles in this portion of the Tennessee Valley from 1770 through 1816. These people, their exploits, and historic significance became intertwined with the life of the old Chief Black Fox.

LESSON 18 – LOCAL INDIAN LEADERS

During Black Fox's reign as chief, eight Cherokee Indian towns flourished along the banks of the River of the Cherokees (Tennessee) in this area. These Indian towns included Mousetown or Moneetown, Fox's Stand, Doublehead's Town at Brown's Ferry, Melton's Bluff, Cuttyatoy's Village, Gourd's Settlement (Courtland), and Shoal Town. The towns were located adjacent to the Elk River Shoals and Big Muscle Shoals at major Indian trail crossings of the river called Chake Thlocko (Big Ford or Great Crossing Place). These Indian towns benefited from the shoals that provided an abundance of food in the form of freshwater mussels.

Black Fox and Doublehead lived in Lawrence County a few miles from each other on the old Brown's Ferry Road. Black Fox lived for a while at Mousetown on the Tennessee River at the mouth of the creek that became his namesake before moving a few miles to the road junction that became his stand. By 1790, Doublehead had established a village at Brown's Ferry on the Tennessee River that became his stronghold until 1802 when he moved down the river to Shoal Town, which was located some seven miles from the eastern end of the Big Muscle Shoals between the mouths of Big Nance, Town Creek and Blue Water Creek. Shoal Town was controlled by Doublehead's nephew and Bench's brother, Talohuskee Benge.

Black Fox and Doublehead were friends and signed numerous treaties with the United States government. Doublehead would sign treaties benefiting Black Fox and Black Fox would sign treaties that benefited Doublehead. John Watts, Doublehead, Black Fox and others signed the Treaty with the Cherokee on July 2, 1791. On October 20, 1803, Black Fox places his (X) between his name and Principal Chief; however, this treaty refers to "our beloved Chief Doublehead". Both Black Fox and Doublehead signed Cherokee treaties of October 25, 1805, and October 27, 1805. Also Doublehead signs the Cotton Gin Treaty of January 7, 1806, that gives the Cherokees a machine for cleaning cotton and places the gin at Melton's Bluff. The treaty also gives the old Cherokee Chief Black Fox $100.00 annually for the rest of his life. The final payment recorded for Chief Black Fox is found as follows: *"Abstract of Disbursements made by Return J. Meigs, Agent of war in Tennessee on account of the Indian Department between the 30th June & the 1st of October 1810…date of payments. July 11th, number of payments. 4. to whom made, Black Fox Cherokee King, Nature of Disbursements. Being the amount of Annual Stipend for the current year received by his proxy, Amount. $100.00."* It is probable that Black Fox was getting in bad health because he had some of his people to pick up the money and died the next year.

Little Turkey preceded Black Fox as the Principal Chief of the Cherokee Nation. Pathkiller succeeded Black Fox as chief of the Cherokee Nation. Doublehead's nephew, John Watts, Jr. was elected Chief of the Chickamamga over him after the death of Dragging Canoe in March 1792. Chief Watts was wounded at Buchanan's Station near Nashville in September

LESSON 18 – LOCAL INDIAN LEADERS

1792 but recovered and led his army the next year against Cavett's Station near Knoxville, Tennessee. The Bench (Robert Benge) acting as an interpreter convinced the people to surrender. Soon as they had surrendered, Doublehead killed every one. The Bench wept because he had given his word and felt that his honor had been betrayed by his uncle Doublehead. The Bench was ambushed and killed in 1794 by Lieutenant Vincent Hobbs. John Watts, Jr. eventually died at Willstown in 1808. Doublehead was assassinated on August 9, 1807. Black Fox died in 1811. Path Killer died in 1828. Thus, as the great Cherokee leaders of the lower or southern faction of Cherokees died, the tribal control and leadership shifted to the upper or northern faction.

After Black Fox was elected chief in 1801, a lot of differences began between the Upper and Lower Cherokees. With the lower towns in this area having secured control of the tribal leadership, they were assured favorable distribution of annuity funds. A delegation of Upper Cherokees complained to President Thomas Jefferson that the Lower Cherokees divide all funds from annuities and land sales among those of their own neighborhood. President Jefferson explained that once the funds were turned over to the authorized representatives of the tribe that it was purely a Cherokee affair. Alexander Saunders proposed that the funds be split between the Lower and Upper Cherokees. Both Black Fox and Doublehead, who were Lower Cherokees, had serious conflicts with Major Ridge, a Cherokee Chief of an upper town. After Doublehead signed the Cotton Gin Treaty of 1806, giving up Cherokee claims to lands on the north side of the Tennessee River except for Doublehead's Reserve between Elk River and Cypress Creek, he was assassinated by Major Ridge, Alexander Saunders, and John Rogers on August 9, 1807.

In early 1808, Colonel Return J. Meigs had convinced Black Fox and Tahlonteskee to seek the Cherokee council approval for exchanging their lands for territory west of the Mississippi. At the fall council meeting of the Cherokee Nation, Black Fox made the proposal as follows, *"Tell our Great Father, the President (Thomas Jefferson), that our game has disappeared, and we wish to follow it to the West. We are his friends, and we hope he will grant our petition, which is to remove our people towards the setting sun. But we shall give up fine country, fertile in soil, abounding in water-courses, and well adapted for the residence of white people. For all this we must have a good price"*. The Ridge was very upset and spoke against Black Fox in such an eloquent manner that the tribal council rejected both Fox and his proposal. Black Fox was reinstate at a later council meeting, but felt disgraced for the rest of his life. However, in the summer of 1809, Tahlonteskee took the offer from President Thomas Jefferson and some 1,131 Cherokees left the Shoal Town area to lands west of the Mississippi River. Tahlonteskee told President Thomas Jefferson that his reason for leaving was the fear of assassination as his uncle Doublehead. Jefferson was the first president to strongly advocate Indian removal.

LESSON 18 – LOCAL INDIAN LEADERS

Today, Fox's Creek is the name of a small tributary to the Tennessee River that flows into the river at the north border of Morgan and Lawrence Counties at an old Cherokee town site of Mousetown or Moneetown. Black Fox's home was located between the drainages of Fox and Mallard Creeks some two miles west of Doublehead's Village, which was on the Tennessee River at Browns Ferry in Lawrence County, Alabama. The location of Fox's Stand was at the junctions of two Indian trails-Browns Ferry Road and Black Warriors' Path. Black Warriors' Path continued six miles northwest to Melton's Bluff which was established by Irishman John Melton, who had married Doublehead's sister Owma. His half blood sons became important in the local early history of Lawrence County. From Fox's Stand, the Brown's Ferry Road continued west some eight miles to Gourd's Settlement (present-day Courtland) on Pathkiller's Creek (present-day Big Nance Creek).

According to General John Coffee's Diary -1816 is the following: *"21st Feb'y 1816. This morning Maj. Hutchings left us to go to meet Gen. Jackson – Mr. Bright surveys and we pass on down the river. When at Huntsville I did not pay my bill – neither did I pay it at Mr. Austin's – I paid Mrs. Austin for buiskit, candles and washing $2.00 – paid Charles Melton 3 bushels corn $1.50 – fodder, $1.00 – whiskey 75¢. Paid to Charles for Reed $2.00. Encamped all night on Big Nance Creek."* From Big Nance, Coffee continues to the mouth of Caney Creek and run a boundary line up the creek crossing Gaines Trace. Coffee continued the line to Cotton Gin Port before starting back to Melton's Bluff on March 2, 1816. This became the Chickasaw boundary in the Turkey Town Treaty of September 1816. Coffee's diary continues, *"6th March, 1816. This day we reached Melton's Bluff about one o'clock. Bought sundry supplies &c Viz; whiskey $1.00-whiskey, $1.371/2- 3 dinners, 75¢ - 20 lbs Bacon 9¢ $2.50 Paid for corn and fodder to Charley Melton $5.00"* It should be pointed out that Coffee specifically mentioned Charles Melton who moved east after the Turkey Town Treaty of 1816 and established an Indian town known as Meltonsville. James Melton became a keel boat guide for Malcolm Gilchrist and his family remained in Lawrence County. David Melton sold Andrew Jackson all the land at Melton's Bluff and some 60 slaves. Lewis' son Moses Melton and Charles Hicks were given by treaty a tract of land on the south side of the Tennessee River. These Melton boys were the half blood Cherokee sons of Irishman John Melton.

On December 20, 1807, John Sevier, Governor of Tennessee, writes to Black Fox concerning a report from Colonel Meigs about the Creek Indians settling on the Tennessee near Elk River. Sevier writes, *"I am informed that the Creeks have built Huts, and is living on the banks of the Tennessee; what business have they there? They have none only to be convenient to kill come of our people, and plunder our Boats as they are going down the River – You know the Creek people are Rogues, and you say steal from and rob your own people; if it be true, why don't you drive them from out of your Country? For a people who both murder & steals, aught not to be Suffered to live in any place – You are Surely able to drive away the few that comes to do Mischief, and disturb the peace of your people and*

LESSON 18 – LOCAL INDIAN LEADERS

ours; If their nation means to protect them in their murdering and plundering excursions, you then know where you can resort to for protection and Strength enough to do yourselves Justice – I state these circumstances to inform You how you aught to conduct towards the white people, who are your Fathers, Brothers, friends, and your good neighbors." It should be noted that Meigs and Sevier confirm that the old Chief Black Fox was still living at the Elk River Shoals some four months after the death of his friend and cohort Doublehead.

The old Principal Chief Black Fox evidently had a son also known as Black Fox that also lived in Lawrence County, AL and his name appears on numerous Cherokee documents after the death of his father in 1811. John Coffee put the following note in his diary, *"**26th July, 1816**. Borrowed Capt. Hammond's large tent- left my old one – breakfasted with the Captain. Started on and got to Wilders where I dined, Bought corn to carry with me – bill $1.50. Went to the river – crossed at Brown's Ferry – paid ferrage &c $1.25. Hired young Wilder to go on to Col. Barnett &c. This night went to **Black Foxe's** and lay all night; bought _ bushels of corn to carry with me. Hired ____ Lancaster to carry six bushels to Major Russell's, for which I am to pay three and half dollars –bought some salt from **Fox**, hired him and McClure to carry the corn to the wagon road about two miles – paid bill at **Fox's** $6.75."* Coffee continued on to Major Russell's (Russellville) to survey Indian boundary and begin his return. Coffee's notes continue, *" **1st August 1816**. This morning we start in towards Madison County – lay all night at the Path Killer's creek near Jones'. **2d August.** This morning we hired Vanpelt to carry letters to Col. Brown inviting him to meet us as Campbell's Ferry on the 12th. Come to the **Black Fox'es** – bought 2 1/2 bushels corn – paid the bill $1.75 –Same day came on – crossed the Tennessee River at Brown's Ferry and came to Wilders where we lay all night."* After the Turkey Town Treaty of 1816 took the Cherokee lands in this area, the young Black Fox moved east into the Cherokee Nation. Other historical references indicate there may have been other Cherokee men with the name Black Fox after the original died 1811. Also another important note is that Colonel Richard Brown was a Cherokee leader during the Creek Indian War and negotiated the Turkey Town Treaty of September 1816 for the Cherokee Nation.

According to <u>Chronicles of Oklahoma</u>, volume 16, number 1, March 1938, by John P. Brown, *"Black Fox died in 1811. He was succeeded by Pathkiller, Nunna-dihi, a very honorable man who was to guide the destinies of the Cherokee through sixteen years."*

Black Fox's death was reported in the <u>Columbia Centinel</u>, Boston, Massachusetts on August 31, 1811. His obituary stated, *"In the Cherokee country, Black Fox, a worthy chief of the Cherokee Tribe of Indians, and a great friend of the U.S."*

According to an article titled <u>A Description and History of Blount County</u> from the Transactions of the Alabama Historical Society on July 9 and 10, 1855, *"Most of the first settlers of Blount as well as those of the adjoining counties, believe that lead mines existed*

LESSON 18 – LOCAL INDIAN LEADERS

in Blount and Jefferson Counties, and that the Indians knew their location and obtained lead from them. Perhaps, this general belief originated from the following circumstances, which occurred in 1810: An old Cherokee Chief, named Black Fox, died in the north of our county, and was buried in an old mound; and in digging his grave, the Indians found some pieces of lead ore. This trivial discovery was magnified and circulated in Madison County, and many intelligent persons in the county believed a lead mine really existed, at, or near the grave of the old Chief. This opinion became so strong, that Alexander Gilbreath, who then resided in Huntsville, was induced to visit the grave of Black Fox. His searching there, proving unsuccessful....Mr. George Fields, at that time fifty or sixty years old, informed him that the Indians knew of no lead mines nearer than those of Missouri and Illinois, and gave it as his opinion, that the lead found in the grave of Black Fox, had been brought from one of those States." It is important to note that Blount County at one time included this area of north Alabama. According to a proclamation by David Holmes, Governor of Mississippi Territory, *"All that tract of country lying south of the River Tennessee, east of the Chickasaw boundary line, north of the high-lands that divide the waters of the Tennessee from the water of the Mobile Bay and west of the Cherokee boundary line shall form one other County to be called and known by the name of Blount, the courts of justice whereof will be held at Melton's Bluff."* Melton's Bluff is in Lawrence County some six miles northwest of Black Fox's Stand.

Black Fox was probably buried near home which was the custom of the Cherokees at that time. For example, Doublehead was killed in east Tennessee and transported back to his home overlooking Blue Water Creek where he was buried. Since Black Fox's family resided at his stand for several years after his death, they probably had his body interned nearby.

Within a few years, several magnanimous and powerful leaders of the Cherokee people of north Alabama were dead. Along with their demise, the colorful lives and exploits faded as the sunsets disappear on the rolling hills and roaring shoals of the great bend of the Hogohegee (Tennessee) River.

Review Questions

1. Who was an important chief to the Cherokee of Lawrence County?
2. Sequoyah was a famous member of which tribe?
3. How did Dragging Canoe get his name?
4. What did the Cherokee call papers with words on them?
5. What did Sequoyah invent?
6. Who owned large farms and a great number of slaves?
7. Who terrorized settlers on his frontier?
8. Who burned nearly two years of Sequoyah's work on the alphabet?

LESSON 18 – LOCAL INDIAN LEADERS

9. Who were Doublehead's brothers?
10. What future Cherokee Chief had a father named Attakullakulla?
11. Who was the great nephew of Doublehead?
12. Sequoyah was also known as whom?
13. What is another name of William Weatherford?
14. Who was the son of Great Eagle?
15. Where in Lawrence County did Doublehead live?
16. Who was a double son-in-law of Doublehead?
17. What was the name of the first Indian newspaper?
18. How long did it take Sequoyah to invent the alphabet?
19. Who assassinated Doublehead?
20. What kind of trade did Sequoyah have earlier in life?
21. Who saved the lives of some 5,000 Indian women and children by surrendering and risking his own life?
22. Who was Doublehead's father?
23. What year was Sequoyah's alphabet completed?
24. Where is Doublehead supposedly buried?
25. Who was one of the early Irishmen that came into Lawrence County during the 1780s with the Cherokee Indians?
26. What were the names of Doublehead's two daughters and also George Colber's wives?
27. Who was the half brother to Sequoyah who signed the 1806 Cotton Gin Treaty?
28. Who was Melton's Bluff named after?
29. Who was Doublehead's nephew who accompanied him on many raids?
30. What year was the Cotton Gin Treaty signed?
31. What were the two towns in this area where Doublehead lived?
32. What year did Doublehead establish his first town on the Tennessee River?
33. The Shoal Town site was in the disputed reserve that was called what?
34. What degree of Indian blood was Sequoyah?
35. In 1806, what treaty was signed that gave up Cherokee claims to land north of the Tennessee River except for Doublehead's Reserve?

LESSON 19 – INDIAN BATTLES

Creek Indian War - The Creek Indian War in Alabama became a part of the American-English War of 1812. The citizens of the still young United States were hemmed in on the Atlantic coast from New England all the way to Georgia. The English and other native Indian people claimed much of the land that the Americans wanted for westward expansion.

In the north, the Americans and the English fought vicious land and sea battles. In Alabama, the soil and the rivers were stained with American and Indian blood. Even though all of the Indian land in Alabama was in danger of being lost, only the hostile Creeks chose to go to war. The war party thought the English were strong enough to help them win the conflict with the Americans.

The first skirmish of the Creek Indian War was at Burnt Corn Creek. The Red Stick Creeks won. Next, was Ft. Mims, also an Indian victory under the leadership of Red Eagle, William Weatherford. After the battle at Ft. Mims, the Americans realized that more settlers in the Indian Territory and on the borders would be in danger if they did not have protection.

Andrew Jackson - The Governor of Tennessee assembled an army of volunteers led by Andrew Jackson, and sent them to Alabama to begin a war of extermination of Creek people – men, women, and children (genocide). The Cherokees, newly trying to develop friendly relationships with the white man and long in conflict with the Creek Indians, began to discuss joining forces with Andrew Jackson. Later, on November 22, 1816, Andrew Jackson became the first white landowner in Lawrence County, Alabama. He established the Town of Marathon in Lawrence County at Melton's Bluff, between Spring Creek and Mallard Creek. Marathon was located at Melton's Bluff on the Tennessee River.

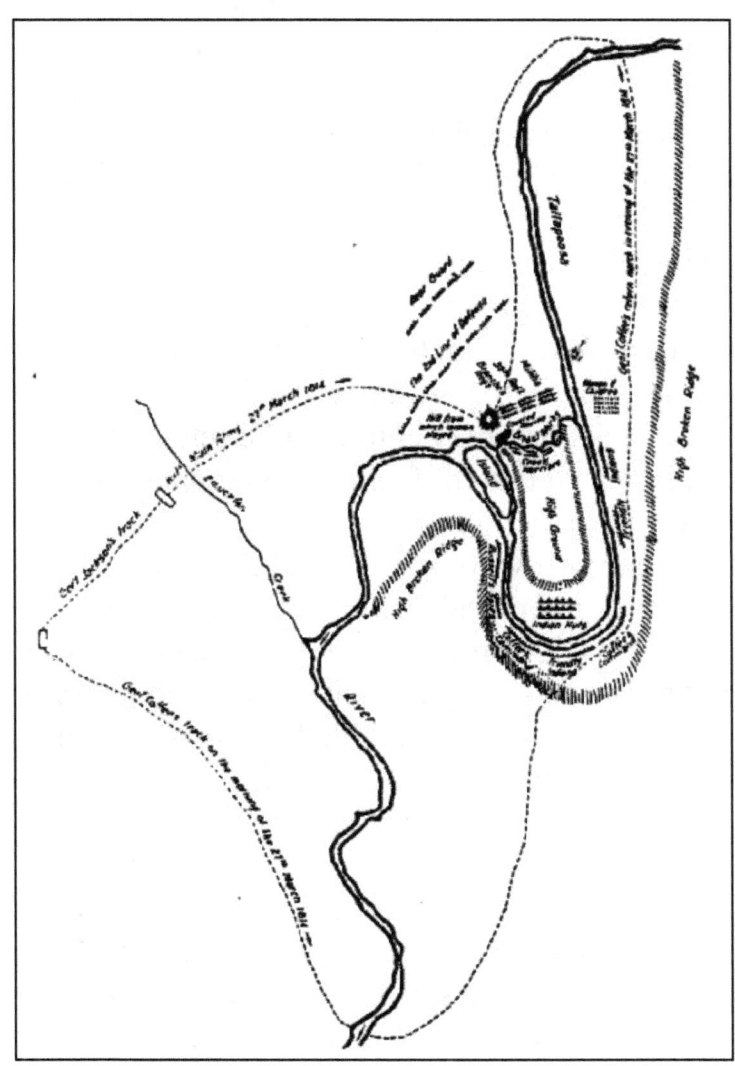

Map of the Battle of Horseshoe Bend

LESSON 19 – INDIAN BATTLES

Chief Junaluska had convinced the Cherokee to remain neutral and not join with Tecumseh's Creek forces. Now, with the challenge from the Tennessee Legislature along with payment for support of their causes, it was hard for the Cherokee to remain neutral. Junaluska recruited some 800 Cherokee warriors to go to the aid of Andrew Jackson in an advance down the Coosa River. Upon their arrival with Andrew Jackson, Junaluska was made captain of the Cherokee men.

The decisive battle of the Creek and Indian War was fought on March 26, 1814. It took place near the Creek village on Horseshoe Bend of the Tallapoosa River, near present-day Alexander City.

Albert James Pickett describes the setting of the battle thusly, "At six o'clock in the morning to the battle, General Coffee with his 700 mounted men and 600 friendly Indians; was detached from the main army and ordered to cross the river three miles below and occupy positions on the south side and along the top of the Horseshoe to prevent the escape of the enemy in the direction where Jackson's main army should attack the breastworks across the heel of the Horseshoe. The Cherokee Indians were assigned positions along the margin of the river while the 700 mounted men were held in reserve on higher ground further back. The enemy Creeks had many canoes tied along the opposite bank across from the Indians' position, to be used for escape in case of emergency. The stage is set for the remarkable action reputed to have been conceived and carried into execution by Junaluska and his comrades. As General Jackson's main army opened fire on the breastworks, the roar of the cannon and rattle of the musketry so aroused the Creeks that they could not be retained inactive on the riverbank. Junaluska become so animated that all fear of danger and death was destroyed in him and he craved to be at the center of action; that after obtaining permission from his superior officer (Colonel Morgan) he, with one assistant, swam the river, cut loose some of the canoes, tied them together and carried them to the other side. They were at once filled with Cherokees. Other boats were brought over, and the entire Cherokee force together with some of the white troops, ferried over. His surprise attack in their rear (of the Red Sticks under command of Chief Menawa) so divided the attention and efforts of the enemy that the main army under Jackson was enabled to take the breast works by storm and led to a completely victorious outcome of the engagement.

This section came from the book History of Alabama, Vol. II.: A short time after the Battle of the Horseshoe, Jackson had built a fort at the site of old Fort Toulouse and named it Fort Jackson. Now, many of the "Red Sticks" began to come in and surrender to General Jackson.

After the Creek Indian War was over in 1814, the Creek land in North Alabama and areas to the south was declared public land. Land-hungry whites rushed in to claim the Creek land. During the war between the Creek Indians and the white settlers, two major battles that may

LESSON 19 –INDIAN BATTLES

be familiar to you: The Battle of Fort Mims and the Battle of Horseshoe Bend. The fight at Horseshoe Bend was the final battle for the Creeks. The 1,000 mighty Creek warriors could not win against General Jackson and his 3,300 soldiers. After the Battle of Horseshoe Bend, most of the Creek land was taken from them. In 1835 and 1836, with some of their chiefs in chains, some 14,000 Creeks were forced to move to Oklahoma. Two groups of Creeks came through North Alabama during removal.

Lawrence County has several things in common with Creek people: (1) Creek land in Lawrence County lay from the High Town Path to the south. (2) Moulton is named after Lt. Michael Moulton who was killed during the Battle of Horseshoe Bend. (3) Andrew Jackson who defeated the Creeks became the first white landowner in Lawrence County, Alabama. (4) The High Town Path, the Creek Nation's northern border, ran across southern Lawrence County. (5) A major Creek trading path, Black Warriors' Path, ran across eastern Lawrence County from Piney Grove, through Oakville, and then to Melton's Bluff on the Tennessee River.

During Indian removal two large groups of Creek people were moved through North Alabama. On December 19, 1835, 511 Creeks came through Lawrence County and were in Moulton on December 19, 1835. Again, in September 1836, 2000 Creeks with all their belongings were marched through our county to Tuscumbia landing. From Tuscumbia, many were moved west by boat and others marched over land driving their livestock.

Battle of Indian Tomb Hollow - The following is a shortened version of the "Battle of Indian Tomb Hollow" which occurred in Lawrence County. The story was published in The Moulton Democrat on November 7, 14, and 21, 1856, some twenty years before Custer's "Battle of Little Big Horn" in 1876. According to the story, the battle occurred in 1776, some 100 years before the "Battle of Little Big Horn".

The author says the story was told to him by one long connected to the Chickasaw Tribe. The final fight is thought to have occurred in the upper portion of the southwest fork of Indian Tomb Hollow within sight and sound of the waterfalls. Now, begins a shortened version of the "Battle of Indian Tomb Hollow."

But never having met with a history of the following scenes and trials of the Chickasaws, in their warfare with their neighbors the Creeks, and having often visited the spots where the following scenes were enacted, and heard the incidents related by one long connected with the tribe, I have been induced to give them publicity.

It was a beautiful day in that loveliest of months, October, the deep old forest had begun to present the first indications of the approaching change of the seasons. The bright scarlet hue of the sumac, the golden leaf of the sassafras, the poplar's dull yellow contrasted beautifully,

LESSON 19 – INDIAN BATTLES

and blended agreeably with the many tints of green of the old wood. This hill is the last of a series of undulations, that gives to the old wood to the east a wavy appearance, whilst to our left, or farthest west, it becomes level and of a low swampy character, made so by the springs, four in number, that gush forth from the base of these hills, and empty their bright waters into the small creek bounding the western border of this flat.

Early, on a bright October morning, eighty years ago (1776), our story opens. The sun had scarce marked a hand's breadth on the horizon, as two Chickasaw warriors approached the largest of the four springs we have spoken of, and leaning their rifles against the black walnut trees, from amidst whose roots the bright waters flowed, drank from the gushing fount ere proceeding to make their frugal morning meal; their simple repast consisting of a handful of parched Indian corn, and a small piece of dried venison; being finished they sat for some time in perfect silence, when the elder of the two warriors arising and taking his rifle said, "The leaf of the sumac is red, and ere its fall, Ittaloknah, the pride of our tribe, must be again in the wigwam of her father.

Then, let us fly with the speed of the deer, for when yonder's rising sun shall have set and rose again, the warriors of the Chickasaws will await us in council."

The Chickasaw, a powerful and brave nation, in the time of which we write, inhabited all of the northern part of the State of Mississippi, reaching from west of the Mississippi River to the meandering creek in Franklin County, Alabama, known as Caney Creek. Such were the boundaries of the nation, yet claiming farther east than this.

Some three days previous to the opening of our story, at the close of a warm sultry day, with the prospect of a stormy night ahead, there sat at the door of a wigwam, situated near the eastern boundary of the Chickasaw Nation, a warrior of this tribe engaged in assisting an Indian youth in fashioning his bow. The youth seemingly some fifteen years of age, stood eagerly watching his aged companion, and ever and anon addressing some question to him. The warrior was a perfect type of his race. Remarkably tall and of perfect form for strength and endurance; he was now passed the meridian of life, and marked with the scars of many and various hard fought battles; yet that eagle eye and those sinewy limbs, spoke forth that age had not yet quenched the fire of his youth, nor destroyed the power that made him ever a brave of renown, and a chief of importance with his tribe. Such was Eagle Eye.

As the sun went down behind a dark and heavy mass of clouds, and the first burst of heaven's artillery was heard in the west, and aged squaw (White Lily) appeared at the door of the wigwam and spoke to the warrior, who now left his work, and began to gaze intently towards the east, as if eagerly watching for someone. The squaw, like the warrior, had passed the meridian of life, yet the remnants of great beauty were plainly to be seen in her features; and a close observer, tho' dressed as an Indian, and an Indian in every action and

LESSON 19 – INDIAN BATTLES

movement, tell that the blood of the white man coursed through her veins. When an infant, captured by a party of Chickasaws from a company of French emigrants ascending the Mississippi, she alone escaped death. Taken to the Chickasaw village at Pontotoc, she was placed under the charge of an aged squaw, and being but two years of age, and reared as an Indian child, she soon forgot her parents, and grew in feelings and acts, as well as looks, a perfect Indian. She had, when about twenty years of age, blessed the wigwam of the Eagle Eye as his bride. They were the parents of but one child - a daughter - whom they called Ittaloknah or Magnolia. She, like the beautiful tree of her native mountains, possessed that grace and perfection of form and fairness of skin that made her sobriquet perfectly appropriate.

"It is Ponioc," said the warrior, as an Indian youth, apparently some twelve years of age, emerged from the brush, and came running towards the group with a countenance bespeaking alarm.

"What makes Ponioc seem as the fleeing fawn, when the panther follows fast on his trail?" said the old warrior to the breathless boy, who had now reached them and stood exhausted by his fright and rapid gait.

"The Creek warrior bears away the light of our wigwam and Ponioc mourns for her he loves," spoke the youth in broken accents.

"What! my child! my Magnolia!" cried the alarmed mother seizing the boy by the arm.

"Yes, Ittaloknah is a captive. I met Kokomah, who bleeding from his wounds, told me to haste to the wigwam of the Eagle Eye and tell the tiding while he returned to the trail.

The nine Chickasaw warriors pursued the Creeks on a Southeastward course for some time, when they separated into parties of two, one however having been detailed to go back to the tribe and inform the council should the eight not return in time to meet them at Tulumah or the four springs, agreeing among themselves to search that day, and if no signs were seen, all to return to the council save two who were to keep up the search until the war party from the council should reach Tulumah, and then report their success, and accompany the party in the invasion of the Creek Nation.

Let us again go back to the time of Ittaloknah's leaving her parents wigwam. Taking Kokomah, she went in the direction of the creek, east of the wigwam, for the purpose of fishing. Having a description of the maiden sufficient for our purpose, let us describe her companion - Kokomah, or Wild cat, as he was called by his tribe, was about thirty years of age, not exceeding four feet in height, with a breadth of chest and length of arm indeed remarkable.

LESSON 19 –INDIAN BATTLES

Like most dwarfs, his features bore the appearance of greater age than really belonged to him. With all the cunning instincts of his race, he had even apparently the instincts of the animal combined with it. Taken by Eagle Eye and by him reared, and treated with contempt by all save the inmates of this wigwam and the Panther, he seemed to hate all save these few, and for them his affections knew no bounds.

Ponioc, who was nearby, hearing the cry of Magnolia, was making to her, when he was met by Kokomah, who, having revived, was hastening to the wigwam to give the alarm, but sending Ponioc, he returned, and crossing the stream he was soon on the trail of his assaulters. Coming in sight of them he found that three more warriors had been added to their number.

Pursing their course still southeast, they did not stop with the fall of night, but continued on their way, until the long uninterrupted march overcame with fatigue, Magnolia; and they were reluctantly forced to stop. It was near midnight when they halted at the place chosen for their rest within a small gorge or hollow of the mountain, where firmly securing their prisoners, the two warriors made preparations for their night watch.

With the same serpent like motion, Kokomah approached the captives, and with his knife severed the bonds that bound the Panther's hands. The Panther, severing the bands that held his feet confined, rushed into the combat; calling to Wild Cat to ascertain his position, and finding him beneath, with his arms pinioned around the Creek warrior, who was striving manfully to relieve an arm, but in vain, the knife of the Panther soon put an end to the combat. Relieving Magnolia, upon consultation they determined to remain in their present position until day. The two Chickasaws now took their post of watch, while the Indian maiden slept.

With the first rays of light the Chickasaws were on their way back to their nation; and with what difference in feeling, from those experienced on the previous night, as they passed over the same trail they were now retracing! Leaving the mountains, they now entered the beautiful valley of land running across the now County of Lawrence in Alabama. When the sun was some two or three hours above the horizon, they met, near Tulamah a party of Chickasaws under the lead of Eagle Eye, who were fast following the trail made by the Creeks and their prisoners the night previous.

The meeting was indeed a joyous one; and as neither party had as yet made their morning meal, they were in the act of going to a small spring nearby, when with the whoop of a set of fiends, a party of Creeks fired upon them from the surrounding trees and brush.

A party of Creeks, some sixty in number, being out in search of the six warriors, who we have seen slain, and finding the bodies of Topeka and his companion, had followed the trail

LESSON 19 – INDIAN BATTLES

of the returning Chickasaws, and had succeeded in making a near approach to the party, unperceived; so much were they engaged with the returned captives. Darting to some cover the Chickasaws, began to battle for life. With the first fire, several of their number having fallen, and the assailing party being more numerous, the odds were greatly against them. Three of the Creek warriors seeing Magnolia, and knowing her to be the cause of the loss of their braves, determined upon her recapture. Gradually advancing to her rear, which reaching, they rushed upon her, one seizing her in his arms, bore her shrieking for aid, farther into that part of the woods occupied by his party; her cry caused her friends to rush to her rescue and in so doing, exposed themselves to the fire of their enemy. This so much weakened their force, that they were compelled to retire, leaving Magnolia again a captive in the hands of their foemen. Returning, towards evening, from the pursuit, they buried their few slain, and scalped their slain enemies, proceeded with their captive homeward. The retiring Chickasaws, collecting their forces found that they had lost twenty of their number.

The place which the Creeks had chosen for their halting place was a large natural amphitheater. Entering it from the north, the sides rose quite abruptly, and gradually enlarging from the mouth, where it was about fifty paces in width for some distance, when having reached the width of two hundred paces, it gradually closed again, and ended in a perpendicular ledge of rock some forty feet in height, over which passed a stream of limpid water. Some six or eight feet from the base of this ledge of rock, on one side it shelved off into a cave of considerable length but shallow. The Chickasaw warriors now approached the point around which the Creeks had passed and disposing their forces so as to open deadly fire upon the unsuspecting Creeks. This was soon done, and pouring a well-aimed fire of rifle ball and arrows upon them with a whoop rushed upon their astonished enemies.

The fight was fast drawing to a close; there now remained only ten Creek warriors to combat, not now for victory, or even life, but to die with as many slain around them as possible; those few were fast falling beneath the Chickasaw knives, for this now was the only instrument of death used by either party.

Magnolia upon the onset of the battle was led into the cave at the head of the gorge, where, unconfined, she was a witness of the terrible conflict. She saw the onslaught of the Creeks upon her father, and also saw him fall; but as the combat thickened around him; she was unable to tell whether he had arisen, and was yet leading the now victorious Chickasaws, or lay a corpse amidst the heap of slain, she saw around the spot where he had fallen. The battle fast receding down the gorge, she determined to allay her anxiety by going to the spot where she had seen her father fall; reaching which, she beheld his lifeless body, with his life blood clotting the grass at their feet with a wild shriek she cast herself upon the inanimate clay.

LESSON 19 –INDIAN BATTLES

A Creek warrior, stunned by a blow from her father's rifle, recovering from it and hearing the battle passing away, was arising from the ground to make good his escape, and hearing the cry of the maiden, and seeing who it was, determined, with a fiendish purpose, to be yet avenged for the loss of his companions.

With the bound of the deer, the Panther sped to her relief. The Creek encumbered by his burden, saw he must fall a prey to his rapidly advancing foe; with a fiendish yell, he raised his knife high above his head; and buried it to the hilt in the bosom of the Indian Maiden; and with wild quivering limbs she sank from the embrace of her murderer. The Panther saw the hellish deed, and it lent speed to his already rapid steps; and ere he reached the summit of the hill, the death of Magnolia was revenged by the knife of her lover.

Returning to Magnolia, who yet lived, but was fast sinking into death, he heard from her why she screamed, and the attack of her murderer. "Bury me with my father, down in the gorge there, where my lovely namesake will bloom in springtime o'er my grave, and where the spirit of Magnolia may wander in the bright light of the summer morn;" sighed the dying maiden."

Dragging Canoe

The white man ere long began to be seen in the country and the red man was fast failing before him. In autumn's sad time of each year, for a long while, an Indian might be seen wending his way to "Indian Tomb Hollow", - Grief had marked his sad features and wan countenance. With the taciturnity of his race, he bore them without a murmur, and when at length he felt his days numbered, he wended his way to the spot of all others most dear to him, and there upon the grave of her he loved so well in life, he breathed his last. The "pale face" now soon occupied the land far and wide - not satisfied with his treatment to the red man during life - his bones were not sacred in death. The grave of Eagle Eye and Magnolia was torn open, and the bones were left to molder in the winds of winter and the dews of summer.

Read, before students arrive, "Ittaloknah" (The Battle of Indian Tomb Hollow). Condense as you like, tell students story or use play to tell story.

Cherokee War - In 1763, the war, known as the French and Indian War, between the French and British ended with the British victorious in controlling most of the eastern North America. In addition to ending the war, a Proclamation Line of 1763 was established to

LESSON 19 – INDIAN BATTLES

protect the Indians west of the Appalachians and to halt encroachment on their lands. The Proclamation Line did not prevent settlers from invading Indian lands west of the line.

Eventually, the Cherokee were forced into making land cessions west of the Appalachians. In 1768, 1770, 1772, and 1773, treaties were made between the government and the Cherokee Indians. The Cherokee were pressured to give up land claims in South Carolina, Georgia, Virginia, West Virginia, Kentucky, and Tennessee. The Treaty of Sycamore Shoals, in 1775, took Cherokee lands through the middle of Kentucky and Tennessee.

Now, with the door to settlement opened, settlers poured into the area north of the Little Tennessee River to the heart of the once powerful Cherokee Nation. As the settlers moved in from the north and east, the Cherokees began moving south and west. By the 1750's, Cherokees were occupying eastern Alabama. By 1770, the Cherokees were firmly established in the area of the Warrior Mountains to the Mussel Shoals.

The Cherokee decline and loss of lands continued after the Revolutionary War partly because of their alliance with the British. The Middle, Valley, and Overhill Towns of the Cherokee were practically destroyed by military movements lead against the Cherokees by men such as Colonel William Christian and Colonel John Sevier. Eventually in 1780, the armies of John Sevier and Arthur Campbell destroyed the Overhill Towns including the Cherokee Capitol of Chota. By this time, a thriving population of Cherokees was occupying the lower Tennessee Valley.

Many of the Cherokee moved south under the leadership of Dragging Canoe, son of Oconostota. The Cherokees under Dragging Canoe settled from Chattanooga to the south and west in five villages referred to as the "Five Lower Towns on the Tennessee"—Running Water, Nickajack, Long Island Village, Crow Town, and Lookout Mountain Town.

Cherokee Chief Doublehead migrated farther southwest along the Tennessee River into North Alabama. Historical evidence indicates Doublehead settled for some 12 years at the head of Elk River Shoals at Doublehead's Village on the south bank of the Tennessee River at Brown's Ferry. Doublehead helped establish the following villages along the Tennessee River in Lawrence County: Moneetown at Fox's Creek, Doublehead's Village at Brown's Ferry, between Fox and Mallard Creeks; Melton's Bluff between Mallard and Spring Creek; Cuttyatoy's Village on an island in the mouth of Spring Creek. Gourd's Settlement; Courtland on Big Nance Creek; Shoal Town at the Blue Water/Town Creek Village just one mile west of present-day Wheeler Dam; and, Oakville at the junction of Black Warriors' Path and the Coosa Path.

In east Tennessee, by the 1780's, the Cherokee were a defeated people trying to survive in a country controlled by a newly established government of the United States. Devastated by

LESSON 19 –INDIAN BATTLES

war, disease, and land hungry American settlers, their days east of the Mississippi River were numbered.

By the beginning of the 1800's, the once flourishing towns along the Little Tennessee River were practically abandoned by the Cherokee people. By 1817, even the lands along the Great Mussel Shoals were taken by the Turkey Town Treaty. Then, in 1830, the Indian Removal Act spelled doom for many Cherokee. Two years after the Treaty of New Echota in 1836, the Army of Winfield Scott attempted to remove all the Cherokee remaining east of the Mississippi. The remnants of the Cherokee and mixed bloods that remained in the east were a scattered and defeated people living in a state of denial of their aboriginal beginnings, but in their hearts holding to their beliefs and staying in the land they loved "Warrior Mountains".

Review Questions

1. Where was the first skirmish of the Creek Indian War?
2. Who fought in the French and Indian War?
3. What is another name for the Indian maiden, Magnolia, in the Battle of Indian Tomb Hollow?
4. Who is Moulton named after?
5. Who was the Indian maiden who was killed at the Battle of Indian Tomb Hollow?
6. Where was the last skirmish of the Creek Indian War?
7. Marathon is located on what river and was founded by whom?
8. Who was called Ittaloknah in the Battle of Indian Tomb Hollow?
9. Magnolia was what type of Indian?
10. What were the two tribes fighting each other in the Battle of Indian Tomb Hollow?
11. When did the Cherokee war end?
12. Where did the Creek-Indian War take place?
13. The Battle of Fort Mims was an Indian victory under the leadership of whom?
14. What year did the Indian Removal Act occur and who was responsible for it?
15. Which chief convinced the Cherokee's not to join forces with Tecumseh's Creek and to remain neutral?

LESSON 20 – INDIAN TREATIES

Our Indian people utilized the Warrior Mountains for years before the coming of the white man. Shortly before the first settlers arrived in the Warrior Mountains, many treaties had taken the last remnants of the native lands.

The Cherokee people of North Alabama were unfairly treated through agreements with the United States. Between 1750-1819, the United States forced or bribed the Cherokees into making twenty-five treaties which took their land. Before the end of the 1830s, the United States had taken all Cherokee lands east of the Mississippi River which consisted of over 50,000 square miles.

Treaty of Sycamore Shoals of March 17, 1775 – The Treaty of Sycamore Shoals involved the ceding of Indian lands in Kentucky and middle Tennessee. These lands were sold to the Transylvania Company.

Treaty of Hopewell of November 28, 1785 – The Treaty of Hopewell set up the boundary line between Indian people and the citizens of the United States.

Chickasaw Boundary Treaty of January 10, 1786 – The Chickasaw Boundary Treaty recognized the High Town or Ridge Path along the Continental Divide in North Alabama as the Chickasaw's southern boundary and Creeks northern boundary. This early boundary between the Creeks and Chickasaws lay primarily along the present-day Leola Road and Ridge Road of Lawrence County's portion of the Warrior Mountains.

The backbone of North Alabama or Tennessee divide was also the boundary line between the Cherokees and Creeks. The boundary line lay along the divide with Chickasaw claims extending eastward to a north-south line drawn between The Path and Hobb's Island or Chickasaw Old Fields just south of present-day Huntsville, Alabama. The north-south line lay along the Huntsville Meridian and formed the eastern boundary of the Chickasaw Nation until the Turkey Town Treaty of 1816. After the December 1801 Treaty, from Ditto Landing or Hobbs Island, the Chickasaw boundary crossed present-day Madison County about 45 degrees toward the northwest to the Tennessee State Line. Prior to 1801, the Chickasaws owned the land from their eastern boundary at the mouth of Flint River to the North and South to the Tennessee Divide.

First Treaty of Tellico of October 2, 1798 - Cherokees ceded land north of Little Tennessee River forcing more Cherokee people to migrate south and west into Alabama.

The 1800s - During the early part of the 1800s some 20,000 Cherokees were living on 43,000 square miles with half of the land in Tennessee, and the rest divided equally between Alabama and Georgia.

LESSON 20 – INDIAN TREATIES

Georgia Compact of 1802 - The United States paid Georgia $1,250,000.00 for their western lands and agreed to obtain land title from the Cherokees.

Wafford Settlement of October 25 and 27, 1805 - The Cherokees ceded in two treaties a large tract of land in central Tennessee and Kentucky with the United States paying $15,600.00 plus an annuity of $3,000.00. Article IV authorized construction of Gaines' Trace through North Alabama. This Treaty was signed by Doublehead.

Cotton Gin Treaty of January 7, 1806 - The Cotton Gin Treaty was between the Cherokee Indians (Doublehead) and the U.S. Government. The treaty identified the tract of land that Moses Melton, the half-blood Indian son of John Melton, lived on and declared the land to be the equally shared property of Melton and Charles Hicks in equal shares. Charles Hicks was noted in Cherokee history as being the first person to show Sequoyah how to write his name in English. In addition, Doublehead and his great nephew, Tahlonteeskee (Talohuskee the Overthrower) controlled the North Alabama area. Talohuskee was the half brother to Sequoyah.

The treaty gave up Cherokee claims to Indian land north of the Tennessee River, except for Doublehead's Reserve, and placed a cotton gin at Melton's Bluff. Doublehead was killed because of the terms of this treaty. Doublehead's Reserve lay between Elk River (Chu wa lee) and Cypress Creek (Te Kee ta no-eh) in present day Lauderdale County. The Cotton Gin Treaty with the Cherokees did not relinquish the Chickasaw claims to the area; therefore, Ft. Hampton was established to remove squatters from Chickasaw land, located primarily in the area of Limestone County known as the Simms Settlement. Fort Hampton was the only fort built in the United States to remove white settlers from Indian lands.

The Cherokees ceded a large part of land north of the Tennessee River, which consisted of nearly 7,000 square miles in Tennessee and Alabama, for $10,000.00, a gristmill and cotton gin, and $100.00/year for Black Fox. The cotton gin was placed at Melton's Bluff. The cotton gin was noted by Anne Royall on January 14, 1818, at Melton's Bluff.

Supplemental Treaty to Cotton Gin Treaty of September 11, 1807 - This treaty extended and defined the cession boundaries as Elk River to the west and the Tennessee River and Tennessee Ridge to the south and north. It also gave the Cherokees hunting rights until white settlement and $2,000.00 in expenses.

Treaty of Ft. Jackson of August 9, 1814 - The majority of the new frontier that now makes up Bankhead Forest was taken from the Creeks at the Treaty of Fort Jackson in 1814. The Creeks did not receive monetary compensation for their vastly large tracts of land from Bankhead Forest to the south near Montgomery, Alabama. This large tract was taken after

LESSON 20 – INDIAN TREATIES

Jackson's defeat of the Red Stick Creeks at the Battle of Horseshoe Bend. The 1814 cession of land was from the High Town Path or Tennessee Divide in North Alabama and extended south for nearly 200 miles.

The Creeks ceded Lawrence County land south of the High Town Path which lies along the Leola and Ridge Roads. The first white settlement near Haleyville was made by Richard McMahon in 1815.

Boundary Treaty of March 22, 1816 - This treaty clarified the Cherokee - Creek Boundary between the Coosa and Tennessee Rivers by recognizing Cherokee land claims South of Tennessee.

Turkey Town Treaty of September 14, 1816 - The Turkey Town Treaty gave up Cherokee and Chickasaw land in the North Alabama portion of the Warrior Mountains. Both tribes had legitimate claims to the land.

According to the terms of the Turkey Town Treaty, the last Indian lands of the Warrior Mountains were bought from the Chickasaws and Cherokees on September 16 and 18, 1816, respectively. The Chickasaws were paid $125,000.00 with the Cherokees being paid $60,000.00 for land that now makes up Colbert, Franklin, Lawrence, and Morgan Counties.

The Cherokees ceded all claims south of the Tennessee River and west from Chickasaw Island in the Tennessee to the junction of Wills Creek and Coosa River at Gadsden. The cession of 3,500 square miles included Franklin, Lawrence, and Cotaco (Morgan) Counties in North Alabama. The Cherokees received $60,000.00 including $5,000.00 for improvements.

The Chickasaws and Cherokees had overlapping land claims with the Cherokees claiming land west to Natchez Trace some 10 to 15 miles west of Caney Creek in Colbert County. The Chickasaws claimed land east to the old official Chickasaw boundary, which runs from the Chickasaw Old fields (Hobbs Island) south to the High Town Path then west along the High Town Path to Flat Rock in present-day Franklin County. From Hobbs Island, the original boundary of the Chickasaw ran north across Madison County from the mouth of Flint River and up the river to the north; however, in December 1801, the boundary traversed northwest 45° across Madison County from Chickasaw Island.

The Cherokee Chief Doublehead and the Cherokees farmed and controlled the Tennessee Valley to Natchez Trace by agreement with George Colbert. Two of Chief Doublehead's daughters married Chickasaw Chief George Colbert. It was thought that by agreement of Colbert and Doublehead, the Cherokee people were allowed to remain within the Chickasaw Territory including lands west of Caney Creek in present-day Colbert County, Alabama.

LESSON 20 – INDIAN TREATIES

The Turkey Town Treaty signed by the Cherokees on September 16, 1816, ceded Colbert, Franklin, Lawrence, and Morgan Counties; however, the U.S. Government established the Chickasaw's new eastern boundary from Franklin County's Flat Rock to Caney Creek in Colbert County until 1832. The High Town Path was recognized as the southern boundary of the cessions for both the Chickasaw and Cherokee, until the Turkey Town Treaty of 1816. The 1816 treaty identified the new cession boundary as a straight line drawn from Flat Rock in Franklin County to Ten Islands on the Coosa River. Previous treaties recognized the Continental Divide along which ran the High Town or Ridge Path.

Reserve Treaty of July 8, 1817 - The Cherokees ceded in Alabama reserves of one square mile family blocks between the Tennessee and Flint Rivers. These "reserves" were Cherokee Indians and mixed-bloods that had accepted reservations under previous treaties and were thus citizens of the United States.

Technically reserves had given up their rights as Cherokee citizens and became individual landowners and citizens of the United States.

Indian Removal Act of May 28, 1830 - Congress passed this act authorizing the exchange of lands in the west for those lands east of the Mississippi River held by Indian tribes. President Andrew Jackson was intent on seeing all Indian people removed from the eastern United States.

Treaty of New Echota of December 29, 1835 - The Treaty of New Echota was signed by a small number of Cherokees. The U.S. Congress ratified the treaty on May 23, 1836. The treaty ceded the entire Cherokee territory east of the Mississippi River.

Trail of Tears of 1838 - The Cherokee people were given two years to move at which time the forced removal known as the "Trail of Tears" began in the spring of 1838. The forced march began in October 1838 and ended in March 1839.

Cherokees on the Trail of Tears – The Rise and Fall

An estimated 4,000 Cherokees died on the forced march to the west. Many of the Cherokees from the east passed through North Alabama during 1838 by railroad. By the

LESSON 20 – INDIAN TREATIES

time of the "Trail of Tears" in 1838, much of the land of the Warrior Mountains had already been claimed by Celtic/Cherokee mix-bloods who denied their heritage in order to remain in the "Warrior Mountains", the land they loved.

Many of North Alabama's Indian people were already mixed with Celtic settlers (Irish, Scotch, and Welsh) and stayed in the hill country of the Warrior Mountains. They denied their ancestry and basically lived much of their lives in fear of being sent west. Full bloods claimed to be Black Irish or Black Dutch, thus denying their rightful Indian blood. After being fully assimilated into the general population years later, these Celtic/Cherokee mixed-blood descendants began reclaiming their Indian heritage in the land of the "Warrior Mountains."

Review Questions

1. What direction did our ancestors travel during removal?
2. How many Cherokees died on the Trail of Tears?
3. The backbone of North Alabama was divided by which tribes?
4. When did the "Trail of Tears" begin?
5. Who forced the Cherokee removal?
6. What year was the Cotton Gin Treaty signed?
7. Who signed the Cotton Gin Treaty?
8. Full blooded Indians claimed to be:
9. What was the forced removal of Indians known as?
10. The United States forced the Cherokees into making how many treaties which took their land?
11. When did the Trial of Tears end?
12. The Turkey Town Treaty was signed in what year?
13. What state did our ancestors move to during the trail of Tears?
14. How much did the United States pay Georgia for their western lands?
15. Who was Sequoyah's half brother?
16. The Cotton Gin Treaty gave up Cherokee claims and placed a cotton gin where?
17. Which treaty was signed by Doublehead?
18. Why was Doublehead killed?
19. What was the only fort built in the United States to remove white settlers from Indian lands?
20. What law did Andrew Jackson have passed on May 28, 1830?
21. What counties were involved in the Turkey Town Treaty?
22. What were reserves?
23. The Indian removal act did what to our ancestors land?
24. The Treaty of January 10, 1786 gave most of North Alabama to which tribe?
25. The first white settlement near Haleyville was made by whom?

LESSON 20 – INDIAN TREATIES

26. What treaty ceded all Indian land east of the Mississippi?
27. The Cotton Gin Treaty was between the U.S. Government and which Indian tribe?
28. How much were the Cherokee paid for their land?
29. Which two tribes had overlapping land claims?

LESSON 21 – INDIAN REMOVAL

Major Ridge

At the time of removal, many North Alabama Indians were already mixed with white settlers and stayed in the hill country of the Warrior Mountains. They denied their ancestry and basically lived much of their lives in fear of being sent west. Full blooded Indians claimed to be Black Irish or Black Dutch and denied their Indian blood. Many years later, the descendants of these mixed-blood Indians still live in North Alabama. Those descendants are you-- students of Indian heritage. You are eligible to attend Indian classes because your parents, or grandparents have reclaimed their Indian heritage. There seems to be a renewed pride in our Indian heritage and so the Cherokee culture will go on here in the old homeland.

1808 Removal - In 1806, Cherokee Chief Doublehead, his great nephew Tahlonteskee (Talohuskee Benge), and other Cherokees signed the Cotton Gin Treaty which gave up Cherokee claims to land north of the Tennessee River except for Doublehead's Reserve. The reserve lay between Elk River (Chuwalee) and Cypress Creek (TeKeetanoeh) in present day Lauderdale County.

The signing of the Cotton Gin Treaty brought the wrath of other Cherokee leaders upon the individuals who signed the treaty giving up Cherokee Lands. Major Ridge, a powerful Cherokee leader, made known that Doublehead and others would pay with their lives for relinquishing Cherokee lands. At a meeting of Cherokee headmen in Tennessee, Doublehead paid with his life at the hand of Ridge, Alex Saunders, John Rogers, and their accomplices. Alex Saunders and John Rogers had ties to Lawrence County and probably profited from the assassination of Doublehead.

After the assassination of Chief Doublehead by his own people, due to the circumstances of the Cotton Gin Treaty of 1806, several Cherokees living in the North Alabama area moved west to avoid the same fate. The following is from "The Cherokees" by Grace Steele Woodard published in 1963 and found on page 131:

> *"However, in 1808, the Compact 1802 was not needed to effect the removal of some 1,130 Chickamaugans to lands west of the Mississippi (today Dardanelle, Arkansas, in Pope County). Jefferson had merely to suggest to Tahlonteskee and other Chickamaugans that if they did not care to remain in the same country with their enemy countrymen, they could remove to Dardanelle Rock. Thus, in the Spring of 1808, Tahlonteskee-fearing assassination-notified President Jefferson that his people were ready to migrate. Following their*

LESSON 21 – INDIAN REMOVAL

migration Tahlonteskee's band of Cherokees called themselves "Cherokees West" or "Old Settlers."

Even though some Cherokees in the Warrior Mountains area left with Tahlonteskee's group in 1809, many Cherokee people still lived in the Tennessee Valley from the river to the High Town Path. Within the great valley of the Tennessee, cotton became the agricultural "king" for making money. With the new government cotton gin at Melton's Bluff and black slaves for farm labor, both the Chickasaws and Cherokees, who shared ownership of the river valley, became wealthy; however, the government and settlers wanted the cotton wealth of the Tennessee Valley which was controlled by Indian people.

1816 Removal - In 1816, with several more years of pressure, the Chickasaws and Cherokees finally relinquished their claim to the remainder of Warrior Mountains. Therefore, due to the circumstances of the Turkey Town Treaty of September 16 and 18, 1816, another contingent of Chickasaws and Cherokees moved west, from the land of the Warrior Mountains and North Alabama. The first documented removal from Melton's Bluff in Lawrence County is found in the following excerpt given in the book <u>Letters from Alabama 1817-1822</u> by Anne Royall on pages 134 and 135 with the Letter XXIV dated January 14, 1818:

> *"Melton's Bluff is a town, and takes its name from a person by the name of John Melton, a white man ceased two years since, at an advanced age... You recollect Rhea whom I have mentioned: he married one of Melton's daughters-a most amiable woman, and very lame. When the Cherokee Indians abandoned this territory last fall, some of them went up the river to the Cherokee nation, there to remain, till boats were provided for their removal to the west, by the government;* <u>*others went directly down the river to Arkansas-of whom Rhea's wife was one*</u>*.*
>
> *The order for their departure was sudden and unexpected. Rhea, at that time was absent from home, but returned on the same day and learning what had happened, was almost frantic jumped into a canoe, and soon overtook the boats. He flew to his wife, and clasped her in his arms. Neither spoke a word, but both wept bitterly. In a few moments, he resumed his canoe and returned to the Bluff, and she went on. They had no children.*
>
> *Whether Rhea was prohibited by the treaty from accompanying his wife, or whether he was under a prior engagement, none here are able to inform me-but certain it is, he is now married to a white woman."*

LESSON 21 – INDIAN REMOVAL

Rhea had moved to Melton's Bluff about 1803 and had married one of John Melton's half-blood Cherokee daughters. According to Royall, he had guided as many as four boats at a time, ten dollars each, through the Elk River Shoals, Big Mussel Shoals, and Little Mussel Shoals for some 15 years. Also, at this time, James Melton, Rhea's half-blood Cherokee brother-in-law, was a river boat guide that piloted boats through the Shoals for Malcolm Gilchrist, one of the early settlers of the Courtland area.

Shortly, after the Turkey Town Treaty was signed, several Cherokees left Melton's Bluff in Lawrence County for lands in the west during the Fall of 1816. In addition, Andrew Jackson did not wait until the dust of the 1816 removal had settled to begin staking his claims to Indian lands and property in Lawrence County as early as November 22, 1816.

1818 Removal - After Jackson had acquired Melton's Bluff which he named Marathon, another group of Cherokee's were facing removal. On January 20, 1818, while at Melton's Bluff, Anne Royall observed some 300 Cherokees camped just two miles east of the Bluff in Lawrence County. These Cherokees were in the process of moving west of the Mississippi River. The following writing was found in Letter XXX dated January 20, 1818 and on pages 154 and 155 of the Letters from Alabama 1817-1822:

> *"Hearing eleven boats had arrived about two miles from hence, and had haulted up the river, we set off, as I said before, in a little canoe, to see the Indians, which are on their way to their destination beyond the Mississippi. Government, agreeably to their contract, having completed the boats, the news of the arrival of the Indians had been received with much interest; but being unable to proceed by water, we quit the canoe, and proceeded by land in our wet shoes and hose.*
>
> *We arrive at the Indian camps about eleven o'clock. There were several encampments at the distance of three hundred yards from each other, containing three hundred Indians. The camps were nothing but some forks of wood driven into the ground, and a stick laid across them, on which hung a pot in which they were boiling meat; I took it to be venison. Around these fires were seated, some on the ground, some on logs, and some on chairs, females of all ages; and all employed, except the old women. There were some very old gray-haired women, and several children at each camp. The children were very pretty; but the grown females were not."*

This group of Cherokees was probably waiting for a rise in the river in order to pass through the Elk River Shoals safely. Keelboats and flatboats waited at the head of Brown's Island until the water conditions permitted safe passage. At Brown's Island, the river channel divided as it passed around either side. Before the channels rejoined on the island's

LESSON 21 – INDIAN REMOVAL

downstream end, rapids on both sides of the island created dangerous situations for boats. At the upstream end of Brown's Island was Brown's Ferry which Ms. Royall said was visible eight miles upstream from Melton's Bluff. At Brown's Ferry, the head of Elk River Shoals, Doublehead lived on a slight hill just west of the ferry and south of the river until 1802.

Indian Removal Act of May 28, 1830 - On May 28, 1830, Congress passed an act authorizing the exchange of lands in the west for those lands east of the Mississippi River held by Indian tribes. President Andrew Jackson was intent on seeing all Indian people removed from the eastern United States.

It should be noted that Jackson later lost the respect of the Cherokee when he ordered their removal from Georgia and Alabama. Jackson had the Indian Removal Act passed in 1830, which later led to the removal of southeastern Indians. After the discovery of gold in Georgia, the greed of the white men created a greater desire for Indian land. In 1828, the Georgia Legislature passed a law that no Indian must deal with gold in anyway and they were under the law of Georgia.

Georgia assumed authority over the Cherokee Nation's capitol at Echota, Georgia. It was then moved to Wills Valley (present day Fort Payne, Alabama). Later, it was moved to Red Clay, Tennessee. Chief John Ross hired a famous Philadelphia lawyer to represent the Cherokee cause before the Supreme Court of the United States. The court ruled this law was illegal and ordered President Jackson to remove the white intruders. President Jackson refused the order. Chief Junaluska upon hearing this said he would have killed him that day at the Battle of Horseshoe Bend if he had known of his attitude. There was a report that Chief Junaluska prevented Jackson from being stabbed by a captured Creek Warrior. This made Jackson's attitude even more bitter for Junaluska to understand.

Treaty of New Echota of December 29, 1835 - The Cherokees gave up all Indian land claims east of the Mississippi River and were forced into removal during 1838-1839.

On December 29, 1835, the Treaty of New Echota was signed by a small number of Cherokees. The U. S. Congress ratified the treaty on May 23, 1836. The treaty ceded the entire Cherokee territory east of the Mississippi River. Most of the members of the signing party of Cherokees were eventually assassinated by Cherokees of the northern faction under the leadership of John Ross. Stand Watie of the southern faction was one of the lone survivors in the signing of the Treaty of New Echota. Stand Watie was also the last Confederate general to surrender at the close of the Civil War.

Treaty of New Echota 1835 - On December 29, 1835, the Treaty of New Echota was signed by a small number of Cherokees. The United States Congress gave formal approval to the treaty on May 23, 1836. The treaty took the entire Cherokee territory east of the Mississippi

LESSON 21 –INDIAN REMOVAL

River. The Cherokee people were given two years to move. At this time, the "Trail of Tears" began. It was the spring of 1838. The forced march began in October 1838 and lasted until March 1839, five months.

Trail of Tears from October 1838 until March 1839 - The Cherokee people were given two years to move at which time the forced removal known as the "Trail of Tears" began in the spring of 1838. The forced march began in October 1838 and ended in March 1839. During the spring and summer of 1838, General Winfield Scott under orders of President Andrew Jackson began placing Cherokees in stockades for removal to the west.

An estimated 4,000 Cherokees died on the forced march to the west. Many of the Cherokees from the east passed through North Alabama during 1838 by railroad. By the time of the "Trail of Tears" in 1838, much of the land of the Warrior Mountains had already been claimed by Cherokee mix-bloods who denied their heritage in order to remain in the land they loved which was the "Warrior Mountains."

The March West - In Georgia and Alabama, Cherokee Indians were forced off their farms and herded into newly built stockades (like an animal pen) which are east of us. Fort Payne, was built to house Cherokees prior to their forced march to the west. In the stockades, the Indians were overcrowded and many were very sick. Close to 2,000 Cherokees died there, before they even left on the long march west.

Many were weak and underfed at the start of the journey. Many were also poorly clothed and barefoot. None were prepared for November's raging snowstorms and icy winds. Sickness and death were everywhere, but the march went on. One of the soldiers wrote, "the exiles (Indians)...had to sleep in the wagons and on the ground without fire. And I have known as many as 22 of them to die in one night of pneumonia due to ill treatment, cold, and exposure."

A traveler who passed the struggling Cherokees reported seeing a Cherokee mother carrying her child, who was close to death. He wrote that when the child died, the mother would have to stop in a strange land and bury her baby in the cold ground. The traveler was deeply troubled. He said, "I turned from the sight with feelings which language cannot express. And wept like childhood then." The Cherokees also wept.

Broken Promises - Treaties signed between the Cherokees and the United States Government had been broken before. It was always the government that broke these treaties. This time was no different. The United States promised the Cherokees they could keep some of their land, but in the end that promise was also broken.

LESSON 21 – INDIAN REMOVAL

A newspaper, entitled "The American History Herald", December 12, 1838, published an article about the Trail of Tears. The author wrote, "And so, the Cherokees struggle west on their Trail of Tears. Some white Americans watch in sorrow. Most seem untroubled by this tragedy. Yet, the ghosts of this disgrace may haunt America for many years to come. What do you think? Who would like to share your opinion of the Cherokee Removal, Trail of Tears, or Broken Promises? Have you been told that your ancestors were on the Trail of Tears? Explain how you would feel if we were forced from our homes today.

Many of North Alabama's Indian people were already mixed with Celtic settlers and stayed in the hill country of the Warrior Mountains. They denied their ancestry and basically lived much of their lives in fear of being sent west. Full bloods claimed to be Black Irish or Black Dutch in denying the rightful Indian blood.

After the Civil Rights Act of 1968 and after being assimilated into the general population, our Cherokee mixed-blood descendants began reclaiming their heritage in the land of the "Warrior Mountains."

Review Questions

1. What does assassination mean?
2. Approximately how many Cherokees died on the Trail of Tears?
3. What was the Trail of Tears?
4. What year was it ok to say you were Indian?
5. Who signed the Cotton Gin Treaty and in what year was it signed?
6. The Warrior Mountains were home to what people?
7. After what act did the Indian mixed-blood descendants begin claiming their heritage?
8. What president wanted the Cherokee's removed?
9. When did the Trail of Tears begin and end?
10. Where were our ancestors forced to move?
11. President Andrew Jackson had what act passed in 1830?
12. What three men killed Doublehead?
13. Which treaty took the entire Cherokee territory east of the Mississippi River?
14. What did our ancestors claim to be while denying their Indian heritage?
15. Which president began placing Cherokee's in stockades for removal to the west?
16. Who was Melton's Bluff named after?
17. What became the agriculture king for making money?
18. Why did some North Alabama Indians, during the time of removal, deny their ancestry?
19. In what year was the Treaty of New Echota signed?

LESSON 22 – TRADITIONAL CULTURAL PROPERTIES

For thousands of years, inhabitants of the Tennessee Valley have looked south to see a beautiful range of mountains rising from the flat middle plain in the heartland of North Alabama. This east-west mountain range has represented many things to modern man, but probably was more important and sacred to our red ancestors than any of our European immigrants.

By the time of Desoto's visit to our state in 1540, our Muscogee people recognized the range of mountains as a tribal and geographic boundary along the Tennessee Divide. The High Town Path or Ridge Path is a prehistoric east-west Indian trail that lies along the divide. The divide begins separating the Atlantic's coastal waters from those of the Mississippi drainage in Maine and continues through the upper Tombigbee watershed in the western portion of Alabama and into Northern Mississippi.

Black Warrior - Probably the most accurate and appropriate name for the North Alabama portion of this vast chain of mountains is derived from the Muscogee people who lived along the forest streams hundreds of years before white people came to our county. The Creek word "taskagu" or "taska," and the Choctaw word "tashka" refer to the English translation of "warrior" with the Muscogee word "lusa" meaning "black." We know from reading Alabama history, Desoto encountered a giant of a man known as "Chief Tuscaloosa" or the Black Warrior; therefore, the name was here long before the first European settlers claimed the land in the southern portion of our county.

Mountains - In early days, the stream forming south from the mountains in North Alabama also became known as the Tuscaloosa River. On a French map dated March 1733, Baron De Crenay, Commandant of the Post of Mobile, identified the southern drainage from our mountains as the Tuscaloosa River. On other early maps, the main river, which drains south, was also called the Tuscaloosa. Later in 1814, a map of Alabama identified the river draining south from our county as the Black Warrior River.

John Bull - In 1829, a frontiersman and famous rifle maker by the name of John Bull, engraved two of his masterpieces from the Warrior Mountains. According to information provided by Mr. Dan Wallace, the exceptional rifle is inscribed on a silver platelet in the stock, "John Bull for David Smith, Warrior Mountain." The inscription on the silver cheek piece is as the following:

"Ann"
this gun is named Charlotte,
from hills and mountains came,
made to delight the heart of man,
with Joy, the labouring Swain,

LESSON 22 – TRADITIONAL CULTURAL PROPERTIES

and from the sportsmen of the day
Victorious bear the prife,
Away"

According to Old Land Records of Lawrence County, Alabama by Margaret Cowart, David Smith entered 79.92 acres of land in Section 36 of Township 7 South and Range 7 West, near Indian Tomb Hollow on September 12, 1818, and 79.92 acres on

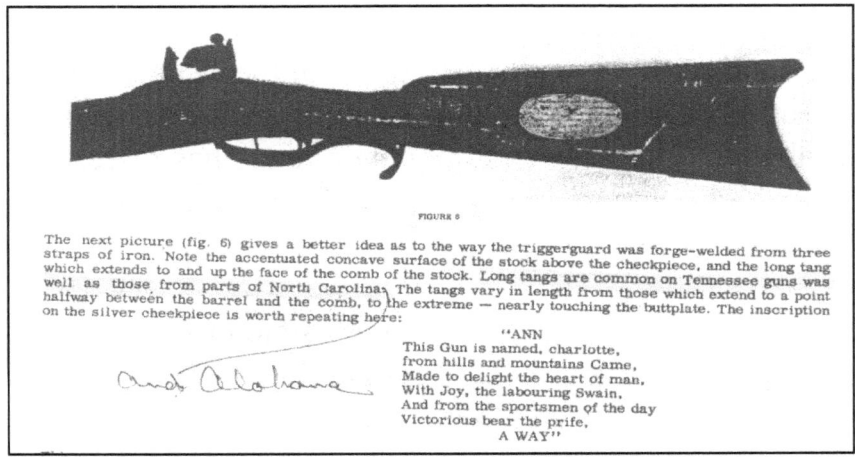

John Bull Rifle made for David Smith

September 28, 1818, in Section 35. He married Charlotte Ann Havens, who was the daughter of James Havens. According to the Havens family legend provided by Spencer Waters, James Havens was buried next to his Indian friends on the side of the Warrior Mountains where the magnolia blooms in the spring. It is highly probable that James Havens was buried in the Indian Tomb Hollow Cemetery,

Warrior Mountains - In his 1899 book, Early Settlers of Alabama, Colonel Edmonds Saunders refers to Lawrence County's southern highlands as the "Warrior Mountains." Later in 1918, when the government began organizing our mountains into a national forest the area was called the Black Warrior. Today, the State Wildlife Management Area is still known as the Black Warrior.

It is a shame that our forest had a name that could be traced back for over 400 years and has been changed to honor a white politician. However, with the Indian pride that has grown strong in North Alabama, our mountains will never take second place. These mountains will always remain the Sacred Land of our ancestors, and be known as the "WARRIOR MOUNTAINS."

Indian Tomb Hollow - Indian Tomb Hollow is located primarily in Section 2 of Township 8 South, Range 7 West in on the northern edge of William B. Bankhead National Forest. In the distant hollows of Indian Tomb, the wood hen can be heard as the evening sun sinks behind the bluffs. Three gracious waterfalls of the southwest fork echo eternal sounds that formed the sandstone canyon containing vertical walls reaching to the sky. Looking down the canyon toward the northeast sandstone bluffs on either side of the canyon causes one to be in awe of the area because of its beauty.

Early settlers and Indian mixed-bloods settled to the north and west of the hollow's southwestern fork. Several folks lived for a while in the old High House located on a small knoll at the southern mouth of Indian Tomb. Families of the Warrior Mountains would enter

LESSON 22 – TRADITIONAL CULTURAL PROPERTIES

the hollow from Chestnut Ridge, Beulah, and High House Hill not only to view and enjoy the beauty of the area, but to dig roots, herbs, and hunt. It was in this same tradition that I, Rickey Butch Walker, was first introduced to the mysterious but beautiful Indian Tomb Hollow.

The late, Mr. G. H. Melson told me of experiences he had as a small boy in Indian Tomb Hollow and was a wealth of information concerning an Indian fight occurring near the mouth of the famous canyon. He tells of his father working on the old plantation and passing down stories through many generations about our Indian people of the area, the black slave cemetery, and the early settlers who called the area home.

Over many years, the Gillespie family has traditionally been drawn to Indian Tomb. Not only does the family consider the area a sacred Indian burial site, but their ancestor, James Richard Gillespie, a veteran of the Creek Indian War, is buried in the Gillespie or Indian Tomb Hollow Cemetery. In addition, Gillespie Spring and Gillespie Creek, which runs through Indian Tomb Hollow, are named after the Gillespie Family of Lawrence County.

My family (Rickey Butch Walker) also has strong ties to Indian Tomb Hollow. My great, great, great grandmother, Mary E. Welborn (Granny Naylor) Segars Naylor, is buried at Beulah, on the western edge of Indian Tomb. My grandfather, Authur Wilburn, lived as a young boy in the hollow and carried me many times to this sacred place. Many of my family are buried within sight of this mysterious place.

According to William Lindsey McDonald's article on Melton's Bluff, "The renowned pioneer and soldier, David Crockett, remembered two occasions when his military unit crossed at Melton's Bluff. The first instance was in October 1813. Actually according to Crockett, he crossed the Tennessee River twice on this first occasion in order to maneuver around the local Indians. After crossing at Huntsville, they moved westward to cross the river again at Melton's Bluff. Crockett described the river at this point as being about two miles wide. The rocky bottom of the river was rough and dangerous. While fording the river, several of the horses became stuck in the rocky crevices and had to be left there while the military command moved onto their destination. Crockett's second crossing at Melton's Bluff was in October 1814. Payroll and muster records reveal that he was a third sergeant in Captain John Cowan's company at the time." According to McDonald, the above information was obtained from the book <u>A Narrative of the Life of David Crockett</u>.

In 1813, David Crockett helped General John Coffee's forces burn the large Creek Indian village known as Black Warrior Town after finding it deserted. Crockett and General Coffee's forces traveled along the Black Warriors' Path through present day North Alabama to destroy the Creek town. James Richard Gillespie, who eventually settled and was buried in Indian Tomb Hollow also served with David Crockett. Gillespie served under Captain Cowan in

LESSON 22 –TRADITIONAL CULTURAL PROPERTIES

1813 during the same period of time as David Crockett. Gillespie attended the muster rolls in Blount County, Tennessee on January 1, 1814.

The ancient beech trees of Indian Tomb are a record of family traditions, which has spanned hundreds of years of time. From early Indian drawings (known as arborglyphs) and settler names, the beeches of Indian Tomb bear record of visitation. The markings also indicate much of the time spent in Indian Tomb was recorded in the numerous beech carvings located throughout the canyon. In addition, the Indian marker tree in Indian Tomb Hollow is a symbol considered sacred by the descendants of those who once roamed the beautiful valley.

A story called the "Battle of Indian Tomb Hollow" or "Ittaloknak" was originally printed in The Moulton Democrat on November 7, 14, 21, 1856. The articles are a beautiful love story that describes a fierce fight in Indian Tomb between the Creek and Chickasaw inhabitants of the Warrior Mountains.

Treasures can be found in Indian Tomb Hollow for all who enter her solitude. The treasures lie not in the destruction of her timber nor the looting of her artifacts, but in beautiful waterfalls, sheer rock walls, virgin timber, and the mysterious closeness of GOD. Four waterfalls lie just beyond the fork of the canyon with the first waterfall's branch being the southwest boundary of the clear-cut. The other three waterfalls are upstream at the end of the canyon. In three different areas along the way, Gillespie Creek flows under huge boulders and has a splendor that only GOD could create. Let's hope that man does not destroy the rest of GOD's handiwork in Indian Tomb Hollow.

In 2001, the U.S Forest Service set aside Indian Tomb Hollow as a traditional cultural property to be protected from future logging operations.

Kinlock Rock Shelter

Kinlock - Kinlock Rock Shelter is located in Section 31 of Township 8 South and Range 9 West. The shelter is one of the largest of its kind with an overhang of sandstone rock some 250 feet wide, 30 to 100 feet deep, and 30 to 150 feet high. The Indian shelter is a premier petroglyph site of prehistoric Indian occupation. The sacred Indian shelter is still actively used by American Indians for ceremonies. Kinlock Bluff Shelter has been deemed eligible to be nominated to the National Register of Historic Places.

LESSON 22 –TRADITIONAL CULTURAL PROPERTIES

You don't need to travel far from your home to experience the beauty of nature. Our mountains offers many beautiful sites to behold. One that's rich with Indian history is Kinlock. Kinlock Falls is probably the best known waterfall or cascading waterfall in Bankhead. Water flows over Kinlock for the entire year, but the waterfall is most beautiful during the spring creating a white cascade among the green leaves. Kinlock Falls is located on Hubbard Creek.

Also, within walking distance, is the Kinlock Rock Shelter. After you cross the bridge, take a left at a gate near Kinlock Spring and walk about a quarter of a mile. Take a right at the old logging trail and follow this down to the shelter. Keep on the trail. Be sure to have a partner if you go there because it is a steep climb down. Kinlock is considered a sacred place to many Indian people so always treat it with respect. It was believed to be used for vision quests.

Teachers may read from <u>Walking Sipsey</u> pages 1, 2, and 3, "The Sacred Fire". This explains some of the feelings of Terra Manasco about the Kinlock Rock Shelter. Also, teachers may read pages 43 through 46 from <u>High Town Path </u>about Kinlock.

Needle's Eye or Windows in King Cove

Sipsey Wilderness - Sipsey Wilderness is found in the southwestern portion of Lawrence County. Many people enjoy the beauty of Lawrence County's greatest resource, the Sipsey Wilderness Area of Bankhead Forest that lies in the heart of the Warrior Mountains. Sipsey River Picnic Grounds are located on Sipsey River near the Cranal Road, the south border of the wilderness. Many people not only hike in the wilderness, but also drive along Highway 33 and the Cranal Road to enjoy the fall colors and splendors of the Sipsey Wilderness.

Sightseeing, hiking, canoeing, and horseback riding are only a few of the many outdoor recreational activities available to Alabama residents, as well as visitors from all over the southeastern United States. The Sipsey Wilderness is the place for those who want to get away from modern conveniences without the sound of traffic, telephones, and TV's, but instead listening to the songs of warblers, the hammering beaks of woodpeckers, the hoot of the great horned owl, the howl of a lone coyote, and the sound of water running over rocks and boulders in the many streams flowing through this portion of the Warrior Mountains. Avid outdoorsmen cherish

LESSON 22 –TRADITIONAL CULTURAL PROPERTIES

the stimulating sounds, sights, and smells that only Mother Nature can provide to those who visit the Sipsey Wilderness.

Ship Rock - Ship Rock is located in the Sipsey Wilderness Area in Section 27 of Township 8 South and Range 9 West. The large rock is located some 200 yards east of the forks of Hubbard and Thompson Creeks in the heart of the Sipsey Wilderness. The site is known as Ship Rock, Herron Point, Boat Rock, Needle's Eye, or the Windows. The following text is a descriptive but symbolic version of the Ship Rock of Sipsey.

Ship Rock is a monument in time and a symbol of persistence before the age of the great reptilian dinosaurs, the age of the gigantic mammals, and the age of the red man who once inhabited her great-forested seas. No time, force, or age is her master, for God is her pilot and only he knows her true destiny. As God spins the eternal swirl of the universe, Ship Rock holds steady while dragging the Warrior Mountains along with the rest of the world.

Narrows Ridge - Narrows Ridge is located in Bankhead Forest in Section 21 of Township 8 South and Range 8 West. While walking south on a ridge from the Northwest Road, suddenly a high narrow strip of land emerges between two beautiful old growth hardwood valleys. The valley to the east was the Borden Creek Canyon and the valley to the west was the Flanagin Creek Canyon. The old settler road along the top of the ridge continued along the slender natural bridge of sandstone rock connecting the two mountaintop ridges, which divided the beautiful creek bottoms. To either side of the old road were the edges of bluffs, which rose some 40 to 60 feet above the two hardwood valleys.

The narrow ridge runs in a north-south direction for approximately 100 yards narrowing to as little as some 12 feet wide. The unique and beautiful ridge is known to most local people as the "Narrows Ridge." Narrows Ridge is now in the Sipsey Addition to the Wilderness Area, which will provide protection for the beautiful hardwood valleys on either side of this natural bridge ridge.

King Cove - King Cove is located Township 8 South, Range 9 West in Sections 22 and 27 of the southwestern portion of Lawrence County. King cove lies adjacent to the forks of Hubbard and Thompson Creeks, which is the beginning of Sipsey River in the western portion of Bankhead Forest. The King Cove extends up Thompson Creek to the forks of Tedford and Mattox (Thompson). Ship Rock is found at the southern end of King Cove and is just east of the forks of Hubbard and Thompson.

King Cove shows evidence of early Indian habitation. Mortar Rock, located to the north across the creek from Ship Rock, contains five mortar holes and a huge nutting stone used by early Indian people. Local folklore tells of numerous arrowheads and spear points picked up in the old creek bottom fields.

LESSON 22 –TRADITIONAL CULTURAL PROPERTIES

The canyon area of King Cove was not heavily settled but farmland lies adjacent to the creek bottoms. Most of the early settler homes were located on the ridges above the cove but still make up the early King Cove Community of the Warrior Mountains.

Parker Cove - Parker Cove is located in Section 30 of township 7 South and Range 7 West and is named from the Parker family who settled the cove long ago. Parker Cove forms the headwater streams of Elam Creek on the north-central edge of Bankhead Forest. The cove still contains three old log houses that were used over 100 years ago. When going south on Highway 33, the main entrance to Parker Cove is along the first steep winding road turning east off of Wren Mountain. The deep cove is visible east of the Wren Mountain portion of the Wilderness Parkway, which runs through the center of the Warrior Mountain.

Borden or Blankenship Cove - The lower portion of Blankenship Cove is still an active cattle-farming site and is located primarily in Section 2 of Township 8 South and Range 8 West on the upper portion of Borden Creek. The Cove was originally called Borden Cove, settled by the family of Christopher Borden. The upper portion of Blankenship Cove extends through the northeast part of Sections 34 and 35 of Township 7 South and Range 8 West. Some of the Borden Family originally settled along portions of the cove adjacent to Borden Creek. The cove was owned by Glenn Whisnant, who bought the property from the heirs of his Granddaddy Willis Blankenship. Two areas of the Blankenship Cove were known as the upper place and the lower place. Willis Blankenship lived on the lower place. David Borden earlier had his home near the Borden Spring in the beautiful Cove.

Bee Branch Canyon - Bee Branch of the Sipsey Wilderness Area is located primarily in Section 26 of Township 8 South, Range 9 West. Bee Branch is a deep canyon located east of Sipsey River. The area is probably the most primeval site in the Warrior Mountains. Most of the canyon was protected by the U.S. Forest Service as early as 1919.

Bee Branch is a forked canyon with seasonal and beautiful waterfalls in each fork. The Bee Branch Falls plunge from some 50 feet above the canyon floor. Both forks are virtually box canyons forming a small creek that flows into Sipsey River. The eastern fork of the canyon features the largest yellow poplar in the Southeastern United States. The whole canyon is a botanical garden of a virgin gorge in the Warrior Mountains.

Tar Springs Hollow - Located in the upper portion of Capsey Creek, once known as Capp's Creek, is a place not found elsewhere in William B. Bankhead National Forest. The creek begins at Cave Springs on Highway 41 and on the Leola Road at Basham Shelter and Spring. The area, not noted for the two-headwater springs, is unique because of the two mineral springs downstream in the middle of the big hollow. This unusual site found on

LESSON 22 –TRADITIONAL CULTURAL PROPERTIES

Capsey Creek is known as Tar Springs Hollow. The road from Poplar Log Cove into Tar Springs Hollow was originally an Indian Trial and called the Double Springs Road or Trail.

Capsey Creek is a tubutary to Brushy Creek, which empties its waters into Sipsey River on Smith Lake. The Tar Springs Hollow on Capsey Creek contains two mineral tar springs which are located about one-quarter mile apart in the southwest ¼ of Section 26, Township 8 South, and Range 6 West.

Glyphs - Our Indian ancestors did not have a written language until Sequoyah invented the Cherokee alphabet in 1821. How then did the Cherokees keep records of the things that happened? (response) One method was picture writing.

Arborglyphs, petroglyphs, and pictographs were all forms of picture writing. Arbor meaning tree, glyph meaning drawing--tree drawing (show example in book High Town Path). The American beech tree was commonly used for arborglyphs because carvings would remain on the bark for hundreds of years. Beech trees were also known as boundary trees because they marked tribal boundaries. The Warrior Mountains (Bankhead Forest) contains many beech trees with Indian drawings.

Petro means rock and glyph means drawing. Petroglyphs, meaning rock drawings, are pictures that have been carved or scratched onto hard surfaces such as rocks, shell, or copper. These symbols can be found in Kinlock Bluff Shelter in our county (show picture in the book Walking Sipsey).

Pictographs are pictures that have been painted on hard surfaces or animal skins. These have been found all over the United States and date back hundreds of years. Animal skins were used by some tribes to draw pictographs. Since animal skins were used to make blankets and clothing, Indian people would draw pictures on their personal belongings. Examples include their names, battles that were fought, deaths, hunger, brave deeds, or anything they wanted told about their everyday lives.

Warrior Mountain Wildlife - Have you ever been to the Warrior Mountains (Bankhead Forest)? What did you see? (trees, paved roads, rock roads, mountains, and animals). What kinds of animals did you see?

We are going to talk about some other animals and plants that once lived in the Warrior Mountains before the 1900's. These animals have since been eliminated. It is very sad to learn that there were certain animals that our Indian ancestors depended upon, no longer live in our forest and are now gone.

LESSON 22 –TRADITIONAL CULTURAL PROPERTIES

Animals - One of the animals that had been eliminated in the Warrior Mountain was the whitetail deer. By the early 1900's there were no more whitetail deer. These deer had to be brought into the forest again from the north. Again in 1990, more whitetail deer from South Alabama were restocked in the forest. Just think what our forest would be like if deer had not been brought in after the first deer were eliminated.

How do you think the first deer were eliminated? (too many hunters were killing too many deer, finally, there were no more deer until they were brought in from another place).

Other animals that once lived in the Warrior Mountains were the elk, bear, panther and three kinds of wolves – gray timber, red, and black wolves. The last of these animals were seen in the early 1900's. Trade between Europeans and Alabama Indians was based largely on the barter of animal skins (furs and hides). An Indian could swap about 30 deer hides for a rifle. All of the commercialized fur trade led to the elimination of these animals in the Warrior Mountains.

Hunting parties, an important part of wilderness life, provided a means of obtaining meat for hungry families, hides and furs which could be traded for goods, and the thrill of the hunt along with the fellowship of friends and neighbors. However, unregulated hunting practices began taking their toll on the native wildlife. Between 1890 and 1910, big game species, which were eliminated from the Warrior Mountains by over hunting probably, included the whitetail deer, black bear, timber wolf, and eastern cougar.

Whitetail Deer - After the last original Warrior Mountains whitetail deer was killed, the herd was restocked with a northern subspecies of deer during the 1920's. Again in the 1990's, deer from South Alabama were restocked in the Black Warrior Wildlife Management Area.

Mr. Rayford Hyatt, past conservation officer of Bankhead, relates an interesting story about the last native deer to be killed in the forest. According to Mr. Hyatt, the last pure bloodline deer was a small racked buck that was hunted for two or three days before it was eventually killed. The deer was killed by James M. Flanagin on Hagood Creek in early 1909. Mr. Amos Spillers, a Cherokee Indian descendant and one of the first conservation officers of Bankhead, had the antlers of the last known native Bankhead whitetail deer, which were seen by many people.

Wolves - The last known timber wolf of Bankhead was killed during snowy weather in the Hurricane Creek area in 1910 by Cherokee descendant William Straud Riddle according to Mr. Hyatt. The wolf had killed several sheep owned by a Mr. Sewell who lived south of Grayson. After hunting and tracking the wolf in the snow nearly all day, the hunt was ended without success. As Mr. Riddle started home toward the western side of Sipsey River, he found fresh wolf tracks in the snow. After tracking the animal a short distance, he saw the

LESSON 22 –TRADITIONAL CULTURAL PROPERTIES

wolf standing next to a huge hollow log where it had denned. Once the wolf was shot and killed, it was taken home and was placed in a standing position before it became stiff. Many people came to see the carcass before it was finally discarded.

At one time three species of wolves inhabited Lawrence County, they were known as the Red Wolf, Black Wolf, and Grey Wolf. In the early days of this county, all three wolf scalps could be used in the payment of taxes. Notice in the following law:

ACTS OF ALABAMA 1835 SESSION. ACT NO. 123 Pages 119, 120

"After passage of this Act, it shall be lawful for Tax Collectors of Franklin and Lawrence Counties to receive all wolf scalps in payment of any county tax due from any person in the county, on prior affidavit made before an acting Justice of the Peace that the wolves were killed in Franklin or Lawrence County, as the case may be - Scalps received at the following rate; all scalps under one year $1.00; all scalps one year and upward $1.50. Tax Collector of each county to return affidavits with scalps to the County Treasurer as money for any county tax due from them as tax collectors - no money to be paid out for scalps; only receive scalps in payment of taxes."

Bear and Panther - The black bear and eastern cougar were eliminated from Bankhead as a breeding population in the early 1900's. Specific information about the demise of the last bear and cougar in Bankhead is unknown, however, many mountaineers tell stories of encounters their grandparents had with bears and panthers during the early 1800's. Reports of bears and cougars still persist to this very day; however, no known population of either exist in the Warrior Mountains. It is estimated that some 30 wild eastern cougars still roam the swamps of southern Florida and ranks as the most endangered animal in the Southeastern United States.

Elk - The eastern elk migrated the Appalachian Mountains into Alabama in the early 1800's. The elk were rapidly eliminated by Indian and early settler hunters. The eastern elk were killed out in the state of Tennessee by 1870. No known record exists on the demise of eastern elk in the Warrior Mountains.

Birds - The passenger pigeons, which are now extinct, were once beautiful birds in the Warrior Mountains. The last passenger pigeons seen here was in 1893. Eight birds were killed before the flock (with over 300 birds) flew away, never to return here.

Another bird which was once native to the Warrior Mountains was the ivory-billed woodpecker. These woodpeckers have not lived in Alabama since about 1906 and are almost extinct due to habitat destruction and needless killings.

LESSON 22 –TRADITIONAL CULTURAL PROPERTIES

Passenger Pigeon - Passenger pigeons were beautiful birds that once filled the skies and woodlands of the Warrior Mountains. Old-timers have passed down stories of passenger pigeons, which were extremely abundant and roosted in mature hardwoods in flocks containing thousands of birds. The passenger pigeons, much larger but similar to an oversize mourning dove, would use the same roosts for years. One such roost existing in the northern portion of Bankhead was near the forks of Thompson and West Flint Creeks, which was at the site of the old Jake Alexander Place (now Dallas Yeager's farm). Other places in surrounding areas immortalized the name of the passenger pigeon by being named "Pigeon Roost."

The pigeons were smoked out at night while on the roost by huge bond fires. They were also shot and killed at their nesting sites. Eventually, this beautiful wilderness bird was eliminated from Bankhead Forest with its last verified flock appearance in Alabama in 1893. Eight birds were killed before this flock containing some three hundred birds flew away never to return to our state. The last known passenger pigeon died while in captivity on September 1, 1914, at the Cincinnati Zoological Garden. This wilderness bird that once fed on the giant chestnut, oak, and beech in Bankhead Forest is now extinct.

Ivory-billed Woodpecker - The ivory-billed woodpecker, another large bird once native to the Warrior Mountains, is on the verge of extinction due to habitat destruction as well as needless killings. The last known ivory-billed woodpecker in Alabama died about 1906. The bird met its fate at the hands of a hunter who probably never considered his kill would be the last of the species reported from our state.

The ivory-billed woodpecker's form was mystic and immortalized by prehistoric Alabama Indians who engraved its image on stone plates, handles of axes, and other ornaments of the Mississippian culture. If our early ancestors who used rifles had cared that much for this bird of mystery, our children today may have been blest not only by sight of the bird but also by the sound of its hammering beak in the hills and hollows of the Warrior Mountains.

Carolina Parakeet – In January 1818, Anne Royall describes flocks of Carolina parakeets in Lawrence County. The Carolina parakeets were probably the most colorful and beautiful birds to inhabit our country. Anne Royall noted they were beautiful birds with yellow and green plumage. They loved very ripe fruit and corn. When one bird was wounded, the others would hover over it making the whole flock easy prey for hunters. Eventually, all the Carolina parakeets were wiped out and never seen here again. They are now extinct.

Plants - The American chestnut was the largest nut producing tree in North America. It was killed by the chestnut blight in the 1930s. The American Indians utilized vast quantities of the American Chestnut. Old growth timber only exists in a few places in the Warrior

LESSON 22 –TRADITIONAL CULTURAL PROPERTIES

Mountains. Trees over 100 years old are considered old growth. Most old growth timber at one time was replaced with pines.

Protection of TCPs - Our ancestors used the natural resources without destroying them. They developed a balanced way of life in harmony with nature. Our Indian people practiced conservation of soil, water, plant, and animal life. This allowed them to live in the same region for century after century with no ill effects. To our Indian people, the land was sacred. All forms of life were equal because each plant and animal was a link in the life cycle chain. To upset this balance could destroy life as it was meant to be. Because of their reverence for the earth, Indians lived in harmony with nature. They felt they had the right to take what they needed but no more. Our society no longer has the same respect for land that it once did.

Raise your hand to give an example of how our environment is being abused? (1)Littering; (2)Pollution-factories, cars, garbage; (3)Clearcutting; (4)Wildfires; (5)Oil spills. Our main focus today is on clear cutting. What exactly do you think clear cutting means as far as the Warrior Mountains is concerned? Why should it bother you as an Indian person? Clearcutting is the process of destroying acres upon acres of timber with the use of heavy equipment such as bulldozers. When an area is set to be clear-cut, nothing is left standing. Several thousand acres of old growth hardwood timber in our own community has been destroyed by clear cutting. Much of the clear cutting in the Warrior Mountains has been done by the U. S. Forest Service. In 2005, it is hoped that the U.S. Forest Service has taken new steps that will protect our public lands from the ravages of clear cutting.

There are many historical sites in the Bankhead National Forest. Much of our heritage lies within the beautiful mountainous areas. Do we want it to be destroyed? How many of you have been through the Bankhead Forest in the last year? You can't help but see the destruction that has taken place over the years. Maybe the healing processes of this public land of ours can begin to recover to its former old growth state.

You need to realize that not all the land being clear-cut is on public lands. Many private landowners chose to sell their timber for money. They are concerned with money in their pocket now. Clearcutting affects the entire environment. Many of the old growth hardwood trees are homes to many animals. What if you went home one day and your house was flattened by a bulldozer?

You would feel confused, hurt, and lost. As these old trees are being destroyed many are replaced with pine plantations. The reason is they grow faster and could be cut again sooner. Some of the trees like the beech tree which was used for Indian markings are hundreds of years old. That means it will take hundreds of years to reach this size again, but the markings are lost forever.

LESSON 22 – TRADITIONAL CULTURAL PROPERTIES

Review Questions

1. Who was John Bull?
2. Name one way our early ancestors kept records of things that happened:
3. Who helped General John Coffee's force burn Black Warrior Town?
4. What type of tree was the Indian marker tree?
5. What does it mean when you cut all of the trees down with heavy equipment?
6. What, in Indian Tomb Hollow, is a symbol considered sacred by the descendant of that area?
7. What is a petroglyph?
8. What is a pictograph?
9. Where did the name "Black Warrior" come from?
10. Identify the early Indian name for the Black Warrior River?
11. Who was the famous rifle maker who made two masterpieces from the Warrior Mountains?
12. The name Warrior Mountains, that has since been renamed after a white politician, can be traced back how many years?
13. Identify the large rock located in the heart of the Sipsey Wilderness?
14. What area on Capsey Creek contains two mineral tar springs?
15. What is an arborglyph?
16. Bankhead National Forest is also known as what mountains in what county?
17. What year did Indian Tomb Hollow become a cultural property?
18. What giant of a man did Desoto encounter who was also known as Black Warrior?
19. Name at least two geographical locations within the Bankhead National Forest?
20. What are symbols found on rocks at Kinlock Rock Shelter called?
21. In 2001, Indian Tomb Hollow became protected from what by the U.S. forest Service?
22. What shelter, in the Bankhead Forest, is one of the largest of its kind?
23. What deep canyon is located east of Sipsey River and is probably the most primeval site in the Warrior Mountains?
24. Where are Indian Tomb Hollow, Sipsey River, and Bee Branch Canyon located?
25. What Creek is Kinlock Falls located?
26. What tree was the largest nut producing tree in North America till killed by blight in the 1930's?
27. How old does a tree have to be to be considered old growth?
28. What is the best known waterfall in the Bankhead Forest?
29. Later in 1814, a map of Alabama identified what river draining south for North Alabama?
30. What shelter in the Bankhead Forest has been deemed eligible to be nominated to the National Register of Historic Places?

LESSON 23 – STATE RECOGNIZED INDIAN TRIBES OF ALABAMA

There are nine Indian tribes in the State of Alabama that have enrolled several thousand Indians. These represent about 13% of the 165,416 persons in Alabama who disclosed that they were of Indian ancestry in the Federal Census of 1980. Most of those with Indian ancestry in Alabama are descendants of the Cherokee, Choctaw, and Creek tribes who were the aboriginal inhabitants of the State. While the majority of the members of these tribes were removed to Indian Territory in the 1830s, a significant Indian minority remained in the State, including Cherokees in North Alabama, Creeks in South Alabama, as well as a sizeable community of Choctaws in Southwest Alabama (Alabama Indian Affairs Commission, 1988). As of February 2006, Alabama has officially nine Indian tribes with only the Poarch Band of Creek Indians being recognized by the Federal government. In addition to the Poarch Band of Creek Indians, the other state recognized tribes are as follows: Echota Cherokee Tribe of Alabama; Cherokee Tribe of Northeast Alabama; Machis Lower Creek Indian Tribe; Star Clan of Muscogee Creeks; Cher-o-Creek Intra Tribal Indians; MOWA Band of Choctaw Indians; Piqua Shawnee Tribe; and, United Cherokee Ani-Yun-Wiya Nation.

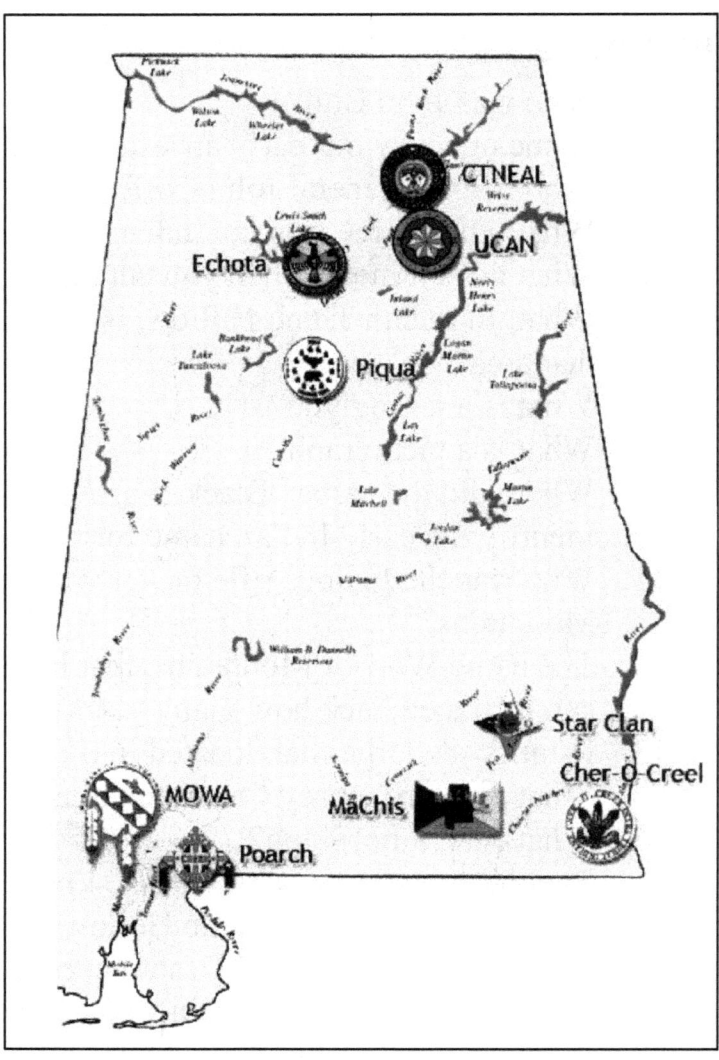

Map of State Recognized Indian Tribes

Poarch Band of Creek Indians – The Poarch Band of Creek Indians descended from the original Creek Nation, which avoided removal and remained in south Alabama. The Creek Nation originally occupied a territory covering nearly all of Georgia and Alabama. The War of 1812 divided the Creek Nation between an Upper party hostile to the United States and a group of Upper and Lower Creeks friendly to the government. The Treaty of Ft. Jackson compelled the Creek Nation to cede much of the territory of those friendly Creeks to the United States including the present site of Poarch. Those Creeks who had actively fought with the United States were permitted a reservation of one square mile. Several Creek

LESSON 23 – STATE RECOGNIZED INDIAN TRIBES OF ALABAMA

families including the Gibsons, Manacs, Colberts, and Weatherfords, secured reservations immediately after the treaty. Congress in 1836 passed an act allowing Lynn McGhee and the others to set aside 640 acres as reservations under the 1814 Treaty of Fort Jackson. The United States continued to protect the Poarch settlement after the removal of the main Creek body to Oklahoma in 1836.

Today, there are nearly 2,200 members of the Poarch Band of Creek Indians, with over 1,500 living in the vicinity of Poarch, Alabama in rural Escambia County. The Poarch Band of Creek Indians is bound by kinship. A leader, that helped to improve the social and economic situation of the Poarch Creeks was Calvin W. McGhee, who pressed for settlement of a land claims case. Also, Eddie L. Tullis, Tribal Chairman as of 1987, led the Poarch Creek Indians in their petitioning the U.S. Government to be federally recognized.

The Echota Cherokee Tribe of Alabama – During the 1990 U.S. Census, 6.7% of Lawrence Countians were listed as American Indian. In the 2000 U.S. Census, 5.8% of Lawrence Countians indicated they were American Indian. The vast majority of North Alabama's Indian people are members of the Echota Cherokee Tribe of Alabama. Many of the North Alabama Echota Cherokees are descended from Cherokee Chief Doublehead and his followers.

The United Cherokee Tribe of Alabama was organized on June 14, 1978, at Daleville, Alabama. B. J. Faulkner was elected principal chief, and Thomas McCloski was elected vice-principal chief. A council of nine people was formed, and the Secretary and Treasurer positions were filled. In 1978, Chief Faulkner opposed the development plans for an industrial park near Northport that would disturb a 1,000-year-old Indian village site and burial ground. In January of 1980, he sought the reburial of 3,000 Indians along the route to be flooded by the Tennessee - Tombigbee Waterway. In 1980, disenchanted members of the United Cherokee Tribe of Alabama formed a new tribe called Echota Cherokee Tribe, Inc.

Joseph "Two Eagles" Stewart was elected principal chief, and Letter of Incorporation was filed in Shelby County and their seal was registered. The tribe filed for and received non-profit status and clans were organized over the State. A newsletter, "Smoke Signals", was mailed to members. Regular monthly meetings were held at the Alabaster Community Center. The governing body of the tribe, consisting of tribal council members, elected officers, principal chief and vice-principal chief, was set in to serve a four-year term. (Cromer, 1984)

The Echota Cherokee Tribe is the largest and one of the most active tribes in Alabama today. The tribe has several thousand members in Alabama and other states. The tribe is affiliated

LESSON 23 –STATE RECOGNIZED INDIAN TRIBES OF ALABAMA

with several Indian education programs in Madison County, DeKalb County, Jackson County, and Lawrence County.

The tribe has a land fund established for the purpose of purchasing land to build a Cherokee meeting ground and museum. Tribal members are active in voter registration drives around the state. The tribe, represented by the principal chief, is a member of the Alabama Indian Affairs Commission and the National Congress of American Indian (Cromer, 1984). The vast majority of North Alabama Indian students are members of the Echota Cherokee Tribe of Alabama.

Cherokee Tribe of Northeast Alabama - The Jackson County Cherokees formed a Tribal Council on May 5, 1981, at North Sand Mountain High School, Higdon, Alabama. Dr. H.L. "Lindy" Martin presided over the meeting which elected the following council members: Jaynn Kushner, Ceil Hicks, Bill Williams, Joe Hunkapiller, Marland Mountain, David Cornally and David Rooks.

The presence of the Cherokee in Jackson County was almost unknown for years even though the tribe had been under the leadership of Chief John Justice, William Keep, James McCony, and Claud Thornhill.

According to Dr. Martin, the Cherokees of Jackson, Alabama, are the descendants of the Cherokee Indians who were led by Chief Dragging Canoe. The Indians had come into Alabama in the early 1780's and settled in an area, which had traditionally been tribal hunting territory. They established five major towns and several smaller villages.

Dr. Martin resigned as chairman of the Jackson County Cherokees in the fall of 1982. In 1983, the tribe changed its name to Cherokees of Northeast Alabama, Inc. Travis Staggs became chairman, and David Rooks became vice-chairman. In 1984, Jaynn Kushner became representative to Alabama Indian Affairs Commission (Cromer, 1984).

Cher-o-Creek Intra Tribal Indians - This group was originally known as The Cherokees of Southeast Alabama In 1982 in Houston County, a group of Cherokee Indians organized into a tribe under the leadership of their elected Chief Deal Wambles. In 1984, the tribe began efforts to establish Indian education classes in their county school system, where tribal members are taught Indian beadwork, dances, and leatherwork.

In 1984, the Tribe held their first Pow-Wow, which drew members and guests from Houston and Dale Counties. The tribal government is made up of an executive committee, the

LESSON 23 – STATE RECOGNIZED INDIAN TRIBES OF ALABAMA

principal chief, the vice-principal chief, the administrative chief, the tribal council, the medicine man, the beloved woman, and the war chief (Cromer, 1984).

Star Clan of Lower Muscogee Creek Indians - *The Yufala "Star" Clan: A Modern Day Tribe with Traditional Values* The Star Clan of Lower Muscogee Creek Indians takes its name from both the Muscogee word "Y'ufala" (Eagle), and the Star, which if found within the Tribal symbol. In the early 1970's, the Tribe chose to relocate its headquarters in the Western sphere of their traditional area of influence. Under the leadership of Chief Larry Johnson, the Tribe moved to Pike County, Alabama.

In 1978, Larry Johnson retired from the office of Chief, and returned to his hometown of Panama City, Florida. It was in October of 1978 that Tommy Davenport was appointed Chief of the Star Clan. During his time in office, he was instrumental in helping to create the Alabama Indian Affairs Commission. He also served on the Commission from its inception. He was Chairman of the Alabama Indian Affairs commission at the time of his death in 1991. At that time, it was the consensus of the Tribe to elect his wife, Erma Lis Davenport, as Chief of the Yufala "Star" Clan. She presently serves in that capacity, continuing the pioneering work that her husband began almost 30 years ago.

Ma-Chis Lower Creek Indian Tribe - In 1985, almost 900 Lower Creeks of Coffee County organized into a tribe under the rules and guidelines of the Alabama Indian Affairs Commission. They were the first tribe in the state to organize under the criteria set forth by the A.I.A.C.

Mrs. Penny Wright was elected as leader of the group, the state's only "female chief." In July of 1985, Governor George Wallace appointed Dr. Johnny Wright, a high school principal from Pike County and member of the Ma-Chis tribe to represent the tribe on the A.I.A.C. Dr. Wright brought to the Board a wealth of expertise in administrative and educational experience. He serves as principal of Pike County High School.

Chief Penny Wright was cited by <u>Women's Day</u> magazine in their fall, 1985 issue, as the only female Indian chief in the United States. Since then, another woman, Chief Mankiller of the Western Cherokee nation has been elected to lead the Cherokees of Oklahoma.

MOWA Band of Choctaw Indians - The MOWA Choctaws of Mobile and Washington Counties, Alabama, get their name from a combination of the two counties where most of these Choctaws reside. They rekindled their great council fire in Washington County in December 1981 after blending in with the general population for some 160 years.

LESSON 23 –STATE RECOGNIZED INDIAN TRIBES OF ALABAMA

The MOWA Band of Choctaw Indians was duly incorporated in 1979 with its tribal office located in McIntosh and purchased 160 acres of land in south Washington County in 1983. There are five officers and fourteen members of the tribe's commission who voluntarily assist the operations of tribal affairs.

Today, there are nearly 6,000 members of the MOWA Band of Choctaw Indians, over 2,500 of whom live in the vicinity of McIntosh, Alabama. All the members are descendants of the original Choctaw Nation who are bound together by a complex network of multigenerational kinship.

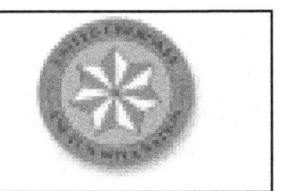

Piqua Shawnee Tribe - Early historical records show that the Shawnee were inhabitants of Lawrence County and North Alabama. They were forced from the Tennessee Valley by the combined efforts of the Chickasaw and Cherokee. Most historians label Shawnee people as nomadic because they have found evidence of Shawnee people moving about in North America, settling in various places and often retaining small family units for long periods of time.

North Alabama has long been the home of many Shawnee people. In fact, some historians state that perhaps the Shawnee people have inhabited Alabama for a longer period of time than any other geographic region. Some archaeologist set the date of 1685 as the first evidence of Shawnee settlement in Alabama. However, oral tradition states that Shawnees have been here much longer than that. Ancient burial sites that use methods common to the Shawnee have been located in several sections of the state.

Now, in the 21st century, there are many descendants who still call Alabama home. Many of their family stories are varied. Some avoided walking the Trail of Tears. Some families escaped into the Cumberland Mountains, others hid in swamps or less traveled places. A careful study of southeastern history will reveal that not all settlers agreed with Andrew Jackson's removal policy. While many people did not escape the removal, some did. After the turmoil subsided some families returned. Many families chose to live in outlying rural areas where there was little government scrutiny and their neighbors weren't too curious. While a lot was lost, family histories and ways were passed down.

It is out of that background that current Piquas live and work to preserve their unique heritage. The tribe consists of several family groups that are interrelated with the majority of Piquas living in Alabama.

United Cherokee Ani-Yun-Wiya Nation - The United Cherokee were recognized by the State of Alabama on July 10, 2001. The United

LESSON 23 –STATE RECOGNIZED INDIAN TRIBES OF ALABAMA

Cherokees are descendants of the Cherokees are descendants of the Cherokees in Northeast Alabama around the Guntersville area. The original Cherokee villages and settlements in the area included Willstown, Creek Path, Gunters, Red Hill, Wasasa Village, Turkey Town, Litafatchee, Brown's Village, and Meltonsville. Gina Williamson from Guntersville serves as the tribal chief and serves on the Alabama Indian Affairs Commission.

Review Questions

1. How many Indian tribes are in the State of Alabama?
2. What year was the Echota Cherokee Tribe formed?
3. A majority of North Alabama Indian students are members of what tribe?
4. Many of North Alabama Echota Cherokees are descended from what chief?
5. Were Shawnee people nomadic?
6. What is the Echota Cherokees newsletter called?
7. The Shawnee inhabited what state for a longer period of time than any other geographic region?
8. The Poarch Band of Creek Indians are bound by what?
9. How many members are in the MOWA Band of Choctaw?
10. What bird is in the center of The Echota Cherokee symbol?
11. The Echota Cherokee Tribe is the largest and the most active tribe in what state?
12. Most Alabamians claiming Indian ancestry are descendants of what three tribes?
13. Which tribe of Indians got their name from an eagle and a star?
14. Who was the elected principal chief when the Echota Cherokee Tribe was formed in 1980?
15. In January 1980, Chief Faulkner sought the reburial of 3,000 Indians along the route to be flooded by what?
16. Who formed a tribal council on May 5, 1981?
17. What tribe was organized on June 14, 1978, at Daleville, AL?
18. How long is the term of an elected governing body of the Echota Cherokee Tribe?
19. Who was the state's only female chief?
20. The Poarch Band of Creeks Indians descended from the original Creek Nation, which avoided removal and remained where?
21. The Echota Cherokee Tribe is affiliated with several Indian education programs such as:
22. What tribe is located near Mobile and Washington counties?
23. What group was recognized by the State of Alabama on July 10, 2001?
24. Out of the nine state tribes of Alabama, which one is federally recognized?
25. Name some of the state recognized tribes in Alabama:
26. What was the name of the first tribe in the state to organize under the criteria set forth by the Alabama Indian Affairs Commission?
27. The Star Clan of lower Muscogee Creek Indians takes its name from what word?

Index

A

Alexander Mound, 122
Alibamos, 67, 73
Anigatogewi., 86
Anigilohi, 86
Anikawi, 85
Anisahoni, 86
Anitsiskwa, 85
Aniwayah, 85
Aniwodi, 85
Apalachees, 73
Archaic, 13, 17, 18, 19, 20, 21, 29, 36, 53, 109
Atlanta, 89, 90, 91
Attakullakulla, 135

B

Bankhead National Forest, 28, 90, 92, 99, 102, 156, 168, 171, 172, 173, 174, 175, 176, 177, 178
Battle of Fort Mims, 74, 136, 147
Battle of Horseshoe Bend, 73, 74, 125, 147, 157, 164
Battle of Indian Tomb Hollow, 73, 147, 152, 170
Battleground Mountain, 91
Bean, Mrs. William, 26
Bee Tree Shoals, 18, 54, 55
Benge, John, 5, 119, 127, 129, 138
Benge, Robert, 4, 129, 133, 140
Benge, Tahlontoiskee (Talohuskee), 127
Benge, Utana (The Tail), 138
Bering Strait, 14, 15, 16
Beringa, 14, 15, 16
Bevill, Tom, 2
Big Muscle Shoals, 29, 53, 55, 119, 120, 137, 139
Big Mussel Shoals, 17
Bird Clan, 9, 85
Black Dutch, 1, 7, 61, 63, 159, 161, 166
Black Fox, 138, 139, 140, 141, 142, 143, 156
Black Irish, 1, 7, 61, 63, 159, 161, 166
Black Warrior Town, 97, 99, 169
Black Warriors' Path, 75, 88, 92, 96, 97, 98, 99, 100, 101, 105, 108, 109, 113, 121, 122, 129, 141, 147, 153, 169
Blankenship, Willis, 173
Blue Clan, 5, 6, 9, 86
Boaz, 93
Bone Polisher, 134
Borden, Christopher, 173
Borden, David, 173
Breed Town, 5, 60
Brown, Joseph, 118, 135
Brown, Richard, 138, 142
Brown's Ferry Road, 89, 101, 108, 139, 141
Browns Ferry, 128, 129, 130, 141
Brown's Village, 91, 185
Burnett, 133

Butler, Kit, 135
Byler Road, 89, 91, 92, 94, 96, 100, 101, 102

C

Campbell, Arthur, 153
Celtic, 4, 5, 7, 9, 11, 12, 26, 42, 50, 60, 61, 63, 66, 76, 77, 88, 90, 125, 127, 128, 129, 159, 166
Charles Town, 5, 89
Charleston, 89, 133
Chattanooga, 90, 153
Cheatham Road, 89, 91, 92, 94, 102, 117
Cher-o-Creek Intra Tribal Indians, 82, 180, 182
Cherokee, 1, 4, 5, 6, 7, 9, 10, 11, 12, 21, 23, 25, 26, 27, 30, 32, 33, 34, 35, 36, 37, 38, 40, 41, 42, 43, 44, 45, 47, 48, 49, 50, 53, 55, 56, 57, 61, 63, 64, 66, 67, 68, 69, 73, 76, 77, 79, 80, 81, 84, 85, 86, 88, 89, 90, 91, 93, 94, 95, 96, 98, 99, 101, 103, 105, 106, 107, 108, 109, 110, 111, 112, 113, 114, 115, 117, 118, 119, 120, 121, 122, 125, 126, 127, 128, 129, 130, 131, 132, 133, 134, 135, 137, 138, 139, 140, 141, 142, 143, 145, 146, 152, 153, 154, 155, 156, 157, 158, 159, 161, 162, 163, 164, 165, 166, 174, 175, 180, 182, 183, 184
Cherokee Country, 91
Cherokee County, 10
Cherokee Tribe of Northeast Alabama, 180, 182
Cherokees of Northeast Alabama, 82
Chickamaugans, 131, 137, 161
Chickasaw, 4, 5, 7, 11, 25, 33, 60, 61, 66, 68, 73, 76, 77, 78, 79, 88, 89, 90, 91, 92, 93, 96, 99, 100, 110, 112, 113, 118, 128, 129, 131, 133, 134, 137, 138, 141, 143, 147, 148, 149, 150, 151, 155, 156, 157, 158, 162, 170, 184
Chickasaw Island, 93, 99, 157
Choctaw, 66, 69, 81, 100, 103, 167, 180
Chota, 10, 21, 153
Christian, William, 153
Chuqualatague, 128
Coffee, John, 97, 99, 112, 113, 117, 141, 142, 169
Colbert County, 55, 76, 77, 78, 94, 132, 157, 158
Colbert Shoals, 18, 53, 55
Colbert, George, 5, 34, 76, 77, 78, 80, 128, 129, 132, 138, 157
Colbert, James Logan, 5, 61, 77
Colbert, Levi, 5, 76, 77, 138
Coosa, 91
Coosa Path, 101, 105, 121, 122, 129, 153
Copena, 14, 121, 123
Copper Town, 91, 92
Cornally, David, 182
Cotton Gin Port, 63, 94, 95, 99, 100, 111, 113, 117, 118, 141
Courtland, 89, 94, 97, 101, 103, 105, 106, 112, 117, 118, 119, 121, 129, 139, 141, 153, 163
Cowan, John, 97, 114, 169
Creek, 1, 4, 5, 7, 11, 25, 59, 61, 66, 67, 68, 72, 73, 74, 76, 81, 88, 89, 90, 91, 93, 97, 98, 99, 100, 102, 103, 118, 136, 137, 141, 145, 146, 147, 149, 150, 151, 152, 155, 156, 157, 164, 167, 169, 170, 180, 183
Crenay, Baron De, 167

Crockett, David, 97, 99, 114, 169, 170
Cullman County, 91
Cuttyatoy, 105, 118, 119, 135, 138, 139, 153

D

Dale Counties, 182
Daleville, 10, 181
Davenport, Erma Lis, 183
Davenport, Tommy, 183
Deer Clan, 9, 85
DeKalb County, 11, 182
Desoto, Hernando, 14, 57, 59, 102, 167
Doublehead, 25, 30, 34, 62, 69, 73, 77, 79, 88, 95, 100, 101, 105, 107, 108, 109, 113, 119, 120, 125, 127, 128, 129, 130, 131, 132, 133, 134, 135, 137, 138, 139, 140, 141, 142, 143, 153, 156, 157, 161, 164, 181
Doublehead's Resort, 120
Doublehead's Trace, 88, 92, 100, 101, 119
Dragging Canoe, 135, 136, 139, 153, 182
Dsugweladegi, 128

E

Eagle Eye, 148, 149, 150, 152
Eastport, 94, 95
Echota, 1, 2, 3, 4, 5, 6, 7, 9, 10, 11, 12, 82, 158, 164, 166, 180, 181, 185
Echota Cherokee, 1, 2, 4, 5, 6, 9, 10, 11, 82, 180, 181, 182
Elk River Shoals, 17, 29, 53, 54, 55, 88, 95, 98, 99, 100, 101, 102, 103, 105, 107, 118, 119, 128, 129, 139, 142, 153, 163
Elyton, 92
Etowah County, 91

F

Falkville, 11
Faulkner, B. J., 10, 181
Flanagin, James M., 175
Flat Rock, 91, 92, 100, 157, 158
Fort Mitchell, 88, 97, 98, 99
Franklin County, 91, 94, 148, 157, 158
French Lick, 100
Ft. Hampton, 88, 109, 156

G

Gadsden, 90, 93, 157
Gaines Trace, 62, 88, 94, 95, 98, 99, 113, 117, 118, 128, 141
Gaines, Edmund Pendleton, 95, 100, 117, 118, 119
Gaines, George Strothers, 95
Gillespie, James Richard, 97, 169
Gist, Nathaniel, 125, 129
Great Eagle (Willenawah), 128
Great Mussel Shoals, 53
Guntersville, 59

H

Haleyville, 92, 100, 101, 157
Hallmark, Charlotte Stewart, 2

Havens, Charlotte Ann, 168
Havens, James, 168
Hicks, Ceil, 182
Hicks, Charles, 69, 110, 113, 125, 127, 138, 141, 156
High Shoals, 91
High Town, 89, 90, 91
High Town Path, 73, 74, 75, 89, 90, 91, 92, 93, 94, 95, 100, 102, 103, 137, 147, 155, 157, 158, 162, 167
High Town Trail, 91
Hillsboro, 97
Houston County, 182
Hubbert, James, 132
Hughes, Mary, 27
Hunkapiller, Joe, 182
Huntsville, 53, 89, 90, 97, 99, 101, 107, 109, 114, 141, 143, 155, 169
Hyatt, Rayford, 106, 110, 175

I

Indian Tomb Hollow, 97, 147, 152, 168, 169, 170
Ittaloknah, 148, 149, 152

J

Jackson County, 11, 135, 182
Jackson, Andrew, 63, 64, 67, 73, 74, 79, 105, 109, 112, 115, 116, 125, 127, 135, 141, 145, 146, 147, 158, 163, 164, 165, 184
Jasper Road, 91, 92
Jefferson, Thomas, 64, 140
Jesus Christ, 19
Johnson, Larry, 183
Junaluska, 125, 146, 164
Justice, John, 182

K

Keep, William, 182
King Cove, 172, 173
Kinlock Bluff Shelter, 170, 174
Kinlock Falls, 171
Kinlock Rock Shelter, 170, 171
Koasatis, 73
Kokomah, 149, 150
Kushner, Jaynn, 182

L

Lauderdale County, 69, 108, 129, 130, 131, 138, 156, 161
Lawrence County, 1, 2, 4, 5, 6, 7, 9, 11, 12, 13, 14, 16, 17, 19, 20, 21, 25, 26, 28, 29, 30, 33, 34, 35, 41, 42, 53, 55, 60, 61, 62, 63, 66, 67, 68, 69, 72, 73, 74, 79, 88, 89, 90, 92, 94, 95, 96, 97, 98, 99, 100, 101, 102, 103, 105, 106, 107, 112, 117, 118, 119, 120, 121, 122, 123, 127, 128, 129, 130, 131, 135, 137, 138, 139, 141, 142, 143, 145, 146, 147, 153, 155, 156, 157, 158, 159, 161, 162, 163, 165, 166, 167, 168, 169, 171, 172, 176, 177, 181, 182, 184
Leola Road, 89, 92, 94, 102, 155, 173
Limestone County, 88, 97, 98, 99, 112, 156
Little Muscle Shoals, 53, 55
Little Mussel Shoals, 18, 163
Little Turkey, 139

Long Hair Clan, 9
Lookout Mountain, 90, 133

M

Machis Lower Creek, 180
Madison County, 11, 142, 143, 155, 157, 182
Magnolia, 149, 150, 151, 152
Manasco, Jim, 102
Marathon, 67, 97, 100, 105, 112, 116, 117, 122, 145, 163
Marshall County, 93, 110
Martin, Dr. H.L. "Lindy", 182
McCloski, Thomas, 10, 181
McCony, James, 182
McGhee, Calvin W., 181
McGillivary, Alexander, 5
McIntoshville, 5, 60
Meigs, Josiah, 117
Meigs, Return Jonathon, 120, 132, 134, 139, 140, 141
Melson, G. H., 169
Melton, John, 5, 61, 99, 101, 102, 109, 110, 112, 113, 114, 115, 116, 117, 128, 138, 141, 156, 162, 163
Melton, Moses, 69, 110, 113, 141, 156
Melton. David, 67, 109, 115, 127, 141
Melton's Bluff, 5, 61, 63, 67, 69, 88, 92, 94, 95, 96, 97, 98, 99, 100, 105, 109, 110, 112, 113, 114, 115, 116, 117, 118, 128, 129, 137, 138, 139, 141, 143, 145, 147, 153, 156, 162, 163, 164, 169
Memphis, 89
Menawa, 146
Mississippian, 14, 21, 22, 23, 24, 177
Mitchell Trace, 88, 97, 98, 99, 100
Mitchell, David Brady, 98, 99
Mobile, 90, 92, 93, 94, 95, 143
Mobile Bay, 90, 92, 94, 143
Montgomery, 67, 156
Moulton, 74
Moulton, Michael, 73, 74, 147
Mountain, Marland, 182
MOWA Band of Choctaw, 180
MOWA Choctaws, 183
Moytoy, 128
Muscle Shoals, 95
Mussel Shoals, 14, 17, 29, 55, 67, 92, 101, 109, 129, 130, 138, 153, 154, 163

N

Nashville, 68, 92, 96, 98, 100, 101, 116, 118, 132, 139
Natchez, 96
Natchez Trace, 95, 96, 108, 132, 157
Naylor, Mary E. Welborn Segars, 169
New Echota, 1, 6, 10, 79, 154, 158, 164
New Orleans, 62, 94, 95, 111, 114, 116

O

Oakville, 19, 97, 98, 99, 101, 105, 109, 120, 121, 122, 123, 129, 147, 153
Oakville Indian Mounds, 2, 97, 98
Oconostota, 153
Old Buffalo Trail, 92, 100, 101
Old Corn Road, 89, 91, 94

Old Indian Trace, 105, 122, 129
Old Tassel, 128, 129, 132
Overall, William, 133

P

Paint Clan, 9
Paleo, 13, 14, 15, 16, 17, 19, 29
Pathkiller, 138, 139, 141, 142
Pickett, Albert James, 146
Piqua Shawnee, 180
Poarch Band of Creek, 180, 181
Ponioc, 149, 150
Prucha, Francis P., 63
Pumpkin Boy, 128, 133

R

Red Clay, 79, 164
Red Eagle, 136, 137, 145
Red Paint Clan, 85
Riddle, William Straud, 175
Ridge Path, 94
Ridge Road, 89, 92, 94, 100, 102, 155
Robertson, James, 132
Rodgers, John, 134
Rogers, John, 69, 128, 131, 140, 161
Rooks, David, 182
Russell County, 88, 96, 97, 98, 99
Russellville, 94, 95, 142

S

Saleechie, 77, 80, 128, 129, 132, 138
Sand Mountain, 89, 90, 93
Saunders, Edmonds, 168
Saunders, Ridge, Alex, 69, 128, 131, 134, 161
Seminoles, 66
Sequoyah, 4, 42, 69, 119, 125, 126, 127, 128, 137, 138, 156, 174
Sequoyah, George Gist, 125
Sevier, John, 132, 141, 153
Sevier, Valentine, 132
Shawnee, 25, 66, 68, 73, 135, 184
Shelby County, 11
Sheridan, Richard C., 99
Ship Rock, 172
Shoal Town, 100, 105, 108, 117, 119, 120, 129, 130, 131, 132, 134, 137, 138, 139, 140, 153
Sipsey Wilderness Area, 102, 171, 172, 173
Sipsie Trail, 91, 92, 102, 103, 117, 118
Smith, David, 167, 168
Southern Trail, 91
Spillers, Amos, 175
Staggs, Travis, 182
Star Clan of Lower Muscogee Creek, 183
Star Clan of Muscogee Creeks, 180
Stewart, Joe, 2
Stewart, Joseph "Two Eagles", 11, 181
Swimmer, Amanda, 45

T

Tahlonteeskee, 156
Tahlonteskee, 130, 131, 137, 138, 140, 161, 162
Tallapoosa, 59, 146
Talo Tiske, 128
Talohuskee, 119, 127, 129, 130, 131, 137, 138, 139, 156
Talohuskee Benge, 119, 127, 129, 130, 131, 137, 138, 139, 161
Taluntuskee, 134
Tecumseh, 68, 146
Thomas, Edwin C., 132
Thornhill, Claud, 182
Town Creek, 100, 101, 105, 110, 118, 119, 120, 129, 130, 131, 138, 139, 153
Trail of Tears, 1, 37, 67, 103, 158, 159, 165, 166, 184
Tukabachee, 67
Tullis, Eddie L., 181
Turkey Town, 63, 79, 90, 91, 93, 99, 137, 138, 141, 142, 154, 155, 157, 158, 162, 163, 185
Tuscaloosa, 59, 92, 100, 101, 102, 103, 118, 167
Tuscumbia, 147
Tuskaloosa, 59
Tuskegee, 125
Tuskiahooto, 77, 80, 128, 129, 132, 138
Twisters Clan (*Long Hair*), 86

U

United Cherokee Aniyunwiya, 82, 180, 184
United Cherokee Tribe of Alabama, 10

V

Vann, 134

Vinemont, 91

W

Walker County, 9
Walker, Rickey Butch, 2, 169
Wallace, George, 183
Wambles, Deal, 182
Ward, Nancy, 26
Warrior Mountains, 11, 28, 45, 63, 79, 88, 89, 90, 94, 98, 99, 102, 121, 129, 137, 153, 154, 155, 157, 159, 161, 162, 165, 166, 167, 168, 170, 171, 172, 173, 174, 175, 176, 177, 178
Washington, George, 128, 133
Waterloo Shoals, 18, 54, 55
Watts, John, 5, 125, 127, 128, 129, 139
Watts, John Jr., 5, 125, 127, 128, 129, 139, 140
Watts, Wurteh, 5, 119, 125, 127, 128, 129
Weatherford, William, 136, 145
Whisnant, Glenn, 173
Wilburn, Authur, 169
Wild Potato Clan, 9, 86
Williams, Bill, 182
Williamson, Gina, 185
Willstown, 125, 133, 140, 185
Winston County, 9, 91, 103
Wolf Clan, 9, 85
Woodland, 13, 19, 20, 21, 102, 121, 122
Wright, Johnny, 183
Wright, Penny, 183
Wurteh, 5, 119, 125, 127

Y

Yuchi, 25, 66, 67, 68, 73

Bluewater Publications is a multi-faceted publishing company capable of meeting all of your reading and publishing needs. Our two-fold aim is to:
1) Provide the market with educationally enlightening and inspiring research and reading materials.
2) Make the opportunity of being published available to any author and or researcher who desires to be published.

We are passionate about preserving history; whether through the re-publishing of an out-of-print classic, or by publishing the research of historians and genealogists. Bluewater Publications is the *Peoples' Choice Publisher*.

For company information or information about how you can be published through Bluewater Publications, please visit:

www.BluewaterPublications.com

Also check Amazon.com to purchase any of the books that we publish.

Confidently Preserving Our Past,
Bluewater Publications.com

www.ingramcontent.com/pod-product-compliance
Lightning Source LLC
Chambersburg PA
CBHW081848170426
43199CB00018B/2844